Denise Levertov
New Perspectives

LOCUST HILL LITERARY STUDIES
No. 28

The Locust Hill Literary Studies Series

1. *Blake and His Bibles*. Edited by David V. Erdman. ISBN 0-933951-29-9. LC 89-14052.
2. *Faulkner, Sut, and Other Southerners*. M. Thomas Inge. ISBN 0-933951-31-0. LC 91-40016.
3. *Essays of a Book Collector: Reminiscences on Some Old Books and Their Authors*. Claude A. Prance. ISBN 0-933951-30-2. LC 89-12734.
4. *Vision and Revisions: Essays on Faulkner*. John E. Bassett. ISBN 0-933951-32-9. LC 89-14046.
5. *A Rose by Another Name: A Survey of Literary Flora from Shakespeare to Eco*. Robert F. Fleissner. ISBN 0-933951-33-7. LC 89-12804.
7. *Blake's Milton Designs: The Dynamics of Meaning*. J.M.Q. Davies. ISBN 0-933951-40-X. LC 92–32678.
8. *The Slaughter-House of Mammon: An Anthology of Victorian Social Protest Literature*. Edited by Sharon A. Winn and Lynn M. Alexander. ISBN 0-933951-41-8. LC 92-7269.
9. *"A Heart of Ideality in My Realism" and Other Essays on Howells and Twain*. John E. Bassett. ISBN 0-933951-36-1. LC 90-46908.
10. *Imagining Romanticism: Essays on English and Australian Romanticisms*. Edited by Deirdre Coleman and Peter Otto. ISBN 0-933951-42-6. LC 91-36509.
11. *Learning the Trade: Essays on W.B. Yeats and Contemporary Poetry*. Edited by Deborah Fleming. ISBN 0-933951-43-4. LC 92–39290.
12. *"All Nature is but Art": The Coincidence of Opposites in English Romantic Literature*. Mark Trevor Smith. ISBN 0-933951-44-2. LC 93–27166.
13. *Essays on Henry David Thoreau: Rhetoric, Style, and Audience*. Richard Dillman. ISBN 0-933951-50-7. LC 92–39960.
14. *Author-ity and Textuality: Current Views of Collaborative Writing*. Edited by James S. Leonard. ISBN 0-933951-57-4. LC 94-15111.
15. *Women's Work: Essays in Cultural Studies*. Shelley Armitage. ISBN 0-933951-58-2. LC 95-6180.
16. *Perspectives on American Culture: Essays on Humor, Literature, and the Popular Arts*. M. Thomas Inge. ISBN 0-933951-59-0. LC 94-14908.
17. *Bridging the Gap: Literary Theory in the Classroom*. Edited by J.M.Q. Davies. ISBN 0-933951-60-4. LC 94–17926.
18. *Juan Benet: A Critical Reappraisal of His Fiction*. Edited by John B. Margenot III. ISBN 0-933951-61-2. LC 96–51479.
19. *The American Trilogy, 1900–1937: Norris, Dreiser, Dos Passos and the History of Mammon*. John C. Waldmeir. ISBN 0-933951-64-7. LC 94-48837.
20. *"The Muses Females Are": Martha Moulsworth and Other Women Writers of the English Renaissance*. Ed. by Robert C. Evans and Anne C. Little. ISBN 0-933951-63-9. LC 95-22413.
21. *Henry James in the Periodicals*. Arthur Sherbo. ISBN 0-933951-74-4. LC 97-11720.
22. *"Miss Tina Did It" and Other Fresh Looks at Modern Fiction*. Joseph J. Waldmeir. ISBN 0-933951-76-0. LC 97-28923.
23. *Frank O'Connor: New Perspectives*. Ed. by Robert C. Evans and Richard Harp. ISBN 0-933951-79-5. LC 97-32626.
24. *Aldous Huxley & W.H. Auden: On Language*. David Garrett Izzo. ISBN 0-933951-80-9. LC 98-11922.
25. *Studies in the Johnson Circle*. Arthur Sherbo. ISBN 0-933951-81-7. LC 98-35292.
26. *Thornton Wilder: New Essays*. Ed. by Martin Blank, Dalma Hunyadi Brunauer, and David Garrett Izzo. ISBN 0-933951-83-3. LC 98-48986.
27. *Tragedy's Insights: Identity, Polity, Theodicy*. Ed. by Luis R. Gámez. ISBN 0-933951-85-X.
28. *Denise Levertov: New Perspectives*. Edited by Anne Colclough Little and Susie Paul. ISBN 0-933951-87-6. LC 00-035705.

Denise Levertov
New Perspectives

Edited by

Anne Colclough Little

and

Susie Paul

LOCUST HILL PRESS
West Cornwall, CT
2000

Library of Congress Cataloging-in-Publication Data

Denise Levertov : new perspectives / edited by Anne Colclough Little and
Susie Paul.
      p.   cm. -- (Locust Hill literary studies ; no. 28)
      Includes bibliographical references and index.
      ISBN 0-933951-87-6 (alk. paper)
      1. Levertov, Denise, 1923--Criticism and interpretation.
    2. Women and literature--United States--History--20th century.
    I. Little, Anne C. II. Paul, Susie. III. Series.

PS 3562.E8876 Z62 2000
811'.54--dc21   00-035705

By Denise Levertov: Excerpts from A DOOR IN THE HIVE, copyright © 1989 by
Denise Levertov. Reprinted by permission of New Directions Publishing Corp. Excerpts from BREATHING THE WATER, copyright © 1987 by Denise Levertov.
Reprinted by permission of New Directions Publishing Corp. Excerpts from
CANDLES IN BABYLON, copyright © 1982 by Denise Levertov. Reprinted by permission of New Directions Publishing Corp. Excerpts from COLLECTED EARLIER
POEMS 1940–1960, copyright © 1946, 1979 by Denise Levertov. Reprinted by per-
mission of New Directions Publishing Corp. Excerpts from EVENING TRAIN, copyright © 1992 by Denise Levertov. Reprinted by permission of New Directions Publishing Corp. Excerpts from LIFE IN THE FOREST, copyright © 1978 by Denise
Levertov. Reprinted by permission of New Directions Publishing Corp. Excerpts
from LIGHT UP THE CAVE, copyright © 1981 by New Directions Publishing Corp.
Reprinted by permission of New Directions Publishing Corp. Excerpts from NEW
AND SELECTED ESSAYS, copyright © 1992 by Denise Levertov. Reprinted by permission of New Directions Publishing Corp. Excerpts from OBLIQUE PRAYERS,
copyright © 1984 by Denise Levertov. Reprinted by permission of New Directions
Publishing Corp. Excerpts from POEMS 1960–1967, copyright © 1966 by Denise Levertov. Reprinted by permission of New Directions Publishing Corp. Excerpts from
POEMS 1968–1972, copyright © 1970 by Denise Levertov. Reprinted by permission
of New Directions Publishing Corp. Excerpts from SANDS OF THE WELL, copyright
© 1996 by Denise Levertov. Reprinted by permission of New Directions Publishing
Corp. Excerpts from TESSERAE, copyright © 1995 by Denise Levertov. Reprinted by
permission of New Directions Publishing Corp. Excerpts from THE FREEING OF THE
DUST, copyright © 1975 by Denise Levertov. Reprinted by permission of New Di-
rections Publishing Corp. Excerpts from THE POET IN THE WORLD, copyright ©
1973 by Denise Levertov. Reprinted by permission of New Directions Publishing
Corp. Excerpts from THIS GREAT UNKNOWING: LAST POEMS, copyright © 1998 by
The Denise Levertov Literary Trust, Paul A. Lacey and Valerie Trueblood Rapport,
Co-Trustees. Reprinted by permission of New Directions Publishing Corp.

"All There Is to Know About Adolph Eichmann" © 1989, Leonard Cohen. Used by
Permission/All Rights Reserved.

"The Road Not Taken" from: THE POETRY OF ROBERT FROST edited by Edward
Connery Lathem. Copyright 1944 by Robert Frost, copyright 1916, © 1969 by Henry
Holt and Co. Reprinted by permission of Henry Holt and Company, LLC.

"For Joe" copyright © 1975 by the Estate of Jack Spicer. Reprinted from THE
COLLECTED BOOKS OF JACK SPICER with the permission of Black Sparrow Press.

To

Patrick David Morrow and Peggy Prenshaw

"The true teacher ... inspires self-trust"
Bronson Alcott, *Orphic Sayings*

and

Robert C. Evans

"Let our figure be of a composite nature"
Plato, *Phaedrus*

Acknowledgments

Anne Colclough Little would like to thank Pat Morrow, who directed her thesis on Denise Levertov. He never accepted less than her best and always believed that her best was good. She would also like to thank Lisa Little and Stephanie and Paul Ladeira, who cheer her on even when they need her time and who always make her proud; Anne and John Stewart, who gave her that great and rare gift—a loving family; Maryem Brewer, whose actions remind others what a virtue kindness is; and for Bob Little, with whom she knows that "the best *is* yet to be."

Susie Paul would like to thank Peggy Prenshaw for the example she set for an undergraduate student in her Southern literature class when she herself was young in her career. She also wishes to acknowledge the loving support of Mike Fitzsimmons, Gene Johnson, her children—Joseph and Amelia, and her friend of 20 years Debra Boyd.

Both editors would like to thank Bob Evans who, despite his bad jokes, sets the standard for collaboration between colleagues and with students. He got this project moving. The editors also thank Paul Lacey, Levertov's literary executor, for his enthusiasm about the project, his guidance, and his graciously sharing his history with and knowledge of Levertov; Debra Boyd and Mary Jane Curry for their help as outside readers; Dennis Herrick and Pedro Ruis Mayor for preparing the musical score for publication; Joe Crowley and Ron Blaesing, who solved the problem of the *verba dicendi*; and Alan Gribben, Head of the AUM Department of English and Philosophy, for his encouragement—as always—with this and other projects.

Contents

Abbreviations

Introduction

In "For Those Whom the Gods Love Less," from *Sands of the Well* (96), the last collection of Denise Levertov's poetry published before her death, the poet-speaker (whose "I" sounds much like Levertov) raises what must be a common question for any artist fortunate enough to have a career that spans half a century:

> When you discover
> your new work travels the ground you had traversed
> decades ago, you wonder, panicked,
> 'Have I outlived my vocation? Said already
> all that was mine to say?'

Like Cézanne and James, "the great ones" whose example offers comfort in this poem, Levertov did indeed travel the same ground from time to time—she returned to themes previously explored, reexamined familiar subjects, revisited memories, repeated significant images. Yet throughout her work, including her last volume, *This Great Unknowing*, published posthumously, her poetry has had the ability to create for the reader the freshness of what she calls in "For Those Whom the Gods Love Less" the "radiant epiphanies [that] recur, recur" (96).

The "radiant epiphanies," or what she refers to in her 1965 interview with Walter Sutton, as moments of "sudden illumination" (Brooker 13), often result from the discovery of something hidden, usually in the natural world. Perhaps the best-known example—so characteristic of her first volumes—is "Pleasures," from her fourth volume *With Eyes at the Back of Our Heads* (17–18), where the speaker "like[s] to find / what's not found / at once, but lies // within something of another nature": "the bones of squid," "the seed" of the "*mamey*," "the butteryellow glow / in the narrow flute from which the morning-glory / opens blue and cool on a hot morning." The surprise that comes from seeing one thing hidden in another becomes a metaphor throughout Levertov's work for the sense of discovery of both natural and spiritual phenomena. Poems like this one are characteristic of Levertov's "apperceptive" poetics in which she uses all the techniques at her disposal—line-breaks, "[r]hyme, chime, echo, reiteration" (*The Poet in the World* 9), and so on—to recreate a sudden illumination for her reader.

Frequently the epiphany comes from seeing something that is visible but somehow unnoticed until the eye catches it, as in "The Garden Wall," in *O Taste and See* (60), where the poet-speaker

> discovered
> the colors in the wall that woke
> when spray from the hose
> played on its pocks and warts—
>
> a hazy red, a
> grain gold, a mauve
> of small shadows, sprung
> from the quiet dry brown.

Here Levertov makes explicit that what she has observed goes beyond the observance of a physical occurrence to become

> archetype
> of the world always a step
> beyond the world, that can't
> be looked for, only
> as the eye wanders,
> found.

"Brass Tacks," from *Footprints* (39–41), ends with an epiphany in a working man's lifted spirits, as he

> saw the rose-colored leaves
> of a small plant growing among
> the stones of a low wall
>
> unobtrusively, and found himself
> standing quite still, gazing,
> and found himself
> smiling. (41)

The muted colors are present but cannot be noticed by the human eye until seen through the mist of water. In this poem the poet-speaker only implies the significance of the moment of awareness, yet the reader understands that occasions like this one are the "brass tacks" that become a kind of "Consolation" to those burdened with the "dailiness" of life (40).

In several poems the poet-speaker attributes to her mother her ability to discover what is hidden or overlooked. For example, in "The Instant" (*Overland to the Islands*) her mother points out through the mist "Eryri ... / Snowdon, home / of eagles, resting place of / Merlin, core of Wales." In "Earliest Spring" (*Life in the Forest* 44–45) on a "boring" walk over ground "dark, scumbled, bare / between clumps of wintered-over stems," her mother shows her first the snowdrop's "thin sharp green darning-needles" that "stitch through the sticky gleam of dirt, // belled with white" (44) and then the crocuses' "filigree veins of violet / traced upon white, that make // the mauve seem" (45). These discoveries are transformative; the "earliest spring of [her] life" changes her from "a baby" to "a child," no longer "bored" but, as Levertov proceeded through a lifetime, "moving step by step, / slow, down the path. Each pause // brings us to bells or flames" (45).

Sometimes the epiphany expresses itself in the unspoken answer to a question like the one that concludes "To Olga," from *Breathing the Water* (25–26). The poet-speaker first asks what her sister had felt on their tardiness—yet again—after wandering "too far out and away, leaving / almost as if / not to return" (25). In response to her older sister's irritation at the younger sister's silence on the long walk home, the poet-speaker asks: "Could it, / could it have been that / you, you were afraid, my brave, my lost / sister?" (26). The halting, repetitive final question, although left unanswered, reveals the insight that the younger sister, now grown, has finally achieved.

At other times a query at the end of a poem is not voiced as a question and no answer is implied. Epiphany comes not in insight gained but in the awareness that—at least in the troubled present—no insight is possible. For example, in "The Cold Spring," from *Relearning the Alphabet* (5–9), a lifetime spent on a journey "towards utopias" (6) does not end at the anticipated "circle of holy stones" (7) but instead on a "plain" (7) in "the cold spring" (9). After asking herself "What do I know?" (5), the poet-speaker names those familiar sights of the natural world about which the "All Day Bird" (simply named here but identified as the artist in "Claritas" in *O Taste and See* [35]) likes to sing:

> Swing of the
> birch catkins,
> drift of
> watergrass,
> tufts of

> green on the
> trees.... (5)

But she concludes, "It's not enough" (6). Although the strife of the
world seems distant as the "truces" end and "the firing resumes"
(6), she finds "the place of pilgrimage" barren: "The spirit's left it"
(7). She can finally offer just a disturbing query so doubtful of a
positive answer that it does not end with a question mark: "what if
my poem is deathsongs" (9). Her only epiphany here is the awareness that she does not know what the future holds.

   Although Levertov's phrase "radiant epiphanies" in "For
Those Whom the Gods Love Less" has luminous connotations,
some of her engaged poetry—often most closely associated with
her poetry of the sixties and seventies—produces somber insights.
In "Thinking about El Salvador" (*Oblique Prayers* 33–34), which
Levertov cites in an interview as one of her best poems (Brooker
122), the poet-speaker describes in disquieting graphic images the
atrocities committed in that country. Each sentence begins by focusing on the decapitations, then notes their stunning effect. In the
first four stanzas the poet-speaker repeats the impact of the
killings on her: for "each person's head they chopped off," "for
each tongue they silence," "for each gaze they cut," for each "blade
of *machete*" held over a neck, she is silenced. But the poem ends
with a starker realization that the cost to her is small compared to
the greater loss:

> the silence
>
> of raped women,
> of priests and peasants,
> teachers and children,
> of all whose heads every day
> float down the river
> and rot
> and sink,
> not Orpheus heads
> still singing, bound for the sea,
> but mute. (33–34)

Here the epiphanies powerfully convey the consequences of inhuman acts, both to the poet and to the victims.

   In some of Levertov's poems the epiphany comes in the guise
of insight, often spiritual insight like that of many of her later poems, that had eluded her, and perhaps others, until that moment.
For example, in "Annunciation," from *A Door in the Hive* (86–88),

the poet-speaker acknowledges that the Virgin Mary has historically been venerated for her "meek obedience" to the
"engendering Spirit" who wants her to bear the Christ-child. What
is more astounding than Mary's obedience, however, is her
"courage" (86), which has been overlooked. With the poet-speaker's remembering that the freedom "to accept or to refuse" is
"integral to humanness," epiphany here emanates from the realization of the significance of Mary's yielding without protest:
"Bravest of all humans, / consent illumined her. / … courage un-
paralleled, / opened her utterly " (88). The moment in which Mary
"perceiv[ed] instantly / the astounding ministry she was offered"
(87) and accepted its burden becomes for the poet-speaker an
epiphany of understanding both free will and the courage required at times of those who, having free will, still consent to the
difficult choice.

Despite the doubts expressed in "For Those Whom the Gods
Love Less," Levertov's work in her last book continues to surprise
readers with "radiant epiphanies," even when she traverses familiar ground. In a dying sunflower that has lost its "bright petals"
("A New Flower" 20), the poet-speaker finds a "ring of green, the
petals / from behind the petals" surrounding "that round cushion
of dark-roast / coffee brown, tipped with uncountable / minute
florets of gold, more noticeable / now that the clear, shiny yellow
was gone." The joy of the discovery is tempered by the images of
the transience of life that end the poem: "a new flower / on this
fall day, revealed within / the autumn of its own brief bloom."
Again the broader significance of the discovery is unstated, but the
poignant parallel of these lines to Levertov's stage of life is hard to
avoid.

In "A Cryptic Sign" (*This Great Unknowing* 21) the poet-
speaker again finds what had gone unnoticed:

> In the crook
> of an old and tattered snag
> something gleams amid the stillness,
> drawing the gaze: some bit of heartwood
> so long exposed….

The heartwood speaks, like the colors discovered in the wet garden wall, "of the world always a step / beyond the world" (*O
Taste and See* 60), the sacredness of the epiphany here revealed in
her simile:

> weather and time
> have polished it, as centuries
> of awed lips, touching
> a hand of stone, rub it
> to somber gleaming.
> 　　　(*This Great Unknowing* 21)

The joy Levertov finds in the natural world and her ability to suggest its significance have not been dimmed by a lifetime of seeing.

She also continues to look back at those transformative moments of illumination linked to her mother. "First Love" (8–9), reminiscent of "The Instant" and "Earliest Spring," recounts the first awareness of the natural world from which she later drew such sustenance. Although she "was barely / old enough to ask and repeat its name" (8), her noticing the flower "Convolvulus" ("It looked at me, I looked / back" [9]) marks an important stage in her perception of that world: "suddenly / there was *Before I saw it*, the vague / past" (8) and then "*there was endlessness*" (9). In "the wholeness / of that attention" she finds what she would always seek: "that once-in-lifetime / secret communion" (9). Although her wistfulness suggests that she never recaptured that particular epiphany, certainly "The Instant" and "Earliest Spring" give evidence of similar occasions.

Like "To Olga," "Roast Potatoes" (*This Great Unknowing* 36–37) looks back in an attempt to define the meaning of an earlier event, the real significance of which was not fully understood at the time. The poet-speaker recalls the "wild / Arabian scenes there'd be each night / across from our 5th floor window" (36). After the unloading of fruits and vegetables at the Wholesale Produce Market, men she "thought of … / as old fashioned hobos" (36–37) would gather around fires to roast "fallen potatoes they'd salvaged, … talking, telling stories, / passing a bottle if they had one" (37). In "From the Roof" (*Jacob's Ladder* 49–50), she had remembered a similar scene, perhaps of the same place: "Crates of fruit are unloading / across the street on the cobbles, / and a brazier flaring / to warm the men and burn trash" (50). The earlier poem describes the scene in passing as part of the atmosphere ("This wild night") of the "new place" to which she suddenly realizes she had been brought "by design" (50). The occasion is joyous in contrast to the "night of misery" that preceded it (49). In the later poem, however, she discovers another significance in the gathering on the street: Although the men roasting potatoes were obviously homeless, the camaraderie of their "fragments of talk and laughter" gave the event a spirit not found among the destitute of today:

> *something*
> —you name it, if you know, I can't ...
> something you might call blesséd? Is that hyperbole? Something kind?
>
> (37)

As she had in "To Olga," she raises a question in reconsidering an event from an former time, but her response here, like the closing line in "A Cold Spring," implies a critique of the troubling age in which she writes:

> Something not to be found in the '90s, anyway.
> Something it seems we'll have to enter the next millennium
> lacking, and for the young,
>   unknown to memory. (37)

Despite her inability to define the quality that distinguishes the past from the present, her epiphany here conveys the significance of the loss. The graphic language, even anger, of some of her earlier engaged poems is absent from *This Great Unknowing*, in which overall she achieves a kind of serenity, but she remains true to her belief, expressed in "Poetry, Prophecy, Survival," that, in addition to helping to develop in others "a passionate love of life," poetry should also be concerned with "raising consciousness and articulating emotions for people who have not the gift of expression" (*New & Selected Essays* 144).

Like "Thinking of El Salvador" and "Roast Potatoes," the illumination that comes in "Fugitives" (*This Great Unknowing* 32–33) is a dark one, again to make others aware of a modern tragedy. Watching the "lava-flow" of refugees "[s]ilent in stumbling haste" to escape from "what seems / an unhelpable land of terror" (32), the poet-speaker knows they are "driven / less by what shreds of hope may cling to their bodies / than by a despair" that—except for their deep-seated impulse to flee to a place of refuge—"might well have left them / paralyzed in the dust, inert before imminent slaughter" (33). The last lines of the poem describe their "grim motion thousand upon thousand, / westward to zones Relief has already fled from" (33), the epiphany ironically conveying the utter hopelessness of their plight.

In "Translucence" (*This Great Unknowing* 48), from which the editors took the title of her last volume, Levertov offers one of the many spiritual epiphanies characteristic of her work, in particular her later poems. The poet-speaker describes the "unconscious light in the faces" of those who possess "the immediacy of new life, Vita Nuova":

> not quite transparent,
> more like the half-opaque whiteness
> of Japanese screens or lampshades, ...
> ... which permits the passage of what is luminous
> though forms remain unseen behind its protection.

The epiphany for the poet-speaker comes in realizing that the "holiness" of the "already resurrected" who radiate this light comes from their humility in "know[ing] of themselves nothing different / from anyone else": "This great unknowing." The poem ends with what demonstrates their unawareness of the gift they offer others:

> They are always trying
> to share out joy as if it were cake or water,
> something ordinary, not rare at all.

These final lines also become another "sudden illumination"—obviously unintended by Levertov—for any reader familiar with the body of Levertov's work—and probably account for the editors' choosing the title of her posthumous volume. Although Levertov is clearly referring to others here, the lines resonate as one remembers with what grace, beauty, and humility Levertov struggled, even in the dark times, to "share out joy."

When we conceived this volume, we envisioned a collection of essays that would celebrate the richness of Levertov's life and work, while also providing new insights for her readers, both students and scholars. Levertov's poems have given her readers those "radiant epiphanies" that only poetry can give, but we hope to enlighten in another way. What scholars and poets have offered us in the form of essays for the volume we believe does just that while also celebrating her life and work. The essays provide new perspectives on Levertov's poetry and thus become a kind of tribute to Levertov's memory. Because Levertov spent so much of her time as a teacher, we also wanted to include collaborative essays between those who teach her poetry and their students. In addition, some of the essays honor Levertov more directly with reminiscences. Although this volume was to be a collection of essays, we soon realized that because of Levertov's impact on other poets, we should also include at least a few poems by others to and about her. The result then is an eclectic, non-traditional approach that

seems appropriate for a poet whose poetry and writings about poetry have influenced others in such varied ways and whose work,
as the essays demonstrate, is so diverse.

In organizing the volume, we wanted to achieve an organic
grouping appropriate to Levertov's method of arranging most of
her volumes of poetry. The first two essays, "Valentines Park: 'a
Place of Origin,'" by Christopher MacGowan, and "Denise Levertov and the Lyric of the Contingent Self," by Victoria Frenkel Harris, relate to the issue of identity and thus serve as a kind of prologue. MacGowan tells the history, describes the current state, and
explains the importance to Levertov of two public parks—
Wanstead and Valentines—that she knew as a child and saw as
important in shaping who she was. Both parks have a rich history,
but Wanstead, the wilder and more mysterious of the two, is associated with adolescence and her sister Olga. Valentines Park,
which figures more prominently in Levertov's poetry, is associated
with childhood, and she refers to it in several poems as "a place of
origin." Valentines also represents promise, a "place of departure
into imaginative journeys," and change, while the wishing well in
Valentines becomes a recurring metaphor for a source of inspiration and revelation.

In a time when the lyric itself is dismissed as part of an outmoded tradition, "Denise Levertov and the Lyric of the Contingent
Self" defends Levertov's lyric for its success in resuscitating that
tradition. Harris acknowledges Levertov's "unabashed sense of
subjective identity" that to some is untenable. Yet because Levertov is not isolated from the world, her "sense of self" is constantly
modified by her engagement with social issues in that world. Although several of Levertov's poems demonstrate the dialogical
relationship of the "contingent self" to the world, "Novella," from
Footprints, offers the fullest and clearest example of the need to
avoid "a painfully vague, distant, and spiritless referentiality."

Following a pattern that loosely suggests the progression often
associated with Levertov's career, the next three sections move
from the temporal world to the spiritual, from the concrete to the
abstract. The three essays in the first grouping relate to the body in
some way, with the final piece also incorporating the spiritual. The
first of these, José Rodríquez Herrera's "Reappropriating Mirror
Appropriations: Female Sexuality and the Body in Denise Levertov," has to do with sexual identity. Herrera shows how Levertov
examines the negative stereotype of the female body imposed on
and often embraced by women and reclaims the language used to

denigrate that body. Exposing women's self-censorship, the silencing that prevents their "acceptance of their sexuality," she advocates truthfulness as a way for women to regain their power. By affirming their sexuality, women can undermine oppressive gender stereotypes and finally judge themselves by images from within.

Jim Gallant's "'In the Black of Desire': Eros in the Poetry of Denise Levertov" also focuses on sexuality in Levertov's poems, a topic often noted but not discussed in detail. In the volumes written during the years of her marriage to Mitchell Goodman, in particular *With Eyes at the Back of Our Heads*, *Jacob's Ladder*, and *O Taste and See*, Levertov celebrates the mysteries of eroticism. She delights in the discovery of pleasure, in the male body, and in the sex act itself, often conveying that delight through natural images. The joy is often undercut by "pain and loneliness," but "harmony and satisfaction" predominate. Near the end of her marriage the poems become darker, with the tentative relationships after her divorce leading to poems characterized by "unfulfilled desire and longing."

Despite Levertov's disclaimers that gender is unimportant in her poetry, Katherine Hanson and Ed Block, in "Gender, Nature, and Spirit: Justifying Female Complexity in the Later Poetry of Denise Levertov," the third essay in this section, add their voices to others who have argued conversely. Hanson and Block trace the complex interaction of gender with nature and spirit in eight poems. In the first two, gender is at the forefront as Levertov attempts to reconcile the tensions, represented by nature and spirit, between her conflicting roles of woman and poet. The next two poems bring the conflicting roles together in portraits of two women, each of whom is associated with the natural and spiritual realms. Although not directly about women, the last four poems examine nature and spirit in feminine terms. By noting the interrelationship of the three elements, Hanson and Block show how Levertov validates the diversity of women's experience.

The next section deals with the more abstract world of the mind: the craft of poetry, teaching poetry, poetry and its relationship to politics, and influences. Robert Creeley's tribute "Remembering Denise," not previously available in print, recalls the times Creeley and Levertov spent together and associates her physical qualities like sure movement and balance with her poetic techniques. In the early years the two poets discussed Williams as they were perfecting their own craft. Later, although drawn together in public events for a time through their link to the Black Mountain school, their lives moved in different directions, leaving only the bonds of poetry and memory to connect them.

Gary Pacernick's "Interview with Denise Levertov" provides an opportunity to hear Levertov's own voice as Pacernick asks about her experience as a poet, seeks her insight on what it means to be a poet in the late twentieth century, and urges her to describe the impact of her Jewish ancestry. Although she has always acknowledged her Jewish heritage and the influence of works like Martin Buber's *Tales of the Hasidim*, she conveys her determination not to be pigeonholed—sometimes with the testiness apparent in other interviews when asked about her feminism—and she is emphatic in stressing the diversity of her background: "I cannot be categorized except as a mish-mash."

Because Pacernick interviewed Levertov by mail, he could not promptly follow up her reference to her gift. His essay "The Question of Denise Levertov's Gift," therefore, attempts to define that gift, focusing on her "psalms," in particular from *O Taste and See* and *The Sorrow Dance*, that find a kind of paradise in earthly experience. In these poems, especially "Stepping Westward," he finds evidence of Levertov's gift in her ability as a poet to be both prophet and craftsman.

Although Levertov had little formal schooling, much of her adult life was spent in the classroom teaching more than a generation of younger poets. She recounts her early experiences in "The Untaught Teacher" (*The Poet in the World* 149–99) and conveys something of the spirit of those classes in "A New Year's Garland for My Students/MIT: 1969–70" (*Footprints* 18–25). Reversing the perspective, Anne-Marie Cusac writes as Levertov's student in "'I take up / so much space': Denise Levertov as Teacher." Cusac pays tribute to the memory of Levertov and sketches a portrait in keeping with the voice one hears in her work: an exacting poet and teacher with little patience for carelessness, a committed activist with the gift to inspire, and a complex human being to whom laughter was essential.

Harry Marten shifts the perspective yet again in his essay "To Take Active Responsibility: On Teaching Denise Levertov's Poems." Marten traces the responses of his students to Levertov's poetry as he uses that poetry to instill in them the joy of learning as well as concern for the broader world. Through "Prologue: An Interim" he helps his students comprehend Levertov's ideas about the need to use language honestly. By varying the linebreaks of

"Four Embroideries: (III) Red Snow," as Levertov does in "On the Function of the Line," he demonstrates the "fluidity" of language and the complex ways it conveys meaning. Through other poems he shows the transforming power of language, the nature of evil, and the burden human beings have to prevent inhumanity.

Also concerned in part with Levertov's engaged poetry, Dorothy Nielsen, in "The Dark Wing of Mourning: Grief, Elegy and Time in the Poetry of Denise Levertov," argues that elegies like those about Levertov's sister Olga result from the same apperceptive process that produced her earlier poems and thus provide a link to her later political poetry, often dismissed by critics. Unlike traditional elegies, which attempt to "conquer" time, Levertov's apperceptive elegies "embrace" it as they focus on the thinking/feeling process, and by doing so, show how her poetry can also encompass the political. The later poems do not issue from declining poetic powers but rather signal a change in tone. Her "protest" poems are often elegies that emanate from Levertov's involvement with the broader political world and reflect the Hasidic concept of ecstasy, which incorporates both joy and grief.

In "The Eye as Mirror of Humanity: Social Responsibility and the Nature of Evil in Denise Levertov's 'During the Eichmann Trial,'" Eric Sterling supplements Levertov's portrait of the Adolf Eichmann trial with accounts by some of his victims and explains how, despite the many deaths Eichmann caused, Levertov shows him not as a monster but as a human being, his crimes against humanity therefore even more despicable. He killed without remorse and later justified his actions by saying he was simply "following orders." Although Eichmann's trial found him guilty for his part in the genocide, Levertov's poem indicts all of humanity for failure to stop the Holocaust and calls for people to forget the differences like those the Nazis despised and acknowledge their kinship to one another.

Levertov has written about the influence of writers like Rainer Maria Rilke and William Carlos Williams on her work, but neither she nor others have explored her relationship to other kinds of art. Emily Archer addresses that deficiency in "Denise Levertov and Paul Cézanne: 'in Continuance.'" Levertov's work has obviously been shaped by intimate knowledge of art and music, although the connection between the creation of her poems and other art forms is difficult to trace. Cézanne's impact on her understanding of the artist's vocation, however, is clear. She learned from Cézanne, at least in part, to persist in her work, to return "to the 'origins' of her own work for renewal," and to look constantly to the physical world for "revelations."

Tammy Hearn and Susie Paul examine the connection between Levertov and Rilke in "Denise Levertov's 'Variations' on Rilke's Themes: A Brief Explication." Comparing three of Rilke's poems from his *The Book of Hours* to Levertov's three "Variations" on his themes included in *Breathing the Water*, Hearn and Paul see the poems "as a conversation between two similar but different theological viewpoints." While Levertov's poems were written much later in life than Rilke's and her spiritual understanding is more mature than his, his poems to which she is responding in *Breathing the Water* are early ones that anticipate the kind of growth as a poet Levertov herself had experienced.

In "Salt and Honey: On Denise Levertov," previously published but not widely available, Sam Hamill focuses on *A Door in the Hive* as a culmination of techniques and themes apparent in Levertov's earlier poems. Hamill compares the "subtle music" of her organic poetry with the more mechanical effect of Frost's "predetermined" forms and examines the influence of Rilke on her work. From Rilke she learned to explore the "imperative mystery" in his poetry that becomes such an important part of hers.

The last section of essays is concerned with the spiritual. Denise E. Lynch's "Seeing Denise Levertov: *Tesserae*" traces the development of Levertov's way of looking at the world around her as it can be observed in the autobiographical essays of *Tesserae*. Many of the essays reveal Levertov's awareness of patterns: visual patterns, patterns of motion, patterns of regeneration and so on. Her ability to develop patterns came early, as she synthesized opposites like "beauty and terror" and "joy and sadness." She later became aware of patterns of loss and sometimes recovery—lost books, animals, friendships, family members—as well as interconnections among people. From her mother Levertov learned to see patterns in both the natural and the spiritual worlds, and from her father she learned to be the prophet of what she saw in those worlds.

During their first encounter Jerome Mazzaro and Levertov observed a flower called the Jacob's ladder, a reminder of her book of the same name, published the year before. In "Denise Levertov and the Jacob's Ladder" Mazzaro recounts that first meeting and traces the image of the Jacob's ladder in a number of her poems, concluding with his own poem in which he associates her with flowers and celebrates her ability to inspire. From its beginning in three passages in Genesis, the image of the Jacob's ladder evolved to signify both the striving of human beings toward godliness and the poet who ascends to a visionary position. The image recurs in a number of Levertov's poems, sometimes conveying doubt that the spiritual is possible and at other times affirming poetry as a means of achieving it.

In "Setting Denise Levertov's High Drama to Music for High Liturgy" Karen Fuchs describes the process of composing music for "On a Theme from Julian's Chapter XX." Guided by Levertov's essays that elucidate how she achieves the music of her poetry, Fuchs explains the decisions that entered into creating her score. She finds Levertov's poem to be the perfect vehicle for conveying Christ's pain and suffering that are commemorated through the Roman Catholic Good Friday liturgy and chose that setting in which to present Levertov's poem.

In "Wisdom Hath Builded Her House," Ann Waldman raises a number of questions about Levertov's spiritual beliefs and the implications for her poetry. In particular, does faith limit or enhance the poet's power? Waldman finds her answer in Levertov's essay "A Poet's View," where Levertov addresses the relationship between her religion and her art, and in selected poems, both early and late, through which the reader can judge the effect of Levertov's convictions on her work.

Paul Lacey's "Wanderer and Pilgrim; Poet and Person" shows the importance of the theme of the journey to Levertov's life and work. In her early poetry Lacey sees her more clearly as the self-assured pilgrim being guided toward transformation by her muse, which is always present although sometimes out of sight. Later, cumbered by concern over the world's injustices, she becomes the wanderer, her destination uncertain and her muse found only in passive waiting. Finally, though still conscious of the world's woes, she becomes "a tested blend of pilgrim/wanderer," guided not only by the muse but also by her Christian faith and the example of others. She has learned the importance of persisting in the journey and has become the example for others to follow.

Despite her careful, detailed explanations of her own techniques and discussions of poetics in general, Denise Levertov had little regard for most "scholarly writing" about poetry, believing instead that the experience of reading the poem—not the essay about the poem—was what mattered; still, we believe that literary criticism at its best enhances the reading of a literary work. While respecting her views, we hope that this volume will serve as a tribute to the life and work of a gifted poet.

Works Cited

Levertov, Denise. *Breathing the Water*. New York: New Directions, 1987.

———. *A Door in the Hive*. New York: New Directions, 1989.

———. *Footprints*. New York: New Directions, 1972.

———. *The Jacob's Ladder*. New York: New Directions, 1961.

———. *Life in the Forest*. New York: New Directions, 1978.

———. *New & Selected Essays*. New York: New Directions, 1992.

———. *Oblique Prayers*. New York: New Directions, 1984.

———. *O Taste and See*. New York: New Directions, 1964.

———. *Overland to the Islands*. Highlands: Jonathon Williams, 1958.

———. *The Poet in the World*. New York: New Directions, 1973.

———. *Relearning the Alphabet*. New York: New Directions, 1970.

———. *Sands of the Well*. New York: New Directions, 1996.

———. *The Sorrow Dance*. New York: New Directions, 1966.

———. *Tesserae*. New York: New Directions, 1995.

———. *This Great Unknowing: Last Poems*. New York: New Directions, 1999.

———. *With Eyes at the Back of Our Heads*. New York: New Directions, 1959.

Moffet, Penelope. "Levertov: A Poet Heeds the Socio-political Call." *Conversations with Denise Levertov*. Ed. Jewel Spears Brooker. Jackson: U of Mississippi P, 1998. 4-27.

Sutton, Walter. "A Conversation with Denise Levertov." *Conversations with Denise Levertov*. Ed. Jewel Spears Brooker. Jackson: U of Mississippi P, 1998.

Contributors

Emily Archer, who holds a Ph.D. from Georgia State University, is an independent scholar, teacher, and poet whose work has appeared in *Cross Currents*, *The Merton Annual*, *Studies in the Literary Imagination*, and *Poetry for Students*, a Gale Research series. Her conversation with Denise Levertov in June 1997, one of the poet's last interviews, appears in *Image*, Vol. 18. She lives in Mount Vernon, New Hampshire, with her husband and two daughters.

Ed Block is Professor of English at Marquette University, Milwaukee, Wisconsin. He is also editor of *Renascence: Essays on Values in Literature*. He received his Ph.D. in English and comparative literature from Stanford University. He has published widely on Victorian literature as well as on the relations of science, literature and values in the Victorian era. His book, *Rituals of Dis-Integration: Romance and Madness in the Victorian Psychomythic Tale* appeared in 1993. He interviewed Denise Levertov for a special Levertov issue of *Renascence* and has presented numerous papers on her poetry and thought.

A friend of Denise Levertov's since the late 1940s, **Robert Creeley** shares with her an intense commitment to the poetics of William Carlos Williams. Creeley has published numerous collections of poetry, prose and criticism, among them *For Love*, *Pieces*, *Later*, and *Life & Death*. He was awarded the Bollingen Prize in 1999 and is a member of the Academy of Arts and Letters.

Anne-Marie Cusac is Managing Editor of *The Progressive* magazine, a former Wallace Stegner Fellow in poetry, and the recipient of a Wisconsin Arts Individual Artist Grant. Her poems have appeared in *TriQuarterly*, *The American Scholar*, *Provincetown Arts*, and other journals. Her investigative reporting for *The Progressive* has won several national awards, including a 1996 George Polk Award.

Karen Marie Fuchs, a senior majoring in Liberal Arts at Auburn University Montgomery, is preparing to become a high school English teacher. Besides her work as a medical transcriptionist for a group of orthopedic surgeons, she is a lifelong musician and, presently, Director of Music for St. Bede's Catholic Church in Montgomery, Alabama.

James Gallant is Professor of English at Elms College in Chicopee, Massachusetts, where he teaches courses in Medieval studies and American literature. His doctorate is from the University of Connecticut at Storrs. He has published articles on Levertov, William Morris, and the Pre-Raphaelites. A published poet, he recalls fondly attending several poetry readings and a writing workshop given by Levertov at Assumption College in the early 1970s.

Sam Hamill is the author of more than thirty books, including celebrated translations from Chinese (*The Essential Chuang Tzu*; *Crossing the Yellow River*; *The Art of Writing*), Japanese (*The Essential Basho*; *Only Companion*; Kobayashi Issa's *The Spring of My Life*), ancient Greek (*The Infinite Moment*), Latin, and Estonian, and a dozen volumes of original poetry, including *Destination Zero: Poems 1970–1995* and *Gratitude*. He is Founding Editor at Copper Canyon Press and directs the Port Townsend Writers' Conference.

Katherine Hanson is a graduate student in the English doctoral program at Marquette University. As editorial assistant for the *Renascence* journal, she participated in the production of a special issue dedicated to the poetry of Denise Levertov. Her primary research interests are American women poets, especially Emily Dickinson, Denise Levertov, and Mary Oliver, and literature and the environment.

Victoria Frenkel Harris is Professor of English at Illinois State University where she specializes in literary criticism and theory, cultural approaches to literature, women's studies, and contemporary poetry. She has published extensively on poet Robert Bly, including her book of 1991, *The Incorporative Consciousness of Robert Bly* (Southern Illinois UP). She has also written on poets Gwendolyn Brooks, James Wright, Adrienne Rich, and Denise Levertov; and her articles have appeared in *American Poetry*, *The Centennial Review*, *Contemporary Poetry*, and *Plainsong*.

Tammy Hearn graduated in 1999 with a Master of Liberal Arts from Auburn University Montgomery, where she is now an adjunct instructor for the Department of English and Philosophy. Interested in all the humanities, but in religion and philosophy in particular, she wrote her master's thesis on the philosophy of Aldous Huxley.

Currently Associate Professor of English at the University of Las Palmas in the Canary Islands, **José Rodríguez Herrera** teaches twentieth-century American literature and literary translation there. After receiving a four-year grant from the Spanish government in 1994 to do research on U.S. women's poetry after World War II, he was invited by Charles Bernstein to the Poetics Program at the State University of New York (Buffalo) where he carried out research involving some of Denise Levertov's manuscripts as well as her correspondence with poet Robert Duncan. In 1995 he made a research visit to the Department of Special Collections at Stanford University to continue his studies of Levertov's manuscripts and her correspondence with other poets, among them William Carlos Williams and Robert Creeley. He has published various articles on Denise Levertov, both inside and outside of Spain.

Paul Lacey has taught English, humanities, and a variety of cross- or multi-disciplinary courses at Earlham College, a Quaker College in Richmond, Indiana, since 1960, and earned his Ph.D. from Harvard in 1966. A distinguished teacher and expert on faculty development, his book *Growing into Goodness: Essays on Quaker Education* (Pendle Hill) appeared in 1999. He is also author of *The Inner War: Forms and Themes in Recent American Poetry* (1972), which includes Levertov, and several other articles on her work. He is Denise Levertov's literary executor.

Anne Colclough Little, who received her Ph.D. from the University of South Carolina, is Associate Professor of English at Auburn University Montgomery. She has co-edited two books and published articles on such writers as William Faulkner and James Gould Cozzens. One of her essays was included in the special Levertov edition of *Renascence*.

Denise E. Lynch is Professor of English at Central Connecticut State University where she has served on the faculty since 1969. She received her Ph.D. from Fordham University with a specialty in seventeenth-century British literature. Her interest in Denise Levertov grew out of peace activities in the 1970s and led to publications in *Sagetrieb*, *The Explicator*, *The Journal of Imagism*, *Connecticut Review*, and *Renascence*. Her other publications include articles on Herbert, Marvell, and Atwood.

Christopher MacGowan, born in London, England, is Professor of English at the College of William and Mary where he has taught since 1984. Since receiving his Ph.D. from Princeton University, he has coedited, with A.W. Litz, *The Collected Poems of William Carlos Williams, Vol. I: 1909–1939* (1986) and edited both *The Collected Poems of William Carlos William, Vol. II: 1939–1962* (1988) and *Paterson* (1992). *The Letters of Denise Levertov and William Carlos Williams*, which he also edited, appeared in 1998, and he is currently preparing a history of twentieth-century American Poetry for Blackwells.

Harry Marten is Edward E. Hale, Jr., Professor of English at Union College. He is author of *Understanding Denise Levertov* and *The Art of Knowing: The Poetry and Prose of Conrad Aiken*. He has also published in *Agenda*, *Contemporary Literature*, *ELH*, *The Gettysburg Review*, *New England Review*, *The New York Times Book Review*, *The Washington Post Book World*, and elsewhere.

Jerome Mazzaro recently retired from the State University of New York at Buffalo where he taught for more than thirty years. He is the author of three books of poetry—*Changing the Windows* (1966), *The Caves of Love* (1985), and *Rubbings* (1985)—as well as books of criticism, including *The Poetic Themes of Robert Lowell* (1965), *Transformations in the Renaissance English Lyric* (1970), *William Carlos Williams: The Later Poems* (1973), *Postmodern American Poetry* (1980), and *The Figure of Dante* (1981). A second article on Levertov's work can be found in Linda Wagner-Martin's *Critical Essays on Denise Levertov* (1991).

Dorothy Nielsen teaches English literature at Brescia College in London, Ontario. She has published articles on ecology and literature, mystical/political poetry, and politics and poetry, concerning writers like Denise Levertov, W.S. Merwin, Gary Snyder, and Timothy Findley.

Gary Pacernick is Professor of English at Wright State University. His publications include *The Jewish Poems* and *Something Is Happening* (poetry); *Memory and Fire: Ten American Jewish Poets* and *Sing a New Song: Post-Holocaust American Jewish Poetry* (criticism). He has also edited the letters of David Ignatow and from 1974 to 1990 edited and published *Images*.

Susie Paul is Associate Professor of English at Auburn University Montgomery where she teaches modern and American poetry as well as the creative writing of poetry. Her own poetry has appeared in *Negative Capability, Georgia Review, Kalliope,* and, most recently, *Amaryllis.*

Eric Sterling, who holds a Ph.D. from Indiana University, is an Associate Professor of English at Auburn University Montgomery. He has published articles on various authors, including Shakespeare, Spenser, Jonson, and Edward Albee. He has recently completed a book entitled *Social Conscience and the Holocaust* and is currently working on a book called *The Ghettos During the Holocaust.* His published articles on the Holocaust include essays on Arthur Miller, Rolf Hochhuth, Shimon Wincelberg, Nelly Sachs, Flannery O'Connor, Janusz Kurczak, and bystanders.

Anne Waldman, poet, teacher, editor, performer, has published over thirty books and pamphlets of her own poetry, including *Fast Speaking Woman* (City Lights), *Makeup On Empty Space* (Toothpaste), *Makeup On Empty Space* (Coffee House), *Kill or Cure* (Penguin Poets) and *Iovis, Books I & II* (Coffee House). She has also edited several anthologies, including *Out of This World* (Crown), *Disembodied Poetics, Annals of the Jack Kerouac School* (with Andrew Schelling) (U of New Mexico), and *The Beat Book* (Shambala). She has also founded and edited several small press publishing ventures, including The World Magazine, Angel Hair Magazine & Books, Rocky Ledge Cottage Editions, and most currently Erudite Fangs (the title comes from avant-garde poet Mina Loy). She has worked collaboratively with other small press publishers in Boulder including last generation press and Brad O'Sullivan's Smokeproof Press. She directed The Poetry Project at St. Mark's Church In-the-Bowery in New York City for a decade. She co-founded The Jack Kerouac School of Disembodied Poetics at the Naropa Institute in Boulder, Colorado, in 1974 (where she still teaches) and moved permanently to Boulder in 1976. As an internationally known poet/performer, she has given readings most recently at The Casa de la Poesia in Caracas, Venezuela, at the City Lights bookstore in Florence, Italy, The San Jose Art Museum in California, and at The Schule fur Dichtung in Vienna. She has received a NEA fellowship and was the recipient of the Shelley Memorial Award for Poetry for 1996.

"Some of the Bone Has Gone Missing"
(Post-Transplant Nurse)

for Denise Levertov

by Lucille Clifton

and so i am limping now,
denise,
only slightly but where
and when i walk
it is more slowly, with less grace

still the same odd girl inside
still moving forward   but i notice
many of us are limping now,
something has gone missing
from us, part of our bone that was
you.

Valentines Park:
"a Place of Origin"

Christopher MacGowan

In the "Autobiographical Sketch" (1984) which closes her *New and Selected Essays* Denise Levertov names two public parks close to her parents' home in the London suburb of Ilford as among the important influences on her childhood and adolescent years. The personal history with which they are associated in the essay matches their role in a number of her poems:

> Romantic and beautiful Wanstead and Valentines parks, frequent expeditions into the Essex countryside with my sister, and my mother's very strong sense of history, developed in me a taste for seeking-out and exploring the vanishing traces of the village Ilford which London had engulfed. (*NSE* 260)

In this prose summary the qualities of Valentines Park and Wanstead Park are combined, but usually they represent distinct kinds of landscape and associations within their shared context of Levertov's early childhood and adolescence in Ilford. The River Roding sometimes serves, appropriately, as a divider between these distinct qualities. The Roding forms the boundary between the western part of Ilford, containing Valentines Park, and the eastern part of Wanstead—in fact running along the eastern boundary of Wanstead Park. (The boroughs of Ilford and Wanstead were combined in 1964 to form the Greater London Borough of Redbridge.)

One early poem that examines this part of the poet's complex heritage is "A Map of the Western Part of the County of Essex in England": "I am Essex born ... / the little streams of Valentines heard my resolves" the poem records. It moves on, via the Roding, which "held my head above water when I thought it was / drowning me," to the "basic poetry" of Wanstead Park and

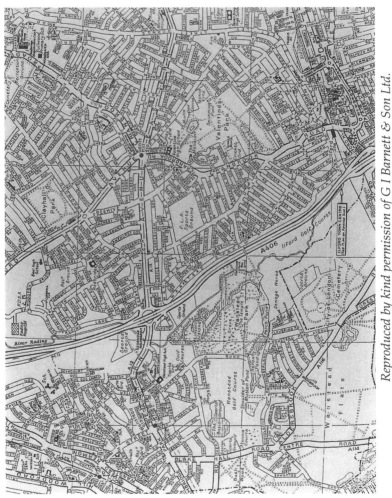

ghostly reminders of that site's history. Wanstead's broader history, "bass-viols among its golden dead leaves," stretches back further than the personal "resolves" committed to the streams of Valentines (*P1* 21). Similarly, in the autobiographical volume *Tesserae*, again contrasting Wanstead Park with Valentines, Levertov calls "Wanstead Park, a more ancient and romantic domain. The interior … was the one place considered out-of-bounds" (60).

Wanstead Park is usually in her work associated with memories of adolescence, and often with personal loss—as in the *Tesserae* essay above, and in the "Olga Poems":

> I never crossed the bridge over the Roding, dividing
> the open field of the present from the mysteries,
> the wraiths and shifts of time-sense Wanstead Park held suspended,
> without remembering your eyes. Even when we were estranged....
>
> (*P1* 209)

Wanstead's rich history and more mature personal associations provide a link to the landscapes of years beyond childhood, such as the Hampstead Heath of "Chekhov on the West Heath" (in *Life in the Forest*). This landscape, like that of Wanstead, fuses personal memories (the continuing friendship with Rebecca Garnett, later mourned in *Evening Train*'s "For Bet" [56], and reading Chekhov) with a fuller history of the place—the poem incorporating some of Hampstead's most famous writers and painters.

In a section of the "Olga Poems" earlier than the memory of Wanstead Park quoted above, Valentines is associated with an escape dream of the two sisters, where a protruding root could be imagined a raised trapdoor descending "long steps to another country / where we would live without father or mother" (208)—although the paraphrased voice is Olga's. In contrast to Wanstead, Valentines is the landscape of late childhood, the beginnings of a sensed power to dream imaginatively—but one connected back often to parents and home, even if by their imagined absence as in the passage above. Valentines Park is also the site of the first of the "wells" that recur in Levertov's poetry, moving from the actual Wishing Well in the park to become through poems across several volumes a rich metaphor embodying multiple levels of time, exploration, self-discovery, and understanding. Valentines Park is a landscape at once both more distant from her mature years than Wanstead, yet one more often returned to. In "The Well," "Living Alone," "The Stricken Children," and "Something More," poems written over thirty-five years, Valentines Park—increasingly and self-consciously a mental as well as an actual site—is "a place of origin," a starting and returning point for reflections upon journeys, loves, identity, and that "Something More" which such a place can reveal, for Levertov, of our final condition.

While the Valentine Mansion, although not open to the public and thus not part of the park's amenities, remains standing in its grounds, the 18th-century Wanstead House—once the home of Richard Rich, a former Chancellor of England and later of Robert Dudley, Earl of Leicester—was demolished in 1824: "through its trees the ghost of a great house" as Levertov describes her experience of Wanstead Park in "A Map of the Western Park of the County of Essex in England." The difference between the status of the mansions is appropriate perhaps for a landscape closer to home and childhood in Levertov's poetry, and the other more associated with loss and an unrecoverable past. The Wanstead manor figures in the history of Henry VII and Henry VIII. In 1553 Mary Tudor, progressing to London to be crowned, paused to receive her sister, Princess Elizabeth, at Wanstead, while both James I and Charles I often visited Wanstead House (*Victoria, Vol. VI* 322–26). The approximately 200 acres comprising the park were purchased by the Corporation of London and formally opened in 1882, the same year that Queen Victoria dedicated adjacent Epping Forest an area exempt from future encroachments of development. Unlike Valentines, which is maintained as an urban public park, Wanstead Park is managed, as an official Corporation of London publication puts it, "with a view to preserving its historic character as a private park." In practice this means preserving the character of the park as if it were a "pasturage for deer and cattle" but without the animals; working with "the long-term processes of nature" as opposed to the formal patterning of Valentines.

Valentines Park has itself a history going back four centuries, although its existence as an urban space is tied to modern development—the engulfing of "village Ilford" by London. The park's 125 acres was less than five minutes walk from the Levertoffs'[1] home at 5 Mansfield Road. Its lake, canal, and formal landscaping cover part of what were once the grounds of a 17th-century estate.

The medieval village of Ilford grew out of an area associated with the manor of Barking and the 7th century founding of Barking Abbey. The estate of Valentines developed out of the 1539 dis-

---

[1]Levertov changed the spelling of her name before the publication of her second book *Here and Now*.

solution of the abbey. The late 17th-century Valentines mansion constructed on the site, probably by James Chadwick, was extensively rebuilt in the 18th century with further changes in 1811, and the house survives in the northern part of the park. (For a photograph see Tasker 87.) According to one local history, the name Valentine derives from a family noted in 17th-century records, including a 1684 mention of John Valentine in Barking Parish Church accounts, and a Christopher Valentine who lived in a small farmhouse around 1605 (*Ilford Old and New* 15).

The large estates that still formed most of 19th-century Ilford began to be sold off at an increasing rate in the second half of the century as Ilford's population numbers exploded—a growth that had accelerated with the coming of a major branch of the Great Eastern Railway in 1839. The population grew from 5,405 in 1861 to almost 11,000 in 1891 and four times that just ten years later. By 1911 Ilford was becoming a dormitory town of London. The area that now forms Valentines Park was saved from development by a combination of the generosity of the last family to occupy the mansion and a community effort to save the grounds for public use.

The modern park developed over a series of stages. In 1898 the town council purchased the lake and some surrounding land from Mrs. Sarah Ingleby, long-time resident of Valentines Mansion, and the following year another eighteen and a half acres. The resulting public space, of forty-seven acres, was named "Central Park" and opened in September 1899. In 1906, upon Mrs. Ingleby's death, her son donated a further ten acres and in 1907 the council purchased another thirty-seven, including the house. A campaign to save at least some of the remaining grounds from development resulted in 1912 in the town's purchase of another twenty-two acres, including the House and outbuildings. The area of the present day park was completed in 1924, the year after Levertov's birth, with the purchase of an adjacent nine acres. (For a history of the manor of Barking, and of the Valentines estate, see *Victoria, Vol. V* 190–92, 211–12.)

The features of the park still combine its two identities, as formal estate and community recreation area. Within the grounds are the boating lake, an aviary, bowling greens, facilities for football, cricket and tennis, a miniature golf course, and a children's play area. But although the grass is well manicured and most of the recreational facilities at least minimally maintained, a number of the park's former facilities have closed, been removed, or changed—including an open air swimming pool, now grassed over. Some of the park's features, including the mansion and some that figure in Levertov's poems, are clearly suffering from neglect, a neglect that itself becomes a theme in "The Stricken Children." The grounds, once kept by a resident Head Gardener, "Pa Taylor," who had started as a gardener's boy under the last private owner of the estate, are now maintained by outside contractors.

In the 1961 poem "The Well," from *The Jacob's Ladder* (*P1* 40–41), Valentines Park is termed "a place of origin." Although the phrase is also used later of the West Heath in "Chekhov on the West Heath," in "The Well" the idea of origin is linked to the childhood discovery of language, communication, "the muse," and love. The narrative centers upon a series of transformations watched from a "bridge of one span" crossing a stream that flows into Valentines lake, and eventually under Cranbrook Road and into the Roding. The actor and teacher in the poem is "the Muse" herself who, watched by the poem's first-person spectator, "wades into deep water" to "fill her pitcher." The Muse's face resembles "the face of the young actress who played / Miss Annie Sullivan," the tutor of Helen Keller (Anne Bancroft both on Broadway and in the film *The Miracle Worker* [1962]). The landscape is transformed "to Valentines," although the allusion to Bancroft has clearly placed the experience itself in the poet's present. The famous moment of communication between Sullivan and Keller, Sullivan spelling out "water" in the palm of her pupil's hand, is then paralleled to the pursuit of the river god Alpheus [Alpheius] for Arethusa, who had been turned into a spring by Artemis. The god's journey and the final mingling of the waters at Ortygia is fused with the flow of Valentines' water into the Roding, and with the poet's present and past experience (across the waters of the Atlantic), as finally "I feel the word 'water'/ spelled in my left palm." Valentines, the name's associations with love also central here, is the "place of origin" in which poetry and language first touch the life of the poet.

Fourteen years later, Valentines Park serves as one end of the spectrum of time covered in the three-poem sequence "Living Alone" (*The Freeing of the Dust* 59 [1975]), itself one of a series about the end of Levertov's marriage to Mitchell Goodman. The poem's opening mood, "anything can happen," carries the poet toward a "home" that is now Somerville, near Boston: "Davis Square and the all-night / cafeteria and the pool hall." And this mood of optimistic, open-ended expectation becomes a "childhood's song … / sung in Valentines Park or on steep streets in the map of my mind / in the hush of suppertime." The memory of Valentines Park, more overtly here a mental landscape, is fused with a landscape of the present, to form a promising "solitude" with love still possible—and through the "song," again with self expression. This mood changes with the silence and threatened barrenness of the second poem in the sequence, a threat relieved in the third poem, which looks to a future that serves as the other end of the spectrum to Valentines' beginning.

The presence of Valentines in this sequence allows for romantic promise. Another poem from the same volume that, fusing continents and times, remembers Ilford but not the park, has quite a different tone. "Don't You Hear That Whistle Blowin' …" describes a dream set in the bedroom of Mansfield Road, only yards from the railroad tracks that changed "village Ilford," evoked by the sounds of a freight train in the Boston night. The connection is broken upon waking, as the marriage is itself breaking.

Where loss is associated with Valentines Park it is a loss for others, deeply regretted, but one from which the poet can "move away, walking fast," as "The Stricken Children" (in *Breathing the Water* [1987]) puts it. This poem is centrally about a Valentines Park landmark, its Wishing Well, and makes explicit the Park's role in Levertov's childhood as a place of "departure" into imaginative journeys, but also its transformation by 1987 into a mental, memory landscape from which she has and will depart for other journeys—journeys that received their initial impetus from this special place. The poem examines the literal drying up and suppressing of that source for a current generation through the condition of the actual well, as she revisits it:

> The Wishing Well was a spring
> bubbling clear and soundless into a shallow pool
> less than three feet across, a hood of rocks
> protecting it, smallest of grottoes, from falling leaves....
>
> This was the place from which
> year after year in childhood I demanded my departure,
> my journeying forth into the world of magical
> cities, mountains, otherness—the place which gave
> what I asked, and more …
>   I returned this year …
> And I found the well
> filled to the shallow brim

> with debris of a culture's sickness—
> with bottles, tins, paper, plastic—(33)

The Valentines Wishing Well lies in the grounds to the north of the mansion, hidden to some extent by shrubbery and a winding path. Local historian Herbert Lockwood notes that "the Well in this form and under this name would appear to have been the creation of early nineteenth century romanticism." But he speculates that the well, also known as "The Bishop's Well," might "echo some more ancient tradition of a sacred or holy well," perhaps evidenced by the "Romano-British burial found in a neighboring field in 1724 … [and] a funerary urn found in the same field a few years later" (Lockwood, letter to CM). The Well remains, in 1999, filled with rubbish, although apparently undamaged. A photograph of the Well from the 1920s is reproduced in Don Hewson's *From Ilford to Hainault* (32) (p. 11 herein). Ironically, the site in Valentines Park now sometimes known as "The Wishing Well" is a conventionally designed, circular brick-walled well beside the lake, dating from 1972 and intended explicitly for fund-raising. By contrast, Levertov's poem remembers "No one threw money in, one had to search / for the right stone." This other well is also, however, presently in something of the condition that "The Stricken Children" describes of the Wishing Well.

The poem, as an endnote in *Breathing the Water* points out, was originally titled "In Thatcher's England," a title Levertov writes there that she found "appropriate but … too restrictive." Nevertheless, the original title suggests more explicitly the extent of time and cultural change since the poet's childhood experience. "Thatcher's England" is far removed from Levertov's England. The association of the Prime Minister with the area itself has a particular personal relevance. Sir Winston Churchill served as adjacent Wanstead and Woodford's Member of Parliament for forty years, while Clement Attlee, Churchill's wartime deputy leader and Britain's first post-war Prime Minister, also lived nearby, both associations proudly claimed in the Borough of Redbridge's publicity, and both politicians, of course, in power during Levertov's last years of living in Ilford.

The wishing well appears again in a more metaphorical guise in a later poem in *Breathing the Water*, titled just like the 1961 poem, "The Well" (37). Here the well is associated with "dark nights of deep sleep / that I dreamed the most, sunk in the well," at the age of sixteen—and the sleep within that well brings a beauty and

The wishing well in Valentines Park in the 1920s.
Reproduced by permission of Brian Evans

power greater than the physical beauty craved in the teenager's waking thoughts.

The metaphor of "the well" takes on an even fuller inclusiveness in the title poem of the last collection that Levertov published in her lifetime, *Sands of the Well* (1996). The poem's spiritual reach is reinforced by the context of its surrounding poems. The site of "the well" is not specified in this poem, but in an earlier section, at the center of the book, "Something More" (63) again recalls Valentines Park and the self-conscious mythology that its landscape has taken on in her work:

> Sometimes I'd make of Valentines, long ago,
> a wilder place than it was—
> the sluice where a man-made lake spilled into Cranbrook
> perceived as a cascade huge in mesmeric power:
> I'd lean my arms on the 'rustic' fence
> and gaze myself into almost-trance.

In this poem the landscape of Valentines is put into the context of the "sly charm of mountain rills in Wales"—a landscape associated elsewhere with her mother's upbringing, appropriate for Valentines' associations with childhood, and part of this volume's juxtaposition of earthly times against the perspective of the spiritual. The fusion of Valentines with Wales also introduces one of the allusions to Wordsworth that thread through Levertov's work at least as far back as "Stepping Westward" in *The Sorrow Dance* (1967). "Something More" particularly recalls Wordsworth's "Intimations of Immortality from Recollections of Early Childhood," in its exploration of a parallel spiritual landscape alongside the landscape of childhood discovery. Wordsworth's "trailing clouds of glory" is echoed in Levertov's "robes of glory," although in Levertov's case characteristically applied to the landscape rather than to the child, in keeping with the poem's insistence upon concrete detail even as it acknowledges adding "something more":

> But even in childhood I knew
> the difference, saw with a double vision.
> And I've found the custom gives, in time,
> new spirit to fact—or restores it. Places
> reveal, as it were, their longings. Inherent dreams.

The poem celebrates the additions that imagination adds to memory "in time" as part of the process of revelation that moves beyond mere fact.

Time has wrought changes in the Park itself as it appears in this poem. The "'rustic' fence" across the bridge is now gone, replaced by a more mundane barrier of metal piping and wire mesh. One artery of the "sluice" whose "stonework channels" the poem recalls carried water that "spilled into Cranbrook" is dry above the bridge, and filled with stagnant water below, although what looks like a later channel nearby still serves as an overflow to Valentines lake. Two photographs from Brian Page and Joyce Piggott's *Ilford Old and New: Volume 3, 1865–1987* (15) (p. 14 herein) show the rustic bridge in 1905 and the modern replacement in 1987.

The role of Valentines Park and its relation to Wanstead Park in Levertov's work is summed up in a key chapter in *Tesserae* (1995). In keeping with the spiritual dimension accorded Valentines in "Something More," the chapter, "The Last of Childhood," is subtitled "For Jean, In This Life or the Next." The story incorporates the range of discovery and loss as played out in the world of childhood, and against the looming complications of adolescence.

The important friendship with Jean Rankin began when both responded to what is apparently the same formal waterfall in Valentines that is remembered in "Something More." The same term, "mesmeric," describes the spot that brought the eight and nine year old together, although here remembered factually as "small" rather than as the huge "cascade" of the poem's accumulated memories and levels of time and place. "Jean and I met in the park, both gazing into a small but mesmeric waterfall" and the friendship continues to be associated with Valentines' waters. "We left notes for each other in a certain hole in the bank of the stream—our post office" (59). Most of the imaginative adventures and games, the chapter recounts, centered around "the weekdays we played in Valentines," although "sometimes on Saturdays we'd go to the outskirts of Wanstead Park, a more ancient and romantic domain" (60). The trivial dispute that ended the friendship, and that across the years Levertov so regrets initiating, occurred in Wanstead Park, not Valentines. "This episode has been, throughout my adult life, a matter of shame and regret to me" (63). Levertov acknowledges that both children were on "the threshold of change," in her own case moving towards the greater influence of her sister Olga. She rediscovered Jean Rankin briefly during the Second World War in London, and again years later in Chicago, but then mislaid a crucial note of her married name. "Who knows—" the chapter concludes, reaching across time from the poet's seventies to the hours in Valentines Park, "maybe she will

Waterfall, Valentines Park, 1905.
Reproduced by permission of Brian Piggott

The same view taken in 1987.
Reproduced by permission of Brian Piggott

read this book, and at least know that I have not forgotten those two years that were the last of our real childhood, and the very best of it" (64). The chapter itself becomes a Valentine, a greeting to be received "In This Life or the Next." As elsewhere in her work, Valentines Park serves as a locus of memory, origin, dreams—and finally a hope that incorporates the actual and the mental landscape into a condition transcending time and space. Rooted in a landscape that arose out of the history of Barking Abbey, childhood dreams become adult faith.

Works Cited

Hewson, Don. *From Ilford to Hainault*. Stroud, Gloucs.: Sutton, 1996.

Levertov, Denise. *Breathing the Water*. New York: New Directions, 1987.

———. *Evening Train*. New York: New Directions, 1992.

———. *The Freeing of the Dust*. New York: New Directions, 1975.

———. *Life in the Forest*. New York: New Directions, 1978.

———. *New & Selected Essays*. New York: New Directions, 1992.

———. *Poems 1960–1967*. New York: New Directions, 1983.

———. *Sands of the Well*. New York: New Directions, 1996.

———. *Tesserae: Memories and Suppositions*. New York: New Directions, 1995.

Lockwood, Herbert H. Letter to Christopher MacGowan, 5 April 1999.

Page, Brian, and Joyce Piggott. *Ilford Old and New: Volume 3, 1865–1987*. Ilford: B Piggott, c. 1987.

Tasker, George. *Ilford Past and Present*. Ilford: Hayden, 1901.

Victoria History of the County of Essex, Vol. V. London: University of London Institute of Historical Research, 1966.

Victoria History of the County of Essex, Vol. VI. London: University of London Institute of Historical Research, 1973.

Denise Levertov and the Lyric of the Contingent Self

Victoria Frenkel Harris

Almost twenty years ago, Charles Altieri described what he perceived to be an "unresolvable dichotomy" between "a poetics of immediate experience," which he associated with the work of Robert Bly, James Wright, and Denise Levertov, and "a poetics acknowledging its status as discourse," which he associated with a group of "younger poets" including Robert Haas, Louise Glück, and Steven Dunn (191). The "crucial differences" between a "poet of discourse" such as Dunn and poets of "immediacy" such as Bly and Levertov "are the presence [in Dunn's work] of a mind willing to achieve seriousness by playing self-consciously with its own metaphoric details and a thematic sense of the poem as artful discourse rather than intense act of perception" (207). Altieri's influential essay marked contemporary criticism and theory's turn away from "lyric consciousness," especially what Tilottama Rajan terms its outmoded model of "a unified person realizing himself through his language" (196). Such a view, Rajan continues, evinces a totalizing "will to transcendental privacy," an "ontology" that "transforms difference into sameness," the regressive "homogenization of the signifier and the signified" (206, 199, 197).

More recently, attempts have been made to recuperate the lyric from charges of ahistoricism, transcendentalism, transparency, and monovocality. Some of the more notable of these attempts may be found in Mark Jeffreys' recent essay collection *New Definitions of Lyric: Theory, Technology, and Culture*. In her contribution to the volume, for example, Dorothy M. Nielsen argues that Levertov's "environmental concerns" forced her to reevaluate "the transcendental individual," which led the poet to forge a paradoxical "postmodernist lyric" that resists "the transcendent lyric subject" while simultaneously acknowledging "the need for a poetic subject" (128, 136). Yet Marjorie Perloff's spirited response to the essays in the collection demonstrates that, in an era presided over by the mantra "Only historicize," rehabilitation of the lyric mode will not be easy. Using Levertov's 1995 lyric "Crow Springs" as an example, Perloff insists that, unlike the Romantic lyric, which "reflected a moment in history when the individual was held to be unique," in our present moment lyric poems must inevitably be viewed as "politically suspect" (250, 246).

> [T]he rhetoric of "Crow Springs" suggests that there is no such thing as cultural construction, no social class, race, or gender. [Levertov's] universal "I" simply addresses other such abstract selves.... Levertov relies on the mere appearance of poeticity ("Look! I'm a lyric poem!") to assert a relationship to nature that is nowhere convincingly rendered. "Crow Springs" is very skill-ful in its choice of adjectives and verbs, but it finally leaves the reader with a "so what?" feeling. So what if these unknown "friends" are gone? So what if the poet sensitively describes the crows' movements? Who really cares?.... The problem—and it is by no means just Levertov's problem—is that the basic human-natural correspondence no longer has much meaning, that the pathetic fallacy cannot be maintained.... [W]hat need no longer be argued, it seems to me, is that lyric poets writing at the turn of the twenty-first century need do no more than record "sensitive" responses to a generalized outerworld. (253–54)

While my own position is closer to Nielsen's than to Perloff's, it seems largely unexceptionable to me that throughout her career Levertov retained an aesthetics of presence, which bears problems addressed by contemporary critiques pertinent to issues of implied innocence and transparency of language that retain immanence and enable access to an unmediated referent. I also recognize that Levertov at times tacitly attempts to align her consciousness as well as her aesthetics unanalytically with a world more hybrid and complicated than such seamlessness acknowledges.[1] I shall argue, however, that while Levertov has retained an unabashed sense of

---

[1]Levertov seems never to have moved far from her 1979 description of a major direction of her poetry: "a development of a fairly tight, not I hope hermetic, but still, rather—not introspective, that's not the word ei-ther—but a lyric poem that derives much of its imagery from somewhere close to the unconscious, a kind of dream level of image." Kenneth John Atchity, "An Interview with Denise Levertov," in *Conversations with Denise Levertov*, ed. Jewel Spears Brooker (Jackson: UP of Mississippi, 1998), 107.

subjective identity, her sense of self is neither immutable nor recidivist, stopping short of—or, for reasons to be touched upon, *exceeding*—the Cartesian subject who is complete(d) and witness, as such, to the world as other. Culture and society, furthermore, are in no way ideally or mythically construed in her poems. Although Levertov may not self-consciously interrogate the notion of subjectivity, the subject expressed in her poems is never self-enclosed but always in process. While she endorses the necessity of vision, vision is never mere passive reception but always an active receptivity that is both modulated by agency and situated within an arena of social involvement and activism.

In *Social Values and Poetic Acts: The Historical Judgment of Literary Work*, Jerome J. McGann suggests that sociohistorical critics problematize referentiality by revising the idea of mimesis as reaction to rather than imitation of the other. Such an "operational rather than a mirroring concept of mimesis" insinuates both speaker and referent (130). "'What may be or should be' is always a direct function of 'what is, hath been, or shall be,' and its theory of representation holds that art imitates not merely the 'fact' and the 'ideal,' but also the dynamic relation which operates between the two" (128). Just as McGann invests the speaker with ethical and aesthetic agency and the world with facts, poetic representation becomes an historicized cite that immanentist critiques might overlook. Likewise, Levertov may be regarded as both a polemical force and a situated being. In a poem foreboding ecological disaster, for example, Levertov admonishes those who rely on the past, whose "feet pull [them] towards / away from now …," whose "fears are only the old fears, antique / anxieties, how graceful; / they lay as cloaks on shoulders / of men long dead, / skirts of sorrow wrapped / over the thighs of legendary women" ("The Sun Going Down upon Our Wrath," *F* 35). Levertov does not figure herself as unimmersed in the plight of contingent, daily existence—a charge aimed often at practitioners of the "lyric consciousness."[2] On the contrary, spiritual strength in her poems is always tested by the complexities of present-day realities. Hypothesizing the capacity of a spirituality informed and motivated by

---

[2]In his essay "'All Wi Don': Tony Harrison, Linton Kwesi Johnson, and the Cultural Work of Lyric in Postwar Britain," for example, Kevin McGuirk maintains that the cultural "exemption" of the "lyric consciousness" is founded on "non-contingent realms of nature, art, or spirit." In Jeffreys, 54.

global concerns, for example, Levertov inquires in "The Sun Going Down" if there were "time to warn you, / if you believed there shall be / never again a green blade ... / if you were warned and believed / the warning, // would your beauty / break into spears of fire, // fire to turn fire, a wall / of refusal, could there be / a reversal...."

She concludes this poem not with a transcendental vision from a decontextualized purview, one indeed removing her from the conditions of potential ecological disaster, but by questioning—while proffering—a vision of spiritual capacity to reverse natural disaster, all the while admitting that she "cannot // hoist [her]self high enough / to see, / plunge ... deep enough / to know" the limits of spiritual powers. Responsibility is, indeed, placed upon the interpreter—both as poet and as reader—to negotiate a subject position when confronted by an other—here, the poet's (as well as the reader's) spirit in dialectic with her situated present and that which she confronts. Positing ecological awareness alongside spiritual hopefulness—contradictory impulses towards the one and the many, alienation and communion, randomness and purpose, mysticism and politics—will not separate Levertov from the highest ranks of poetic heritage and the promissory mission of eking out the numinous from the realities of that which is contingent, ordinary, and troublingly perilous. Levertov's oeuvre is replete with lyric divagations from the worldly to the spiritual.[3] Yet she never exempts herself "from participation in the anarchic world"[4] by evoking the traditional lyric transcension of historical contingency.

Levertov may be seen, therefore, as attesting to the urgency of maintaining an ongoing cultural conversation in a dialogue that has enabled large modifications of what might be seen—in one sense—as a poetry of sensibility,[5] and these changes have entered the postmodern arena of global, ethical, and ecological concerns negotiated through her strong sense of an ability to focus, forge,

---

[3]See my "The Incorporative Consciousness: Levertov's Journey from Discretion to Unity," *America: Exploration and Travel*, ed. Steven Kagle (Bowling Green: Bowling Green State UP, 1979), 166–90.

[4]The phrase is McGuirk's, in Jeffreys, 54.

[5]According to Jonathan Holden, lyric poetry must be seen as "a poetry of sensibility" because its context, "however obliquely, always refers to the same ultimate source, the author." *The Rhetoric of the Contemporary Lyric* (Bloomington: Indiana UP, 1980), 67.

and resist—continually greeting and reinterpreting while maintaining a confidence about a resilient sense of subjective identity and an unwavering commitment to aesthetic purpose. An activity of othering and interpreting charges the aesthetic operation with an ethical component. The reader as well must wrangle with the portrayal of the interpretation, forcing an act of either endorsement or refusal when facing this aesthetic artifact. Refusal initiates alternative constructions, which resist passivity as well. An image exists in the world, and using the capacity to construe images confounds the positions of realism, referentiality, and objectivism while instigating agency. Bearing witness, furthermore, involves paradigmatic contingency rather than the more Romantic notion of isolated creation. As David Hickey states in *The Invisible Dragon*, "images can change the world" (39). To reckon with also requires recognition, but both dialogism and aestheticism as expectations are revised by a speaker whose priorities are imposed upon our constructions of the world. To create from an arena of recognition implicates the culture in the creature—the imagination continually reigniting with regard to its lived contingencies rather than in isolation from them. The most intelligent reading, consequently, requires the reader most informed of and/or by the intertextual content—an aesthetics, in other words, that is intolerant of any project attempting to be divorced from historical and cultural conditions.

Here, Levertov's insistence upon authoredness (pace Barthes) is an ethical corollary, a symbolic presence at the least, to withstand and resist that which appears to her as—at best—an ethically muddled and—at worst—a doomed population of troubled cultures. One may see, in her early delight in finding out that her Hebrew name, Daleth, means doorway, passageway, for example, a metaphoric portrayal of her resistance to figuring herself as completely socially-constructed while concomitantly accepting the notion of flux. In "To Kevin O'Leary, Wherever He Is" (*F* 26), Levertov rejoices at the discovery of the Hebrew meaning of Denise:

> my name in Hebrew, and its meaning:
>   entrance, exit,
>   way through of giving and receiving,
> which are one.
> Hallelujah! It's as if you'd sent me
> in the U.S. mails
> a well of water,
>   a frog at its brim, and mosses;

> sent me a cold and sweet freshness
> dark to taste.
> > Love from the door,
> > Daleth.

The poem's progression shows Levertov's interpretive processing of that which could easily be taken as received and rather objective denotative knowledge. Her figuring, however, leads to a realization that her place in the poem is central. The reciprocal motion of a passageway apparently stirs up enough creative energy in the poet for her to forge an image that is particular, a cold and sweet freshness, that appeals to the senses of touch, taste, smell, and sight. Her central position in this gesture—occupying a space where centripetal and centrifugal energies meet—locates an authoring source for a synaesthetic mingling, one drawing in and tasting darkness. Moreover, a terrain of the imagination, such synaesthesia itself supplements our reality. Yet, this doorway image has, it seems, much to do with investing the notion of authorship with responsibility—always dealing with that which is incoming and outgoing situates one in a position to continually address a new set of givens and what to make of the givens, this setting of perpetual defamiliarized other being one that resists subsumption as well as totalization. Later, in "The Life of Art" (*DH* 85), Levertov writes: "The borderland—that's where, if one knew how, / one would establish residence." Here, subjectivity denotes more than a swerve from fixity, but—if fixed—it is so only by being persistently the locus of change. She wishes continually "to go / just that much further, beyond the end / beyond whatever ends: to begin, to be, to defy" ("Beyond the End," *HN*). Again, in *With Eyes at the Back of Our Heads*, Levertov avers that the artist "*maintains dialogue with his heart, meets things with his mind*" ("The Artist" 4).

Levertov thus uses poetic identity as resistance to historical vicissitudes, a resistance abetted by the aesthetic impulse to incarnate rather than to refer. But, once the other becomes imaged, its poetic architecture supplants transcendental reference. Thus, what seems to be a recursion here to a transcendental category of truth, even spiritual life, turns out to be an investment that must be negotiated. Time and again, Levertov describes the artist's impulse toward truth as one of having a desire for honesty but in terms always mediated by time and place, of acknowledging experience as an integer involved in constructing any such goal, thereby necessitating physical and psychic provisions to be continually modified. In "Joie de Vivre" (*F* 38), for instance, Levertov disqualifies herself as a candidate for the pose of a unified, hermetic subject, saying that although "[a]ll that once hurt / (healed) goes on hurting," it does so "in new ways." Although it may be "[o]ne same heart /— not a transplant—," conditioning is constant. So, even "cut down to the stump," it now "throbs, new, old." Symbolically, the importance of understanding the past must be always dialectically in friction with the present. This kind of depth would prevent the perpetuation of what Robert Bly calls in his wonderful metaphor a "sibling society." Twenty years after *Footprints*, in her volume *Evening Train*, Levertov retains the unity of a speaking subject, but one whose history continually riffs with that which she encounters presently. In "The Two Magnets"(*ET* 17), for example, Levertov reveals her attentiveness to the natural scene while bearing respectful knowledge of its historical reception: "Where broken gods, faded saints, (powerful in antique presence / as old dancers with straight backs, loftily confident, / or old men in threadbare wellcut coats) preside casually / over the venerable conversations of cypress and olive." To the layering of mythic knowledge, Levertov adds the unavoidable associations that her own personal history brings: "[T]here intrudes, like a child interrupting, tugging at my mind, / incongruous, persistent, / the image of young salmon in round ponds at the hatchery / across an ocean and a continent...." This reservoir contains layers of memory, history, and imagination, leading Levertov in the second stanza to ruminate that America, though now her home, calls her to loved images in dreams and of past centuries. Finally she realizes that she is still the same person, but one engaging foundational knowledge as a fluctuating palimpsest in her living journey, portraying both her present, sensory west coast residence and an image connoting the blurred edges of that which is unknown: "Part of me lives under nettle-grown foundations. / Part of me wanders west and west, and has reached / the edge of the mist...." Levertov concludes with a spiritual affirmation: she watches the salmon, suggesting that there will be another form of being for these salmon when this form of their lives will end.

While Levertov's conclusion surely gives testimony to spiritual beliefs in the transcendental, such that she confidently asserts them, the poem reveals an interactive, revisionary, accumulated mental and physical life. Thus, even though this lyric speaker has firm commitments to a world beyond this one, she negotiates the past and the present, the past in the present, throughout the course of her life. In her 1996 collection, *Sands of the Well*, the collection in

which Levertov most explicitly embraces religion, she still understands her life to be one dialogically engaged in the arena of everyday events and her spiritual beliefs to be a force that exists dialectically with the phenomenal world—modifying how she situates herself but providing a realm of belief to which everyday life
will remain incommensurate. When the deep truths which Levertov aspires to know are imaged, it shall be seen, even in her
sundry catalogues, those images are referential to a variousness
portrayed specifically while in a composition resisting a rational
totalizing scheme. My inferences, of course, reveal no imbroglio
but illustrate difference only apparent within a frame of expectation, a randomness perceived only through a context of order. The
catalogue subsequently to be described, therefore, is housed in a
poem replete with history and expectations regarding both composition and reception. But, if a poem can be also a testimony to
what could be, this poem displays what McGann describes as a
dynamic relationship existing between fact and ideal (McGann
129–30). The poem gives materiality, in other words, to an ethics of
care, a pursuit of what may or should be through a context of what
is. Thus, although the hermeneutic circle of phenomenal and
noumenal can never be closed, Levertov retains her commitment
to both worldly activism and spiritual resource. In "Sojourns in the
Parallel World" (*SW* 49), for example, Levertov seems to posit "the
exercise of virtue" as an engagement with a transcendental category, in a realm outside the contingencies of dailiness:

> We live our lives of human passions,
> cruelties, dreams, concepts,
> crimes and the exercise of virtue
> and beside a world devoid
> of our preoccupations, free
> from apprehension....

Yet, she presents that world as natural—a material reality affected
by but existing outside of our human agendas—while figuring us
as a part of this wider berth of nature. This is a "world / parallel to
our own though overlapping." We participate in the larger world
of nature by letting go of activities of domination, "[w]henever we
lose track of our own obsessions, / our self-concerns, because we
drift for a minute, / an hour even, of pure (almost pure) / response to that insouciant life." Then, Levertov portrays particular
images that are not outside the ken of human experience, but that
require an open receptivity. Being of this world, however, Levertov endorses harmonious coexistence with that which is other than

human, but cannot herself avoid the lens of prosopopoeia through which to figure them—even in her attempt to anoint her portrayal with a randomness symbolizing nondomination: "cloud, bird, fox, the flow of light, the dancing / pilgrimage of water, vast stillness / of spellbound ephemerae on a lit windowpane, / animal voices, mineral hum, wind / conversing with rain, ocean with rock, stuttering / of fire to coal." This apparent randomness signifying an open reception of the other is undercut by the humanizing intellect. Incommensurate to the task of exceeding the boundaries of human knowledge, Levertov nonetheless is touched by some degree of otherness, when "something tethered / in us, hobbled like a donkey on its patch / of gnawed grass and thistles, breaks free." Apparently, Levertov senses a difference enabled by elasticizing boundaries, endorsing receptivity—but all the while remaining fixed in time and place.

She is capable of change, then, though that change retains anthropomorphizing syntax even as she attempts to align herself with the larger nonrational natural environment. Her parenthetical cautionary statements in the poem signal an awareness of such rootedness. Her conclusion, thus, may be false. She does not enter a transcendental space, and her own figuration belies her assertion that "[n]o one discovers / just where we've been, when we're caught up again / into our own sphere." Yet, Levertov still realizes herself to be a poet in the world when she parenthetically avers: "(where we must / return, indeed, to evolve our destinies)." What I suggest is that although she attempts to release rational motive, Levertov remains canny—her humanness always distinguishing her from images in her own nature catalogue. She retains, however, a strong subject position that is bolstered rather than rebuffed by her attempt, concluding "but we have changed, a little." Levertov may never access a transcendental moment, and she surely won't articulate one; but her strong spiritual investment is one that she acknowledges as provisional for going beyond a vista circumscribed by humdrum tasks. This other is, therefore, in dialectical difference from the speaker. The speaker, however, continually aspires to being virtuous by being inspired by a belief system that strengthens one to resist many of the facts and dominant paradigms confining a totally socially-constructed identity. To attest to being not of the worldly is no humanist escape if one conducts a life of vigilant interactiveness.

This, too, is her aesthetic theory joining her impulse towards a dialogical speaker's presence—resisting not only an isolated artist but also an uninformed and uninvolved speaker who skates across surface features of the present moment without being able to evaluate what may be lost or gained—a soundbite mentality unequipped for an informed honesty. Again, in "Joie de Vivre" (*F* 38), Levertov admonishes the artist: "[b]ring paper and pencil / out of the dimlit into / the brightlit room, make sure / all you say is true." Here, Levertov rejects the dimness of otherness—abstracted distance of an isolated artist, an uninformed and uncrafted artist—without the equipment and provisions for seeing more clearly. Life as a continuum requires copious and ongoing attentiveness. It cannot be rendered through abstracted memory, but neither can it be reduced to an amnesia for anything but the present day. Levertov's version of honesty requires facing the present through an increasingly deep reservoir of historical, cultural awareness—a richness that fixes one neither in the past nor the present, but involves perception continually modulating perception. Thus Levertov presents herself as a single being, but one who is neither a transcendental subjectivity nor an abstract cogito. Yes, there may be an organicism to her sense of self, but its parts cohere through the modulations of a participatory, intelligent, earnest activist, attempting to construct an ethics and make sense of the world's pastiche.

Furthermore, the iconic rather than representational aspect of literature—the fact that it exceeds conceptual reference—is also realized contingently only, rather than transcendentally. The celebration of an understanding, by the end of "Joie de Vivre," incubates into form—an invention that resists worldly reference as it enacts its own ontology—what Levinas has characterized as a work's capacity to "overflow concepts."[6] Since the etiology of concepts is our lived reality, initiating that which is not yet known forces us to reckon with what exactly characterizes this rub with our own sense of the real. As seen, Levertov's joy comes from her realization that she occupies an intersection of ingoing and outgoing energies. As symbolic site of reception and invention, Levertov becomes inventively enabled and images her position synaesthetically, a nonreferential construal that itself attests to the joy of harmony. Reading this lyric, however, in order to get the artifact at all, one must understand its historical and literary contexts, figuring its alternative to precedent—an iconicism

---

[6]See, for example, Emmanuel Levinas, *Otherwise Than Being: Or Beyond Essence*, trans. Alphonso Lingis (The Hague: Nijhoff, 1981).

instantiating itself in the face of and differing from cultural pulls in other directions. While Levertov clearly identifies herself here as a lyric poet, both dialogism and aestheticism enable her lyric. Likewise, the reader—situated in her or his own societal givens— responds to the defamiliarization as dialectic-in-and-with-culture. This process—for both the poet and her reader—can be defended as coalitional, not universal; not natural, but requiring agency. In this regard, poetic utterance creates an opacity that requires interpretation, thereby invoking motive, voice, response; but the matter does not yield to social constructions, textuality, therefore, exceeding complete externality.

Situating herself, again, at/as the vortex of reception and invention in "The Faithful Lover" (*ET* 20–21), Levertov positions a layered knowledge of art against an awe of nature, but finds even such awe to be mediated through culturally determined terministic screens. When she recalls that Ruskin, upon viewing the Alps, "all unawares / came face to face / with the sublime," she posits this response as clearly going beyond either aesthetic or sensory terms: "unmistakeably not clouds, / surpassing all that engravings had promised." This epiphanic moment changed him from "docile prig … to a man of passion, / whatever his failings." However transcendental the Alps are as signified to Ruskin, Levertov reaches an alternate conclusion when she "[p]lay[s] with a few decades," and tries "to imagine Ruskin in the New World," witnessing Yosemite. Where would he fix his response, she wonders of Ruskin—one whose "loyalties already [are] divided /—Rock Simple or Rock Wrought, / strata of mountains, strata of human craft, / tools of Geology or tools of Art." When she wonders if anything could sweep "him wholly into its torrents of non-human grandeur," she concludes by suggesting the unavoidable realities of contingency in her suggestion of his recourse to Art:

> Or wouldn't Art have pulled him back in the end
> to layered history felt in the bones,
> (even Geology a fraction of that insistence, loved
> for its poetry of form, color, textures,
> not as a scientist loves it)?

In her italicized invention, Levertov offers her own lyrical rendering as

> *rich tessellations* or the *shadowy Rialto*
> *threw its colossal curve slowly*
> *forth … that strange curve, so delicate,*

> *so adamantine, strong as a mountain cavern,*
> *graceful as a bow just bent—?*

In conclusion, Levertov suggests that even a return to the world of nature is always mediated through the contingencies and layers of one's historical and cultural moment:

> Back to where Nature—even the Alps, still so remote,
> unsung through so many centuries—
>
> lay in the net or nest of perception,
> seen then re-seen, recognized, wrought in myth.

Clearly this is a response to vision as that which is not removed from one's lived and affiliative moment, but conditioned by it. Indeed, even perception is not articulated phenomenologically—driven toward a *ding an sich* and capable of bracketing context. No, perception cannot be innocent, but exists rather in a "net or nest"—a *différence*. Significantly, Levertov concludes this poem in couplets, perhaps the form most signifying the hold of rationality, while invoking images that most obviously spill over that which would even attempt linguistic containment—love, awe, wilderness, sublime. Yet, even here, Levertov signifies change rather than containment—through a dialectic filter of perspective: "Seen then re-seen, recognized, wrought in myth." Thus, even nature wrought, to Levertov, bears knowledge of historical precedent, as she acknowledges unavoidable revisionism in re-seeing and re-cognizing the artifact through historical, cultural, and aesthetic lenses.

The percussive effect of renegotiating that which seems given with that imagined is a revitalization necessary, for Levertov, to effect honesty and vigor in both love and language. In her notes to the volume of poems selected upon religious themes, *The Stream and the Sapphire*, Levertov reminds us to remember the roots common to the words *kinship* and *kindness*. Such percussive effect exists in reciprocal exchange, with involvement and not in a sapped and enervated memory. Levertov's poem "Novella" (*F* 6–7) particularly exemplifies her commitment to commitment, an ethics necessitating engagement rather than isolation, a requirement for one to diverge from the enervation that is involved in resorting to tired linguistic constructions or memories, and, by extension, to broader and globally threatening abstract agendas. The poem begins—

> *In love* (unless loved) is not *love.*
> You're right: x needs—

> with azure sparks down dazedly
> drifting through vast night
> long after—
>
> > the embrace of y to even
> begin to become z.

Love in the poem is incarnated here through the maintenance of energy, specifically of reciprocal love energies between x and y. "*In love*," which opens the poem, implies unidirectional motion, which seems entropic compared to reciprocal in-love x greeted by the in-love y. Only then can "in love" become "love." Love energy imbued with spirituality—Levertov's characteristic spark emanating from a substance which could not naturally issue such light-fire—delightfully captures a slow, sensual, melodious, and delicious lingering in the magical love image of "azure sparks down dazedly / drifting through vast night / long after."

The spiritually-sparked love enabled through reciprocal energy would drain if the flow were unidirectional. Levertov's artist must continually refocus to maintain clear perception of the male lover.

> … Example:
> a woman painter returns,
> younger than she should be, from travels
> in monotone countries
>
> and on arrival, bandages of fatigue
> whipped off her eyes,
> > instantly
> looks, looks at whose shadow
> first falls on her primed (primal) canvas
> (all the soul she has left
> for the moment)—:
>
> At once the light
> (not the gray north of journeys)
> colors him! Candle-gold,
>
> yet not still, but shivering,
> lit white flesh for her (who preferred brown)
> and hair light oak or walnut
> was mahogany on the dream-pallete.

Levertov's placing of "instantly" on a line by itself attests both to her investment in immediacy and her sense that such re-vision requires participatory agency. Reiterating her spiritual light image, Levertov portrays shimmering light shining from the artist's canvas, impossible in referential imaging, a light "not the gray north of journeys." This instance of spirituality is founded upon the intuitive medium of a "dream palette," thus attentiveness is augmented by intuition and the image shines from the canvas in a way that could only be inspired. Again, inspiration results not from reclusiveness but from involvement, caring involvement.

Setting the stage in the present, Levertov says the artist begins to transpose this spiritual-intuitive illumination to the canvas by painting "what she sees." The painter, operating in the fluctuating present, must quickly adapt artistic presentation to immediate perceptions. "Now" must overcome "then"; a dialectic of perception revising memory—always dialogic and perspectival, as "she sees" it. Yes, Levertov is invoking the spiritual ingredient of love, but the spirit is not housed in an archaic binary, the artist being required to take care and maintain attentiveness: "the object / moves, her eyes change focus / faithfully, the nimbus / dances." But the scene alters when reciprocation ends. When "y, embarrassed, / and finally indifferent, turns / away," the effect is crucially devastating to the artist.

> ...Talking (he is a poet)
>
> talking, walking away, entering
> a small boat, the middle distance,
>
> sliding downstream away.
> She has before her
>
> a long scroll to paint on, but no room
> to follow that river.   The light's going.

By leaving a space after the lines where the poet is "sliding downstream away," the poet places the artist in the middle of her dilemma of that loss and the ensuing recognition that "The light's going."

Here is the crucial turning point. The love dwindles without "y's" mutuality; he's gone, sapping the energy of commitment, leaving "the painter / [who] paints what she sees" to become the poet of distance and memory who "continues // to paint what she saw." Since the attention demanded by perceptual involvement is eliminated, and the techniques of memory and craft remain, the painter can proceed only "to paint what she saw." Y becomes a "brushstroke now / in furthest perspective." Indeed, the joy of illumination resulting from the interactive present care involved in happily refocusing diminishes into a sadness of the pain of eyes

straining when the symbolic light transmutes into symbolic dull-
ness: "it hurts // the eyes in dusk to see it." The artist laments that
"No one, / indeed, will know that speck of fire." The lack of re-
ciprocity that enervates and finally ends the love is metaphoric of
Levertov's sense of the involvement of ethics in the aesthetic. Re-
moval of the artist from the swell of present tense commitment,
from the vigor of an interpretation invested dialogically in the
ever-unfolding present moment, leaves the rendering to a
painfully vague, distant, and spiritless referentiality.

What is enabled and what is lost in Levertov's aesthetics has
everything to do with one's investment in one's cultural and historical moment, with the acknowledgment of intertextuality and
misprision, the past conceptions vexed by an insistent renegotia-
tion of—in Levertov's case—a strong sense of subjective identity
continually mutable but retaining its commitment to the perhaps
metaphysical aspects of spirit and love yet engendered in a vigorous and vigilant agent working for global concerns. What becomes
manifest through reciprocal, interested care, through commitment
to love and virtue, augurs renewal and preservation that is invigo-
rated by agency, not reliant upon distanced suppositions or inheri-
tances. The absence of presence changes the reality: x in the presence of love is simply not the same x who feels its absence. So, x
has not even begun to become z, the incarnation of the loved x. Indeed, she is not even the same x, for though she remains "a
painter," she is left "not perhaps / unchanged."

A defining difference is that she is "Older." "We'll take //
some other symbol to represent / *that* difference," she states—perhaps the more soulful sounding "a or o" will do. Bereft of spirit,
the artist retains only memory of y—memory being at best static,
but inevitably losing vividness. Y of course no longer remains the
same as the image from the past. Since the memory, then, is not
only imperfect, so the artist's reproduction of the image from
memory becomes dishonest. Terms have changed, energy dwindles, and memory hosts only an image increasingly disparate from
the changing and aging object of that memory. Such an imperative
to be involved in order for love to continue is metonymic of the
ethical and aesthetic demands that Levertov also places upon herself regarding the form and content of social and aesthetic prac-
tices. This loving woman is, after all, an artist whose portrayals become weak and dim in their complete reliance upon referentiality.
Levertov retains vigorous lyrical commitments, as seen in the
conclusion of this poem: going toward the long and soulful sound

of strong vowels "to represent that difference—a or o." Yet, she deftly defies attributing naturalness to her signifiers by suggesting that the artist chooses, will "take some other symbol to represent," and finally that this sound will be no other than of choice, "a or o." Not arbitrary for sure, but the fact that there is a choice being made—of one or the other long vowel sound—resists any presumption of inevitability, and thus insists upon agency. The passivity of accepting any given construction of reality must continually be vexed by engagement. Indeed, in concert with poststructuralist thought in resisting both neutral objectivity and reclusive subjectivity, Levertov's dialogism pertains as well to Levertov's notions of honesty, and in this regard, she, too, interrogates the capacity of language to hold the present. Once again, we see that Levertov advances the necessity for earnest and ongoing witness, commitment, and dialogue. Indeed, Levertov avers that the very moment one labels x as x, the thing so labelled becomes something a little bit different. Honest rendering doesn't result from waning commitedness.

Throughout her career, Denise Levertov maintained her allegiance to the conventions of the lyric form. As I have attempted to suggest, however, the subjectivity figured in Levertov's lyrics is seldom a universal "I," the traditional autonomous lyric self, but very much a poet in the world, a situated subject enmeshed in material and historical contingency. Are Levertov's lyrics therefore "postmodernist," as Dorothy M. Nielsen argues? Perhaps. But we should remember that "postmodernism" is a critic/theorist's term, part of our tool chest, not Levertov's. "Keep in mind," Levertov told Jewel Spears Brooker in 1995, "that I was (and remained) a solitary reader, unexposed (thank God) to academic requirements and critiques and analyses" (184–85). Levertov, that is, did not consciously participate in postmodernist critiques of the Enlightenment concept of the coherent self as essentialist, universalist, and/or humanist.[7] At the same time, Levertov's active involvement in such social issues as the Vietnam War and in global concerns pertaining to human rights and ecology may have helped her avoid the lyric's conventional ahistoricism and wariness of others.[8] While Levertov's poems never wholly elide lyric subjectiv-

---

[7]A point that Nielsen also makes. See her essay in Jeffreys, 137.

[8]As, say, Robert Bly's early lyrics did not. See my discussion of the "unpopulated" nature of Bly's early lyrics of silence and solitude in Chap-

ity, they do distance themselves from its more abstract manifestations, reorienting lyric form from the monologic toward the dialogic, from the transcendental to the material, from universal stasis to cultural process, and from an autononous to a contingent self. Without acknowledging the various theoretical positions involving *différence*, Levertov never rested content with conclusions, never ceased her pursuit of living and rendering a life that undergoes continual questions, that is always devising and revising the ethical, spiritual, and aesthetic implications of commitments that—neither neutral nor natural—require continual acts of choice. And attentiveness: "Aware," the concluding poem in her posthumously published book of poetry, Denise, Daleth, passageway, ends by saying she "liked the glimpse," "liked the sound," but "Next time / I'll move like cautious sunlight, open / the door by fractions, eavesdrop / peacefully" (*TGU* 62). She necessitates that her readers, as well, resist passive reception—investing the matter of poetry with interpretive and coalitional energy. Unlike, say, the experiments of the L=A=N=G=U=A=G=E poets, Levertov's lyrics of the contingent self do not relinquish lyric traditions pertaining to matters such as sensibility and voice. They invigorate that tradition, however, while providing theorists with further occasions to rethink subjectivity and the vexed status of the lyric.

Works Cited

Altieri, Charles. "From Experience to Discourse: American Poetry and Poetics in the Seventies." *Contemporary Literature* 21.2 (1980): 191–224.

Atchity, Kenneth John. "An Interview with Denise Levertov." *Conversations with Denise Levertov*. Ed. Jewel Spears Brooker. Jackson: UP of Mississippi, 1998. 101–8.

Bly, Robert. *The Sibling Society*. Reading: Addison-Wesley, 1996.

Brooker, Jewel Spears. "A Conversation with Denise Levertov." *Conversations with Denise Levertov*. Jackson: U of Mississippi P, 1998. 182–89.

Harris, Victoria Frenkel, ed. *The Incorporative Consciousness of Robert Bly*. Carbondale: Southern Illinois UP, 1992.

Hickey, David. *The Invisible Dragon: Four Essays on Beauty*. San Francisco: Art Publishers Press, 1994.

---

ters 1 and 3 of *The Incorporative Consciousness of Robert Bly* (Carbondale: Southern Illinois UP, 1992).

Holden, Jonathan. *The Rhetoric of the Contemporary Lyric*. Bloomington: Indiana UP, 1980.

Jeffreys, Mark, ed. *New Definitions of Lyric: Theory, Technology, and Culture*. New York: Garland, 1998.

Levinas, Emmanuel. *Otherwise Than Being: Or Beyond Essence*. Trans. Alphonso Lingis. The Hague: Nijhoff, 1981.

McGann, Jerome J. *Social Values and Poetic Acts: The Historical Judgement of Literary Work*. Cambridge: Harvard UP, 1988. 130.

McGuirk, Kevin. "'All Wi Don': Tony Harrison, Linton Kwesi Johnson, and the Cultural Work of Lyric in Postwar Britain." *New Definitions of Lyric: Theory, Technology, and Culture*. Ed. Mark Jeffreys. New York: Garland, 1998. 49–75.

Nielsen, Dorothy M. "Ecology, Feminism, and Postmodern Lyric Subjects." *New Definitions of Lyric: Theory, Technology, and Culture*. Ed. Mark Jeffreys. New York: Garland, 1998. 127–49.

Perloff, Marjorie. "A Response." *New Definitions of Lyric: Theory, Technology, and Culture*. Ed. Mark Jeffreys. New York: Garland, 1998. 245–55.

Rajan, Tilottama. "Romanticism and the Death of Lyric Consciousness." *Lyric Poetry: Beyond New Criticism*. Eds. Chavia Hosek and Patricia Parker. Ithaca: Cornell UP, 1985. 194–207.

1

I move among the ankles
of forest Elders, tread
their moist rugs of moss,
duff of their soft brown carpets.
Far above, their arms are held
open wide to each other, or waving--

from "From Below" (by Denise Levertov
from *This Great Unknowing*)

Reappropriating Mirror Appropriations: Female Sexuality and the Body in Denise Levertov

José Rodríguez Herrera

"Appropriations: Women and the San Francisco Renaissance," a chapter included in Michael Davidson's *The San Francisco Renaissance: Poetics and Community at the Mid-Century* (1991), opens with a reference to Levertov's first visit to the highly influential poetic arena of the San Francisco Bay Area at the end of the 1950s. To celebrate such an occasion, her long-time friend and poetic mentor, Robert Duncan, had arranged a meeting of local poets in his house. With this formal gesture, Duncan wanted to introduce Levertov to the poetic circles of what came to be known later as the San Francisco Renaissance. Jack Spicer was among the local poets invited and, while there, took advantage of the occasion to read one of the poems of his new series, *Admonitions,* apparently intended for the illustrious guest of honor, though the content of the poem he read, Davidson ironizes, "was anything but honorific" (172).

> People who don't like the smell of faggot vomit
> Will never understand why men don't like women
> Won't see why those never to be forgotten thighs
> of Heden (say) will move us to screams of laughter,
> Parody (what we don't want) is the whole thing.
> Don't deliver us any mail today, mailman.
> Send us no letters. The female genital organ is hideous, We
> Do not want to be moved.
> Forgive us. Give us
> A simple example of the fact that nature is imperfect.
> Men ought to love men
> (And do)
> As the man said

It's
Rosemary for remembrance. (62)

In a letter accompanying *Admonitions*, as Davidson tells in his book, Spicer compared his poems to mirrors, "dedicated to the person I particularly want to look into it" (55). It was in response to this berating indictment against women and their sexual organs, said to have been read by Spicer with "extraordinary venom,"[1] that Levertov wrote her infuriated "Hypocrite Women." By writing the poem, Levertov showed her reluctance to resign herself to the mirror *imago* given by Spicer. Instead, as Davidson argues further, she looked "into that mirror and turned it back on the one holding it" (173). Nor did she use the mirror for the self-indulgence of her gender, and so bemoans in the poem "the numbness women induce as an evasion of sexual and spiritual commitment, and the self-hatred which such denials engender" (Showalter 348).

> Hypocrite women, how seldom we speak
> of our own doubts, while dubiously
> we mother man in his doubt!
>
> And if at Mill Valley perched in the trees
> the sweet rain drifting through western air
> a white sweating bull of a poet told us
>
> our cunts are ugly—why didn't we
> admit we have thought so too? (And
> what shame? They are not for the eye!)
>
> No, they are dark and wrinkled and hairy,
> caves of the Moon … And when a
> dark humming fills us, a
> coldness towards life,
> we are too much women to
> own to such unwomanliness.
>
> Whorishly with the psychopomp
> we play and plead—and say
> nothing of this later. And our dreams,
>
> with what frivolity we have pared them
> like toenails, clipped them like ends of
> split hair.
>
> (*OTS* 70)

---

[1]Robert Duncan *dixit.*

In the poem Levertov criticizes women's frivolous, hypocritical self-denial since they consciously repress their authentic selves for the sake of compliance with gender stereotypes. "Hypocrite Women," as Levertov once acknowledged in an interview, was written then "in some recognition of how these stereotypes do in fact oppress one as a woman" (Levertov, "Conversation" 23). Indeed, patriarchal constructs on ideal femininity and the female body demand women's hatred, or at least their denial, of their own sexuality. Much worse, this self-hatred is only compounded by self-censorship of the female unconscious in order to conform to gender stereotypes. Censorship of the female unconscious effects the silencing and self-trivialization of the true needs of the self/body. Self-censorship is actually enacted in the poem as a crisis of language in women, i.e., an inability to speak their selves truthfully. Women's dissociation from truthful language, the split of the self from language, is noticeable in the profusion of *verba dicendi* in the poem—"how seldom we *speak*," "why didn't we *admit* / we have thought so too?" "And *say* nothing of this later" (73). These verbs are an attempt, on the part of the poet, to expose the annihilation of language and consciousness by self-induced censorship. In the end, self-effacement and the silence which comes after the repression of language not only belie truthfulness but also bespeak self-deception for, as Adrienne Rich warns in "Women and Honor: Some Notes on Lying," an essay first published in 1975, "lying is done with words, and also with silence" (186).

Silence, then, as the logical outcome of self-delusion, pervades the poem: on the one hand, women's unfailing condescension towards their male partners entails, Levertov hints, their eschewing of their own self-doubts to "mother" the male's doubt, however "dubiously"; on the other hand, female submissive compliance with the patriarchal construct of ideal "womanhood" demands dismissiveness of the consciousness of the self to "truly" abide with ideals. Thus, when no longer fertile ("And when a dark humming fills us, a / coldness towards life"), Levertov lashes out, "we are too much women to / own to such unwomanliness." Hence, women's silencing of their own doubts is accomplished through lying to their own bodies and, by implication, to their own selves.

> We have had the truth of our bodies withheld from us or distorted; we have been kept in ignorance of our most intimate places. Our instincts have been punished: clitoridectomies for

lustful nuns or difficult wives. It has been difficult, too, to know
the lies of our complicity from the lies we b   ved. (Rich 189)

This "clitoridectom[y]" of the female ins ɪncts to which Adrienne Rich refers, reverts in the poem to a self-ɪutilation which is
not only physical, but also spiritual, a mutilɪtion of the soul as
well, as announced by the *psychopomp*, a beɪ.ɪg whose function in
Greek mythology was to serve as the Hermes of souls.

> This guide of souls, possibly Hermes, the traditional psycho-
> pomp of Greek mythology, is waiting to lead the women
> forward to mystery or to transformation. The god, of great im-
> portance to spiritual development, playing a key role in the
> myth of Psyche, is assailed by a teasing display of charm, which
> the women use as a deliberate strategy of refusal. They refuse
> their own capacity for growth, and they refuse to be faithful to
> their deepest selves. (DuPlessis 201)

The female flirtatiousness with the psychopomp bespeaks her neglect of the true needs of the self and its progress. At stake is a
spiritual realization that will be irrevocably marred if not seriously
assumed. In DuPlessis's words, "by their self-censorship, women
deny themselves the challenge of soul-making" (198). A second
form of masked self-mutilation, however, is the repression of a
female, potential consciousness figuratively exemplified in the
poem in the "dreams" frivolously "pared like toenails." Underlying this imagery is the female's self-imposed incarceration in her
own body and her incapacity to transcend it with a view to her
self-realization. If only concerned with pruning their physical appearance, women refuse both the spirituality and the self-consciousness that is predicated upon the acceptance of their sexuality. As Showalter argues, Levertov "is using the familiar details of
physical maintenance, the constant paring and pruning of wom-
en's daily existence, to suggest the excision of female sexual con-
siousness" (350). Through self-censorship and denial of their own
bodies women have desexualized their consciousness and, by way
of it, their own chance for an identity based on the recognition of
the female body and its needs.

Harkening back to Jack Spicer's poem, what it comes to signal
then is that even at the outset of the liberal hipster movement at
the beginning of the sixties, the female body continued to act as
the privileged "locus of repression." And this because Spicer's
words are not at odds with at least one of the strategies of surveil-
lance of female sexuality that Foucault coined as the "hysterization
of women's body," which he locates in the wake of the eighteenth

century, and whereby the female body came to be viewed as "being thoroughly saturated with sexuality" (Foucault 104). If woman is so attached to her discursive[2] sexuality that she cannot escape from being "nothing but her sex," it follows that she is not fit for higher activities such as thinking and reasoning and, thereby, she can not transcend the physicality of her body. Fated to perform only the "basest" and "lowest" functions with her body, to which she is forever attached and beyond which she can not go, she is left prey to the contempt of the opposite sex. Acting accordingly, Spicer locates the female sexual organ as the site of hideousness and the basis for man's misogyny. Nothing else, so it seems, has he seen to account for man's misogyny and his repudiation of women apart from the imputed ugliness of the female genitals.[3] But, as Davidson rightly argues, "Spicer's unqualified misogyny becomes a vehicle by which Levertov asserts an authority repressed by women" (173). Authority is reasserted in Levertov's poem through a bold use of language that reappropriates the taboo words concerning female sexuality. Making use of a simple but forceful diction, Levertov unashamedly reinscribes the sexual and exploits the untold secrets of the body. Thus, as a disclaimer to Spicer's misogynist remark, one in tune with the Beat ethos[4] that "the female genital organ is hideous," Levertov states even more boldly: "our cunts are ugly." Yet, perhaps, it should not have been, she disparages, for "a white sweating bull of a poet" to have said so.

Nonetheless, just as Virginia Woolf strove, as she herself once said, to tell "the truth about my own experience as a body" (62), so does Levertov struggle to substitute truth-telling for shameful self-

---

[2]I am using here, for my own purposes, Foucault's conception of sexuality as always already permeated by discourses of one sort or another.

[3]Spicer's "the female genital organ is hideous" is his own staggeringly reductionist way of explaining that "men ought to love men" and not women; but Spicer's injunctions do also lay bare, by the same token, his recalcitrant essentialism: if woman is nothing more than the hideousness of her sex, that means then that her biology, which she can not transcend, is her destiny; in other words, she is mired in the immanence and the "baseness" of the pansexuality that Spicer, not unwittingly, has predicated of her gender.

[4]In the same book, Davidson points out that "the Beat ethos relegated women to the role of sexual surrogate, muse, or mom; it did not raise them to a position of artistic equality" (175).

censorship thus hoping that she is creating, as Rich said, "the possibility for more truth around her" (200). This need for truthfulness, so evident in the poem, had been reclaimed in an earlier poem, "The Goddess," whereby the poet, who lies half asleep in Lie Castle, is awakened to truth by the female deity.

> She in whose lipservice
> I passed my time,
> whose name I knew, but not her face,
> came upon where I lay in Lie Castle!
>
> Flung me across the room, and
> room after room (hitting the walls, re-
> bounding—to the last
> sticky wall—wrenching away from it
> pulled hair out!)
> till I lay
> outside the outer walls!
>
> There in the cold air
> lying still where her hand had thrown me,
> I tasted the mud and splattered my lips:
> the seeds of the forest where in it,
> asleep and growing! I tasted
> her power!
>
> The silence was answering to my silence,
> a forest was pushing itself
> out of sleep between my submerged fingers.
>
> I bit on a seed and it spoke on my tongue
> of day that shone already among stars
> in the water-mirror of low ground,
>
> and a wind rising ruffled in the lights:
> she passed near me returning from the encounter,
> she who plucked me from the close rooms,
>
> without whom nothing
> flowers, fruits, sleeps in season,
> without whom nothing
> speaks in its own tongue, but returns
> lie for lie!
>
>   (*EBH* 43–44)

The poet gleans[5] from the goddess the power to speak in her own tongue telling the truth about herself. Rather than simply paying "lipservice" to the idea of truthfulness embodied in the goddess, the poet is violently forced to taste her power and to experience in her own self the import of such a decisive influence. After this mighty encounter with the goddess of truth, the self is left emparented with the power that comes from truth-telling.

In "Song for Ishtar," the poem that opens *O Taste and See* (1964), the poet, having been empowered to truthfulness by her goddess, sets out to subvert the oppressive stereotypes of femininity and female sexuality. To do so, the poet takes on the identity of a pig, an animal said to have been sacred to Ishtar, the Babylonian moon goddess, so as to fornicate with her in a shining encounter. Also, the moon goddess is reimagined as a sow to allow for the poet/pig's at-one-ness with her. This at-one-ness of the sexual encounter is seen in the divinity's shining through the hollow of the poet/pig who/which, in correspondence, breaks into an orgasm of "silver bubbles." The pig's body is depicted in terms similar to what Janet Wolff calls the "grotesque body," which has "orifices, genitals, protuberances" (124). This grotesqueness is opposed to the "classical body," which "has no orifices and engages into no base bodily functions."

> The moon is a sow
> and grunts in my throat
> Her great shining shines through me
> so the mud of my hollow gleams
> and breaks in silver bubbles
>
> She is a sow
> And I a pig and a poet
>
> When she opens her white
> lips to devour me I bite back
> and laughter rocks the moon

---

[5]I am indebted to Mary K. Deshazer for the particular use of this verb with the meaning of learning to be at one with the female divinity and deriving sustenance from this alignment with the Muse in her spiritual manifestation as the goddess (see Deshazer 1986, 164); in the case of this Levertov poem, the poet "gleans" from the goddess the poetic sustenance that allows her to speak in her own tongue telling the truth about herself.

In the black of desire
we rock and grunt, grunt and
shine.

(*OTS* 3)

The poet revolutionizes the genteel tradition of the clean female body by incarnating herself into a grotesque body, nothing
less than a pig, and by situating the scene of the fornication in a
muddy, dirty surrounding, most probably a pig sty. Far from re-
pressing her sexual drives, the poet/pig is bold enough to
exteriorize them uninhibitedly in her grunting intercourse with the
moon goddess. On the other hand, the poet, through intercourse
with the moon, benefits from the folk belief in the fertilizing power
of the moon to achieve what Pope called "an epiphany of self-
fertilization, whereby the poet creates out of her own self and
power" (88).[6]

"Abel's Bride," from *The Sorrow Dance* (1967), recaptures the
theme of the obliteration of the female body. As in "Hypocrite
Women," the female sex stands for that which is unsighted, "not
for the eye," and also that which causes women's incurring self-effacement. The poem shows a woman who "fears for man [because]
he goes / out alone to his labours," i.e., a woman "mothering man
in his doubts." This time, however, the bride, if only momentarily,
pauses to mother herself in her own doubts, facing the mirror, that
is, facing her true self.

Woman fears for man, he goes
out alone to his labors. No mirror
nests in his pocket. His face
opens and shuts with his hopes.
His sex hangs unhidden
or rises before him
blind and questing.

She thinks herself

---

[6]Ishtar, who in ancient times bore the titles of "Opener of the Womb"
and "Silver Shining," fertilizes the poet's hollow with her creative moon-
beams so that "it breaks in silver bubbles"; on the other hand, partheno-
genesis and homoeroticism are effectively conveyed to the reader by the
overtones of a poem which "suggest a retreat not only from men's gender
expectations but from men as sexual partners. The woman alone, or in
partnership with her muse, is explosively sexual. The poet has reached a
fullness of creative and natural independence in her raucous, shining
identification with a female cosmos" (Pope 88).

> lucky. But sad. When she goes out
> she looks in the glass, she remembers
> herself. Stones, coal,
> the hiss of water upon the kindled
> branches—her being
> is a cave, there are bones at the hearth. (13)

The man needs to look through no *speculum*,[7] for his sex lies unconcealed, either hanging "unhidden" or phallically erect "before him / blind and questing." But the woman, whenever she looks at herself in the mirror, sees her sex as a wound, a mystified grotto—"her being is a cave"—and not a hanging and therefore evident protuberance.[8] And this, she knows, is what she is fated to and yet can not do away with. Thus, this woman is one of those women whose genitals the poet called "caves of the moon" in "Hypocrite Women." That is, she is the woman "whose cave-shaped anatomy is her destiny" (Gilbert 94). This image brings the poem to a pessimistic end for when the *speculum* gives her a vision of her own body oppressed by her sex,[9] the erotic fire in the hearth hisses, because banked; the remnants of her sacrificial, burnt-out flesh are "the bones at the hearth."

In "Fantasiestruck," a later poem, from *Life in the Forest* (1978), Levertov returns to the theme of the female's incarceration in her own body. In the poem, she invents for Caliban, the earthbound spirit of Shakespeare's *The Tempest*, an imaginary half-sibling born a bastard to Prospero and the "blue-eyed hag" Sycorax. Like Caliban, who was confined by his master Prospero to a rock, and the airbound Ariel, imprisoned by Sycorax in a cloven pine and freed later by Prospero's art,[10] Caliban's imaginary half-sibling is also imprisoned yet "that tree being / no cloven pine but the sturdy wood / her body seemed to her."

> 'My delicate Ariel'—
> can you imagine,

---

[7]I use this term because it is redolent of the medical apparatus for introspection of the body, especially used as a tube to facilitate inspection of an open conduit.

[8]See also Spivak's introduction to Derrida's *Of Grammatology* (1976).

[9]This in the Freudian sense of a castration complex.

[10]In Shakespeare's *The Tempest*, Prospero addresses Ariel with these words: "It was mine art, / when I arrived and heard thee, that made gape / The pine, and let thee out" (74).

Caliban had a sister?
Not ugly, brutish, wracked with malice,
but nevertheless
earthbound half-sibling to him,
and, as you once were,
prisoned within a tree—
but that tree being
no cloven pine but the sturdy wood
her body seemed to her,
its inner rings revealing
slow growth,
its bark incised
with hearts and arrows,
all its leaves wanting to fly, and falling—
       and ever in spring again
       peering forth small as flint-sparks?

Spirit whose feet touch earth
only as spirit moves them,
imagine
       this rootbound woman
Prospero's bastard daughter,
his untold secret, hidden from Miranda's
gentle wonder.
       Her intelligent eyes
watch you, her mind
can match your own, she loves
your grace of intellect.
But she knows
what weight of body is, knows her flesh
(her cells, her magic cell)
mutters its own dark songs. (79)

The sister is earthbound, and this circumstance, as Kinnahan asserts, "suggests the restrictive association traditionally and derogatorily made between woman and nature" (139). However, "the poem proceeds to invert this devalued link" (139), and it does so by attributing to the sister the higher capacities for intelligent reasoning and not the brutish, vile features of Caliban, her half-sibling. But it does not escape the sister that her body is a burden and so she is unfit to do the airy, graceful errands of Ariel. It follows then that because she cannot transcend the prison of the body, she is only useful as a shade to the airy spirit. She "loves / to see him pass by," but "she grieves that she cannot hold" him (*LF* 79). She

> knows it is so and *must* be;
> offers the circle of her shade,
> silvery Ariel,
> for your brief rest. (79)

"A Woman Alone," from the same volume, depicts an old woman still with a reserve of fear but learning now to free herself from incarceration in her own body. Unlike "Abel's Bride," where the woman remains alone in her home fearing for man who ventures out to his labors, this old woman no longer fears for man nor her own loneliness. What frightens her instead is how to deal with the aging of her body in mirrors and photographs.

> She has fears, but not about loneliness;
> fears about how to deal with the aging
> of her body—how to deal
> with photographs and the mirror. She feels
> so much younger and more beautiful
> than she looks [...] (16)

The mirrors and the photographs remind her that she is growing old; but this woman wants to grow wise as she grows old, "moving into joy and inner beauty, even though—perhaps even because—men no longer figure centrally in their lives" (Pope 96). The woman feels that the mirrors and the pictures do not truthfully reflect her body for "she feels / so much younger and more beautiful" inside of her. Thus, the old woman, by negating the mirror, also impedes incarceration in the physicality of her body. What happens is that too often this incarceration is imposed on women by the tyranny of the *imago* given in poems such as Spicer's "For Joe, " poems presumptuously intended to be mirrors for Levertov and for all the rest of her kind. "A Woman Alone" reacts against this imprisonment of the female body in the outward projections of a mirror, and it does so by reappropriating the mirror and laying bare before it the split between her outward self reflected in the mirror and the non-specularized inner self. Hence, rather than resigning herself to outward projections in a mirror, the woman fully rejects them because she feels that they do not map her inner self.

Most importantly, though Levertov denied in an interview that this was a feminist poem, one can truly construe it as a feminist gesture.[11] In this same sense, by writing a poem on a lonely

---

[11]I am subliminally, even ironically now that I am made conscious of it, paraphrasing Spivak's "in what it seems satisfying to me to construe as

woman, Everywoman, dealing with her old age and interiorizing the aging of her body as a woman's experience alone, Levertov shows that "her poems are feminist not by virtue of excluding all except female experience but by that of including all experience as women's" (Gish 258). This old woman no longer desires to "mother man in his doubt," nor does she mourn for old lovers. For now, being wise enough, living carelessly and dimly remembering past moments of pleasure, she can unashamedly and joyfully— "untainted by guilt"—mother herself in her own solitude.

> [...] At her happiest
> —or even in the midst of
> some less than joyful hour, sweating
> patiently through a heatwave in the city
> or hearing the sparrows at daybreak, dully gray,
> toneless, the sound of fatigue—
> a kind of sober euphoria makes her believe
> in her future as an old woman, a wanderer,
> seamed and brown,
> little luxuries in the middle of life all gone,
> watching cities and rivers, people and mountains,
> without being watched; not grim nor sad,
> an old winedrinking woman, who knows
> the old roads, grass-grown, and laughs to herself ...
>
> [...] Now at least
> she is past the time of mourning,
> now she can say without shame or deceit
> O blessed Solitude.
>
> (*LF* 16–17)

Works Cited

Davidson, Michael. *The San Francisco Renaissance: Poetics and Community at Mid-Century*. Cambridge: Cambridge UP, 1991.

Deshazer, Mary K. "'A Primary Intensity Between Women': H.D. and the Female Muse." *H.D.: Woman and Poet*. Ed. Michael King. Orono: National Poetry Foundation, 157–71.

DuPlessis, Rachel Blau. "The Critique of Consciousness and Myth in Levertov, Rich, and Rukeyser." *Feminist Studies* 3.1–2 (1975): 199–221.

---

a ~~feminist~~ gesture, Derrida offers a hymeneal fable. The hymen is the always folded (therefore never single or simple) space in which the pen writes its dissemination" (Derrida lxvi).

Foucault, Michel. *The History of Sexuality. Vol. 1. An Introduction.* London: Penguin, 1981.

Gilbert, Sandra M., and Susan Gubar. *The Madwoman in the Attic: The Woman Writer and the Nineteenth Century Imagination.* New Haven: Yale UP, 1979.

Gish, Nancy K. "Denise Levertov." *American Poetry: The Modernist Ideal.* Eds. Clive Bloom and Brian Docherty. Hampshire: Macmillan, 1995. 253–70.

Kinnahan, Linda A. *Poetics of the Feminine: Authority and Literary Tradition in William Carlos Williams, Mina Loy, Denise Levertov, and Kathleen Fraser.* Cambridge: Cambridge UP, 1994.

Levertov, Denise. "A Conversation with Denise Levertov." *Ironwood* 4. Eds. Anthony Piccione and William Heyen. (1973): 21–34.

———. *Life in the Forest.* New York: New Directions, 1978.

———. *O Taste and See.* New York: New Directions, 1964.

———. *The Sorrow Dance.* New York: New Directions, 1966.

———. *With Eyes at the Back of Our Heads.* New York: New Directions, 1959.

Pope, Deborah. "Homespun and Crazy Feathers: The Split-Self in the Poems of Denise Levertov." Ed. Linda Wagner-Martin. *Critical Essays on Denise Levertov.* Boston: G.K. Hall & Co, 1990. 73–98.

Rich, Adrienne. *On Lies, Secrets and Silence: Selected Prose 1966–1978.* New York: Norton, 1980.

Shakespeare, William. *The Tempest.* London: Penguin, 1968.

Showalter, Elaine. "Killing the Angel in the House: The Autonomy of Women Writers." *The Antioch Review* 32.3 (1971): 339–53.

Spicer, Jack. *The Collected Books of Jack Spicer.* Ed. Robin Blaser. Los Angeles: Black Sparrow Press, 1975.

Wagner-Martin, Linda, ed. *Critical Essays on Denise Levertov.* Boston: G.K. Hall & Co, 1990.

Wolff, Janet. *Feminine Sentences: Essays on Women and Culture.* Cambridge, U.K: Polity Press, 1990.

Woolf, Virginia. "Professions for Women." *Women and Writing.* Ed. Michèle Barret. New York: Harvest Book, 1979. 57–64.

"In the Black of Desire":
Eros in the Poetry of Denise Levertov

James Gallant

> "In the black of desire
> we rock and grunt, grunt and
> shine."
>
> ("Song for Ishtar")

Denise Levertov's "Song for Ishtar" (*OTS* 3) is an explosively sexual poem. As the moon-sow (her muse) "opens her white / lips" to "devour" Levertov, the poet (as pig) bites back, savoring the push and thrust of the sexual act. The moon, whose "great shining shines through" the poet, is an erotic muse, representing the desire inherent in the creative act. The imaginative "act of the mind" transforms the fertile darkness of the body, so that "the mud of my hollow gleams / and breaks in silver bubbles." In this moment of unbridled joy, the poet celebrates her sexuality and creativity, "and laughter rocks the moon."

"Song for Ishtar" has been frequently anthologized. Yet criticism of Levertov's work has never adequately considered Levertov's erotic and sexual themes, although from the earliest reviews, critics have noted the sensuous and sensory dimensions of Levertov's work. Ralph Mills, Jr., in an essay which still stands as one of the most perceptive studies of Levertov, writes of her concern with "material reality" (101), her "delighted involvement" in the quotidian (109), her celebrations of the mysterious in everyday life. Yet he, like most other critics, focuses on the spiritual nature of Levertov's apprehension of reality, which he categorizes as "meditational" (109).

Thomas Duddy's essay "To Celebrate" considers the way "random moments of ordinary experience" (116) in Levertov take on a rich and sensuous quality. He notes, for instance, how her description of "The Coming Fall" which "ascends / into the genitals" (*OTS* 39) is "a sexual awakening" which reflects her "spontaneous delight in the body's ripeness and more generally a joy in the life of sensation" (Duddy 120). Duddy's essay ignores Levertov's most erotic poems, in part because he chooses to focus on poems which "enact apperception" rather than those "in which celebration is an accomplished fact" (122).

Finally, both Diane Wakoski and Sandra Gilbert have written studies of Levertov's "feminine" poetic, which include some comments upon the erotic dimensions of the poems, though neither essay focuses upon sexual issues. Gilbert sees Levertov as a revolutionary woman-poet: "It is precisely in her womanhood … that her artistic power lies" (344). Wakoski views Levertov's early poetry as a celebration, among other things, of the "sexual, Dionysian creative powers of the feminine self and world" (7).

It is worth noting that the greatest number of Levertov's most highly charged erotic poems were written in the first major period of her creative production, that is, from 1958 to 1965, the years in which she wrote *With Eyes in the Back of Our Heads*, *The Jacob's Ladder*, and *O Taste and See*. These are the years when Levertov discovered her voice and established her central themes. They are also the years of harmony in her marriage to Mitchell Goodman. In this period of creative and personal energy, Levertov seems to have been especially receptive to erotic experience.

Yet sexual themes are present even in Levertov's earliest work, written before she moved to America. "Folding a Shirt," a poem from 1946, hardly noticed among Levertov's early lyrics, is a central text for understanding her eroticism. The poem begins: "Folding a shirt, a woman stands / still for a moment, to recall / warmth of flesh" (6). As the woman touches the sleeve, her hands "recall / a gesture, or the touch of love." That memory evokes a moment of longing that blends desire and fear, as

> she leans against the kitchen wall,
>
> listening for a word of love,
> but only finds a sound like fear
> running through the rooms above. (6)

Though the fear dissipates, she "cannot put desire away." The longing remains with the woman as she

> … puts away
> the bread, the wine, the knife,
> smooths the bed where lovers lay,

> while time's unhesitating knife
> cuts away the living hours,
> the common rituals of life. (6)

Although its tightly controlled rhythm and rhyme reveal a young author who has not yet found an authentic form, the poem establishes some key elements of Levertov's erotic themes. The folding of the shirt opens the door of the woman's consciousness to the dark, mysterious, erotic realm. A flood of feelings and desire urgently overtakes her ("she cannot put desire away"), leading her to a climactic ecstatic moment, one celebrated in part because it is so fleeting. In the moment of joy is also a realization of despair, of pain and loneliness. Here, time, the kitchen knife, "cuts away" the moment of pleasure.

In "Folding a Shirt," Levertov expresses through the persona of the "woman" feelings and themes which she develops and enlarges upon in a more personal way in her later poems. For Levertov, to know the erotic is to find what is hidden, to taste the "nectarine" of pleasure in order to see what lies within, to open the "flesh / rose-amber and the seed" and break apart the coarser leaf to find the "juicy stem of grass" (*CEP* 91). In the poem "Pleasures" in *With Eyes in the Back of Our Heads*, Levertov says, "I like to find / what's not found / at once, but lies // within something, of another nature" (*CEP* 90).

Thus, in "To the Snake," as Levertov strokes the "cold, pulsing throat" (*CEP* 131) of the snake, wearing it as a wreath around her neck, she is reaching out to the darkness, to the gods; she enfolds herself in that which is pleasurable precisely because it is so dangerous. When she removes the snake, the moment of joy leaves "a long wake of pleasure." She returns "smiling and haunted" to a "dark morning."

In "Love Song," Levertov contemplates the hidden, darker regions of her husband's body. Exploring and savoring, she delights in "the way your beauty grows in long tendrils / half in darkness" (*OTS* 6). The rarely seen sexual hairs reflect the rootedness of the body in the earth. In "Our Bodies" (*OTS* 72), Levertov surveys the male and female anatomy, noting how "nipples, navel, and pubic hair / make ... // a sort of face":

> ... taking
> the rounded shadows at
> breast, buttock, balls,
>
> the plump of my belly, the

> hollow of your
> groin, as a constellation. (72)

The male's genitalia "leans from earth to / dawn in a gesture of / play and // wise compassion" (72). The joyful, whimsical attitude toward the body speaks of Levertov's sureness of her sexuality, as does her assertion that the geography of the body has a sort of cosmic harmony.

There is, indeed, in Levertov's poetry a worship of the male body. In her description, Levertov uses an elevated language of praise that is a female equivalent of that which male poets have used for centuries to describe the female body. Wholly unaffected, spontaneous, and non-sexist, Levertov's rhetoric of praise creates some astounding metaphors, as when, in the poem's final sequence, her lover's back says to her "what sky after sunset / almost white / over a deep woods to which // rooks are homing, says" (73). Perhaps no poem, however, better expresses Levertov's awe before the sacred mystery of the erotic and the physical than does her "Psalm Praising the Hair of Man's Body":

> Hair of man, man-hair, hair of
> breast and groin, marking contour as
>   silverpoint marks in cross-
>   hatching, as river-
>   grass on the woven current
>   indicates ripple,
> praise.
>
>   (*OTS* 82)

In a passage such as this, the imagery of the natural world and of the body blend together with perfect (organic) harmony and ease. The words fall from her tongue as if they were inspired in a moment of "spontaneous overflow" of emotion and poetic vision.

Levertov's early erotic poems are characterized by an utter lack of self-consciousness and by an utter joy in the sexual act. "Luxury," one of Levertov's best erotic poems, begins as she and her lover are walking "by the asters," breathing in "the sweetness that hovers // in August about the tall milkweeds, / without a direct look, seeing / only obliquely what we know // is there" (*JL* 52).

By trusting the senses and putting the mind in abeyance, a genital consciousness takes over: "a sense / of languor and strength begins // to mount in us" (52). The erotic urge soon becomes irresistible. As the couple approaches a river pool "flashing with young trout," the poet sees the skin of her beloved: "the sun

// on my whiteness and your / tawny gold" (52). With a sidelong glance she takes in the naked body of her lover and reflects on the "iridescence // on black curls of sexual hair" (52). The poem appears to end at the beginning of a sexual act.

"Eros at Temple Stream"(*OTS* 55) picks up where "Luxury" leaves off. Levertov and her lover stand "on a warm rock to wash." The act of washing is sensuous and pleasurable:

> slowly
> smoothing in long
>   sliding strokes
> our soapy hands along each other's
> slippery cool bodies....

In the quiet wood, the mounting desire becomes a powerful and unstoppable force:

> our hands were
> flames
> stealing upon quickened flesh until
>
> no part of us but was
> sleek and
> on fire. (55)

Levertov uses line-breaks and enjambment to add to the erotic push and shove of experience here. The sensuous sounds of "slowly" and "sliding" are picked up again at the end in "sleek and on fire."

Levertov sees the sexual relation of male and female as a mystical bond or communion that is possible only when both lovers fully give themselves to the darkness, to the mysterious forces of eros. In her poem "Hymn to Eros" she pleads:

> that we may be, each to the other,
> figures of flame,
> figures of smoke,
> figures of flesh
> newly seen in the dusk.
>
>   (*SD* 21)

Yet even in Levertov's most easily achieved erotic moments of joyful merging there is often a disturbing undercurrent, a note like that in "Folding a Shirt," when time or life "cuts away" the erotic moment. The poem "Bedtime" (*SD* 17), for instance, begins with a strong sense of at-oneness: "We are a meadow where the bees hum, / mind and body are almost one." The reader may hardly notice that Levertov adds "almost," yet the note of qualification is picked up in the haunting last lines of the poem, which bring her soaring poetic spirits crashing back down to earth: "though the fall cold // surrounds our warm bed, and though / by day we are often lonely" (17). As Levertov's lines of joy, of faith and hope are frequently countered by words of sorrow, of doubt and despair, so too her moments of erotic communion and merging are often accompanied by a sense of loneliness and incompletion. Thus while the remembered joy at the end of "To the Snake," for instance, brings light to the "dark morning," the poem's last line emphasizes the darkness of the morning rather than the lightness of Levertov's being.

A gradual darkening of the erotic vision can be seen in the work from the late 1960s onward. In a sense Levertov's erotic themes are transferred into the energies of revolutionary commitment, and, later, into her religious and spiritual themes. For instance, the poem "About Political Action in Which Each Individual Acts from the Heart," moves from physical connection and intimacy to a moment of revolutionary communion (*CB* 86). The "lesson" of sexuality is that "great energy flows from solitude, / and great power from communion."

Overall, Levertov's erotic poems of the 1950s and 1960s emphasize harmony and satisfaction, while those of the middle and late 1970s, the years during and after her divorce from Mitchell Goodman, more often than not focus on unfulfilled desire and longing. The poems in *To Stay Alive* and *Footprints* contain flashes, fragments of spontaneous joy. "Leather Jacket," for instance, in *Footprints* (1970), describes an unexpected moment of sensuous pleasure:

> She turns, eager—
> hand going out to touch
> his arm. But touches
> a cold thick sleeve.
>   (*F* 28)

Still, even in this brief poem, the sensation of pleasure is mixed with the ambiguous shock of the cold sleeve. More often in the later poems the moment of joy does not arrive. The poems set up erotic expectations that are not fulfilled. In a pair of poems from the 1970s, "What She Could Not Tell Him," from *Freeing of the Dust*, and "The Poem Unwritten," from *Footprints*, Levertov describes messages which cannot be said or sent, desires and passions which have not been fully shared. In "What She Could Not Tell Him," Levertov seeks to explore the geography of her lover, to savor his sexuality:

> I wanted
> to know all the bones of your spine, all
> the pores of your skin,
> tendrils of body hair.
> To let
> all of my skin, my hands,
> ankles, shoulders, breasts,
> even my shadow,
> be forever imprinted
> with whatever of you
> is forever unknown to me.
> To cradle your sleep.
>
> (*FD* 18)

Yet the poem is all pent-up desire, all "what she could not tell him." In "The Poem Unwritten," for instance, Levertov writes of a poem unsaid, the poem

> of my hands upon your body
> stroking, sweeping, in the rite of
> worship, going
> their way of wonder down
> from neck-pulse to breast-hair to level
> belly to cock—.
>
> (*F* 30)

Although this poem is, in fact, written, the feelings remain unwritten, left in the mind. The years create a debris field, "a forest of giant stones, of fossil stumps, / blocking the altar" to Eros (*F* 30).

Certainly an important hurdle for Levertov in the 1970s was the disintegration of her marriage to Mitchell Goodman. The years alone, and the years of unfinished and inchoate relationships, certainly account for the fragmentary and uncertain nature of the erotic language in her poems. *The Freeing of the Dust* contains numerous images of loss and lack of connection—letters crossing in the mail, trains passing in the middle of the night, a turnpike "grossly / cut through the woods" (*FD* 4).

Relationships begin with the hope for communion but end with the despair of isolation. A sequence of poems called "Modulations for a Solo Voice" in *Life in the Forest* (Levertov in a note states that it could be subtitled *Historia de un Amor*) begins by reflecting on the early days of a relationship, the "Easy days, nights when our bodies / were learning each other" (*LF* 81). The poem "From Afar" expresses passionate and frank desire: "it is you I want, to look / with love into me, / to come into me" (*LF* 67). Levertov

> wanted to learn you by heart.
> There was only time
> for the opening measures—a minor key,
> major chords, arpeggios of desire that ripple
>   swifter than I can hum them.
>   (*LF* 68)

In this sequence, Levertov seems to recreate her earlier erotic poems which celebrate the male body, almost conjuring up a joyful erotic experience:

> Halfawake, I think
> *silky hair, cornsilk, his voice*
> *of one substance with his words, with*
> *his warm flesh.*
>   (*LF* 69)

Yet the opening sequence cannot be sustained. Disruptive and discordant rhetoric moves the poem away from the altar of Eros to a forest of loneliness and isolation. The world outside seems to dampen the erotic mood. In one poem, she compares her feelings of lack and loss to those of inmates in "crowded / prisons" who "can feel more than / I know" (*LF* 70). At one point, she turns the anger on herself: "I am angry with my eyes for not seeing you," she writes. "I am angry with everything that is filling / the space of your absence" (*LF* 72).

The thought of death, which preoccupies Levertov throughout *Life in the Forest*, seems to negate her erotic dreams and deconstruct her sexual desires:

> my lover talks of two years from now …
> In two years I may be richly
> gone into compost.
>   (*LF* 74; Levertov's ellipses)

In a dream, she imagines herself in a chateau looking after her lover's daughter. The lover enters the room "searching for me, for now at last / we can meet alone for an hour" (*LF* 76). In the dream "of sadness … of seeking each other" (*LF* 76), the lovers do steal away. Yet Levertov makes us focus on the obstacles that block desire rather than on the consummation of the relationship. Images of erotic communion ("This man has shared my bed, our bodies / have warmed each other and given each other / delight" [*LF* 78]) give way to ones of disconnection: "our bodies / are getting angry with us for giving them to each other / and then / allowing something they don't understand to / pry them apart" (*LF* 78). Thoughts of her lover's warmth ("the tense and slender / warmth of your body" [*LF* 87]) are replaced by "the bluest, furthest distance" (*LF* 87) within him. Indeed, the colossus ("perfection, nectarine of light" *LF* 81), made large by the power of eros, has become a flawed ("bruised") being, made small by his thoughtlessness, by his treating her as a "secondclass citizen" (*LF* 81).

In "Lovers (I)" (*OP* 12), one of the most powerful erotic poems of the later work, Levertov recalls and re-enacts moments of passion from her past. She remembers the words of former lovers, but "what they tell is gone." With astounding clarity and precision, she recollects her own sexual feelings: "Another led me / under the wing of / the waterfall. Light / was fine mist / my skin was myself." Indeed, in this poem, the past becomes more real than the present. As an earlier poem, "A Woman Alone" in *Life in the Forest*, suggests, while Levertov has difficulty recalling exactly which lover it was with whom she experienced a particular moment of pleasure, the moment itself is permanently etched in her mind. She lovingly remembers "that moment of pleasure, of something fiery / streaking from head to heels, the way the whole / flame of a cascade streaks a mountainside" (*LF* 16).

The poem "Holiday" in *Candles from Babylon* is a celebration of a relationship of Levertov's later years, one which appears to have the sort of autonomy Levertov needs to stay in balance: "it's just that / I wasn't lonesome / before I met you" (*CB* 63). Levertov reaches out once again for the erotic experience, seeks to share with her lover what she has kept in her "pocket," some part of herself that she is still willing to share. Basking in the sun and stretching in enjoyment of her surroundings, Levertov loses herself in the moment of pleasure. Her erotic bliss leads to a sort of childlike pledging: "Let's be / best friends: I'll love you / always if you'll love me." It also leads to a spontaneous hymn of sheer delight, "To Eros," a startling and thrilling sequence which calls to mind the exuberant creative energies of "Song for Ishtar":

> desire hungers
> for wine, for clear plain water
> good strong coffee,
> as well as for hard cock and
> throbbing clitoris and the

> glide and thrust of
> sentence and paragraph in and up to the
> last sweet sigh of a
> chapter's ending.
>
> (*CB* 64)

Although savoring a "hard cock" in the same breath as a strong cup of coffee may perhaps minimize the pleasures of the body, Levertov is here able to glory in her sexual being, enjoying the moment with full knowledge that in the end she will "move into separateness." Even though the poem ends with images of "landlocked" separation and the inevitable "*I miss you*," Levertov appears here to have regained her footing, to have rediscovered her center:

> No one confirms
> an other unless
> he himself rays forth
> from a center.
>
> (*CB* 66)

Levertov's commitment to the erotic quest is what makes her work stand apart from that of many of her contemporaries. Sandra Gilbert writes that "in an age of psychic anxiety and metaphysical angst, Denise Levertov's most revolutionary gesture is probably her persistent articulation of joy—joy in self, delight in life, sheer pleasure in pure being" (335). To this comment I would add that Levertov's value also lies in her heroic persistence in the pursuit of erotic joy even when her pleasures and relationships so often lead to bitter disappointment.

In a sense all of Levertov's work involves a search for some sort of solace from existence's difficulties, for candles in Babylon. Ronald Jannsen has written that the "transformative powers of light and energy" (273) dominate Levertov's work. Certainly sexual energy and eros, the desire to preserve and enrich life, contribute to Levertov's transforming power. Always drawn to the transcendent, Levertov is equally drawn to the physical, to "touch, mass, weight, warmth" (*OP* 13). As she writes in *Breathing the Water*, "What we desire travels with us" (83).

Works Cited

Duddy, Thomas. "To Celebrate: A Reading of Denise Levertov." *Criticism* 10.2 (1968): 138–52.

Gilbert, Sandra, "Revolutionary Love and the Poetics of Politics." *Parnassus* 12–13 (1985): 335–51.

Jannsen, Ronald R. "Dreaming of Design: Reading Denise Levertov." *Twentieth Century Literature* 38:3 (Fall 1992): 263–79.

Levertov, Denise. *Breathing the Water*. New York: New Directions, 1987.

———. *Candles in Babylon*. New York: New Directions, 1982.

———. *Collected Earlier Poems 1940–1960*. New York: New Directions, 1979.

———. *Footprints*. New York: New Directions, 1970.

———. *The Freeing of the Dust*. New York: New Directions, 1975.

———. *The Jacob's Ladder*. New York: New Directions, 1961.

———. *Life in the Forest*. New York: New Directions, 1978.

———. *Oblique Prayers*. New York: New Directions, 1984.

———. *O Taste and See*. New York: New Directions, 1964.

———. *The Sorrow Dance*. New York: New Directions, 1966.

Mills, Ralph J. "Denise Levertov: Poetry of the Immediate." *Contemporary American Poetry*. New York: Random House, 1965. Rpt. in *Denise Levertov: In Her Own Province*. Ed. Linda Wagner. New York: New Directions, 1979.

Wakoski, Diane. "Song of Herself." *Women's Review of Books* 5 (Feb. 1988): 7–8.

Gender, Nature, and Spirit:
Justifying Female Complexity in the
Later Poetry of Denise Levertov

Katherine Hanson and Ed Block

This investigation of gender, nature, and spirit in the later poetry of Denise Levertov is the result of a genuine collaboration. Though each author has written different parts of the paper, the structure, readings, and insights grew out of a joint effort to understand Levertov's later poetry. This collaboration included taped readings of and responses to the poems, and extended discussions of those responses. We hope that the paper reflects the genuinely dialogical nature of our enterprise.

Denise Levertov was from the beginning a poet of nature. "Spirit," too, is at least implicitly present from as early a poem as "Sarnen" (*CEP* 3), where the favorite image of a mountain intimates something beyond the merely concrete. Gender manifests itself as well in many of those early poems. Critics of Levertov's poetry have framed the issue of gender in a number of useful ways, and it is from some of those perspectives that our paper takes its departure. This study will attempt to show how in her best poetry, Levertov explores issues of gender, nature, and spirit often blending them in complex ways within the same poem. She layers her observations and perceptions, one upon the other, in order to perplex, challenge, and enchant the reader at the same time. Her poetry reveals the attempt to understand her place in the world relative to a changing, even fluid combination of the issues of gender, nature, and spirit.

Levertov's public statements on the subject would seem to argue that gender issues are an insignificant and incidental part of her poetry. In a short piece presented at a 1982 MLA symposium entitled "Genre and Gender in Poetry by Women" (*NSE*) she emphatically denies that she "ever made an aesthetic decision based on gender" (102). In this address she states that it is acceptable for a woman poet to use her experiences as a woman as subject matter, but, that to serve poetry as an art, a poem must eventually rise above "any inessential factor—including gender" (103). However, to read her poetry, and to appreciate how she uses the experiences of her life, fusing issues of gender, nature, and spirit in implicit and suggestive ways, one would have to agree with Sandra Gilbert that, even though "Levertov is not an aggressively feminist writer, her rigorous attentiveness to the realities of her own life as a woman has inevitably forced her to confront the contradictions implicit in that condition" (207). Gilbert admires Levertov's poetry for its "persistent articulation of joy" (201) and believes that Levertov is most politically feminist in the attempts she makes "to analyze and justify female complexity" (209).

Rachel Blau DuPlessis sees in Levertov's "Hypocrite Women" an expression of the belief that women feel "cold, moonstruck, [and] self-absorbed" because they repress what they feel in order to maintain a peaceful facade, and, "[i]n doing so, they hide the intensity of the conflict from themselves" (219). This conflict is clearly present in many of Levertov's poems, even as she is denying this "inessential factor" of gender. The "intense self-questioning and internal debate" which DuPlessis sees in Adrienne Rich's mythic poetry (22) also emerges in many of Levertov's poems. In a reading of "In Mind," George Bowering sees "Levertov ... looking for a way to be a complete woman and poet, spiritually whole in a world that looks fragmented" (253). In her poetry, Levertov seeks a way to find this completeness as a woman, struggling to reconcile the often conflicting roles of woman, poet, nature lover, and spiritual questor to understand the world and her place in it. Although Levertov attempts to dismiss the relevance of her gender, gender is there as she struggles to pull together her various roles and identities, reconciling the "double bind" that Susan Juhasz so skillfully describes in her 1976 study, *Naked and Fiery Forms: Modern American Poetry by Women, A New Tradition*. Juhasz sees the strength in Levertov's poetry as coming from "its recurrent ambivalence and frequent flashes of vibrant strength ... aris[ing] out of an engagement with her feminine experience" (58). It is our contention that despite such ambivalence, nature and spirit, together with the demonstrably apparent emphasis on gender, represent a useful set of related issues discussion of which will help readers—

as it has helped the authors—understand the varied ways in which Levertov's poetry justifies the complexity of female experience.

Levertov's ambivalence reveals itself early (1957) in "The Earthwoman and the Waterwoman" (*CEP* 31–32). Two very different archetypal women are portrayed in this poem. The earthwoman is the ideal mother who stays home, nourishing her children with good cooking, seemingly satisfied in her "warm hut" and "her dark fruitcake sleep," while the waterwoman, who is the creative one, goes off dancing, neglecting her children (for they are thin), exhibiting a carefree attitude that borders on the irresponsible. Yet she is the more fascinating character with her "moonshine children" who are serenaded by her gay but sad songs. The earth mother with her "oaktree arms" and her children "full of blood and milk" is substantial and solid. The earthwoman who makes "cakes of good grain" appears to be satisfied with who she is, content to stay at home and curl up in her "dark fruitcake sleep." The waterwoman, on the other hand, is not satisfied. She is still searching, and—as a consequence—may appear light, imaginative, carefree, wistful, yearning. She is more appealing than the earthwoman in many ways. She has more freedom of movement, is more complex, romantic, magical (as in a fairy-tale), going "dancing in the misty lit-up town / in dragonfly dresses and blue shoes." It is her image that ends the poem. A tension exists between the two women, yet they are separate, disconnected, mythical, and not quite real.

The spiritual element in this poem is elusive and not religious in any strict sense. Spirit is embodied in the imaginative waterwoman, an enigmatic creature of fancy. The contented earthwoman is good to her children in physical ways but is not described as imaginative. She is of the earth: solid, material. The waterwoman's children have a joyous, creative songstress of a mother who perhaps nourishes her children in spiritual ways, though we are never directly told that. Her imaginative quality makes this mother sad, however, because her creativity takes her away from her children and impels her to search for a life outside of the traditional realm of home and hearth.

"The Dragonfly-Mother" (*CB* 13–15) represents a first, tenuous attempt at integrating the separate personalities depicted in "The Earthwoman and the Waterwoman." The poem dramatizes the tension between a female speaker's personal integrity as engagé poet to her integrity as an artist: the tension between an activist's broken promises and a poet's need to keep faith with herself. The dragonfly-mother is a "messenger" and the poet's source of inspiration. Gender as an issue is less prominent than in "The Earthwoman and the Waterwoman," but identification of the "dragonfly-mother" with the "Waterwoman" introduces paradoxes that include both implicit gender and explicit nature and spirit issues. An "alien" figure of "irresponsible" inspiration, the dragonfly-mother engages directly with the speaker of the poem, creating a dialogical relation which is both more "intimate" and more "personal" than the objective contrast of characters presented in the earlier poem.

In striking contrast to the waterwoman, the dragonfly-mother is associated with the sort of "earthy" images that, in the previous poem, would have been exclusively part of the earthwoman's world. The dragonfly-mother listens "to the creak of / stretching tissue, / tense hum of leaves unfurling." But, like the waterwoman, she is also associated with air and water as one "who sees in water / her own blue fire zigzag." Like the waterwoman, too, the dragonfly-mother is cold and swift. But the dragonfly-mother is also like an old friend who "sat at my round table" where she and the speaker "told one another dreams" like two old friends. In her close relation to nature, and her more intimate relationships with others, the dragonfly-mother is more like the earthwoman. In this complex blending of the two earlier characters, therefore, the dragonfly-mother represents a tentative model of integration. As if to confirm this integrative power, near the end of the poem's second stanza the speaker describes the dragonfly-mother as hovering over a river. Like the Holy Spirit hovering over the waters of chaos, the dragonfly-mother becomes a creative force who listens even as she tell her own stories, and who listens so actively to others' stories that she contributes a measure of her own creativity.

The third section of the poem returns to the issue of broken promises, leading to the crux of the poem. Having slept and dreamed, the speaker awakes and says:

> I kept a tryst with myself,
> a long promise that can be fulfilled
> only poem by poem,
> broken over and over.

Like the promise, the syntax of this stanza is broken and ambiguous. What is it that is "broken over and over"? It seems clear that faithfulness to the imagination can only be achieved *through* repeated failure. The poem dramatizes an ongoing paradox: the tension between everyday duties and the call of imagination. A woman-poet breaks her promise either way. If she gives a speech, she breaks faith with her muse. If she keeps a tryst with a messenger from the world of imagination, she breaks faith with the world of action.

At the end of the third-last stanza the speaker becomes like the dragonfly-mother. The importance of this impersonation cannot be overemphasized. The speaker says:

> I too,
> a creature, grow among reeds,
> in mud, in air,
> in sunbright cold, in fever
> of blue-gold zenith, winds
> of passage.

Assimilating in paradoxical fashion the archetypal images of earth, air, fire, and water, the speaker, like the dragonfly-mother herself, assimilates features of the earthwoman and the waterwoman and experiences transformation.

The final stanza resolves the poem's key tensions. It enacts the insights which the dragonfly-mother might have visited upon the poem's speaker. Repeating images from the second stanza, the speaker once again appropriates and transforms the dragonfly-mother's insights and influence:

> There is a summer
> in the sleep
> of broken promises, fertile dreams,
> acts of passage, hovering
> journeys over the fathomless waters.

This stanza brings together the worlds of dragonfly-mother and activist poet. "Broken promises," it seems, bring "fertile dreams" and "acts of passage." Like the dragonfly-mother, or the Holy Spirit, the poet is ready to connect disparate elements through "hovering / journeys over the fathomless waters."

Seen in light of the next two poems, "The Dragonfly-Mother" anticipates Levertov's strategy of invoking a female muse to describe and enact female complexity. But looking backward, we can also see that the poem expresses some residual guilt and ambivalence. Long after she had given up the "neo-romanticism" of the 1940s and 1950s, Levertov's poetry continues to reflect—in images with a distinctly romantic flavor—upon the conflict between the everyday duties of mother and activist and the life of the imagination. Reflecting these themes in a structure that subsumes gender as it intimates the relation to nature and spirit, "The Dragonfly-Mother" represents a step further along the poet's journey toward fuller, more complex integration of Levertov's life and poetic gift.

"In Memory: After a Friend's Sudden Death" (*BW* 23) begins a process of reversing the emphasis on gender and nature. An elegiac recollection, the poem significantly re-arranges the gender, nature, and spirit equation as it celebrates a woman who becomes another complex female muse. The poem's structure implies a dialogue between the speaker's perception of the woman and the impressions of the woman's other admirers. The poem's situation is also striking and unusual, and this dimension adds to the powerful effect and a heightened sense of female complexity.

Concrete details make the situation clear: two mature women in a sauna; one surely and the other presumably naked. The situation explains and makes possible a celebration of the female body. The poem evokes a vivid physical impression as it suggests the woman's "inexhaustible" spiritual dimension. It does so by imagining the woman stepping into the "fragrant redwood sauna" and from there into a "welcoming whirlpool." Like the earlier poems discussed, this one is built on a number of opposing images. The poem contrasts the woman's beauty and gentleness with her strength. Other tensions involve the impression of both youth and age, the virginal and the fertile, the body and the mind. A central allusion even establishes a contrast between life and art. Multiple suspensions in the syntax create tension between the woman's words and her works and the impression of her physical appearance. Though the event described took place in the past, before the woman's death, the poem realizes a compelling sense of presence, and this complex presence is created in part by the host of archetypal feminine images.

Nature and spirit come together in the poem's first lines: "Others will speak of her spirit's tendrils reaching / almost palpably into the world." The phrase, "her spirit's tendrils," implicitly connects nature ("tendrils") with spirit and gender. Presenting this "nature" analogy as the view of "others," the speaker recollects instead the appearance of the woman's body in the sauna. Four pairs of lines create the impression of A.N. as both "young" and "nearing fifty"; "vestal" and fertile, having "borne daughters and a son." The allusion to "a 15th century widehipped grace, / small waist and curving belly" recalls such late medieval works of art as Van Eyck's "Giovanni Arnolfini and His Wife." This allusion further complicates the relation between the (imagined) present of the woman's appearance and the past of artistic creation. The image of "breasts with that look / of inexhaustible gentleness" further suggests a medieval ideal of beauty, while "inexhaustible" implies both fecundity and infinity.

The final three stanzas of the poem change course again, proposing further complexity. "And I will speak," she says, "not of her work, her words, her search." As if imagining the dialogue of others who would speak about A.N., the next five lines suggest by negation an almost shadowy dimension of the woman's life. These lines, a significant syntactic suspension, prepare for the final affirmation of the poem: "the great encompassing *Aah!*" with which A.N. enters "the welcoming whirlpool."

Viewed as something between a tableau and a moving picture, the woman's image, as the poem creates it, suggests a complex dynamism that results from contradictory images of the feminine. There are still two women: the speaker and the woman spoken about. But the woman spoken about has become (anticipating Beatrice in the next poem to be discussed) another female muse. Identified with spirit, the woman spoken about nevertheless rises out of nature, exemplifying it only to return, figuratively, to nature, as she steps into the water. Like a reverse image of Botticelli's *Birth of Venus*, "In Memory" memorializes the mystery of the now-departed friend.

Another elegy for a woman friend, "Missing Beatrice" (*BW* 24) is a tribute to Beatrice Hawley, a poet friend of Levertov's. But the name "Beatrice" evokes historical and literary images of an ideal woman—Dante's ideal beauty and muse. The name also evokes the idea of the woman who gives, the name's Latin origin meaning "joy bringer." This woman evokes for Levertov complex natural and elemental images elevated to a spiritual and timeless level. The four elements are again present in this paradox of a woman, dissolving the boundaries between life and death, between hot and cold, between knowing and mystery. This Beatrice is a woman who burns from within with a "Goodness [that] was a fever," comforting "Anyone" with whom she came into contact. Remembering that, simultaneously, Beatrice's goodness is fire (the warmth of the earthwoman) and her innocence so pure that it is "that cold" (as in both the waterwoman and the dragonfly-mother), the natural metaphor that unites these two seemingly opposite elements is the peat, cut from a bog, used to make the fragrant fire (now extinguished) on the hearth.

The peat, a substance that comes from the cold, wet bog, is consumed when burned, producing the fragrant warmth that comforts. Beatrice's innocence (water/cold) is like "peat-bog water, subtle and dark." Her kindness/warmth seems inexhaustible (echoing the "inexhaustible gentleness" of A.N. in "In Memory")— as if she is "an endless supply" of "turf from a bog." This woman is portrayed as an earth mother, consumed by others because of her giving nature. Yet she is also like the poet and the others. Beatrice's passing leaves the speaker with "words / cupped in our hands to drink." This is not the simple earthwoman of the earlier poems, for Beatrice is both warming and cold, both of the earth and of the spirit—"fragrant still"—with an innocence that is both pure, yet "subtle and dark."

This is a woman of such complexity that she is a mystery, even to those who thought they knew her well and who now realize that "we never / really saw you." The speaker does not explain (out of a sense of "reserve," perhaps) how Beatrice's innocence, which is described as pure and cold, can also be "subtle and dark" at the same time. How can we reconcile the fact that this innocence came from her knowing "more than was good for [her]"? This complex woman leaves the speaker wondering how she could have had such a profound influence and yet remained such a mystery. Beatrice's words live on, providing a positive influence. But the speaker regrets the loss of the real person of Beatrice. This poem embodies a struggle to comprehend the mysteries of humanity, of nature, and of spirit. The physical presence is gone, but the poetry and the spirit of the woman remains.

Instead of an actual woman, a scene of nature—Lago di Como in 1989—inspires Levertov in "The Reminder" (*ET* 67). Yet the place remembered is a composition of the mind, an idyllic and romantic picture inspired by the visions of others as well as her own, recorded by "language, paint, memory transmitted." It is a picture that evokes images of the feminine. The water (an archetypal association with woman), the terraces with outstretched wings, the "Mountains delicately frosted," and the lake viewed through a haze "that is not smog" and that "gentles the light" create a feminine vision of "an earthly paradise." The view is as much a product of the imagination as it is a real place. The first half of the poem is devoted to this vision of beauty.

The lake is largely judged by its surface qualities, the way women are often judged in our culture, but the image is an illusion, a misinterpretation of "our own crude gaze." The perception of what is beautiful in nature and in women is influenced by the visions of others. Women often do not trust their own perceptions—"our own crude gaze" is not sufficient. But the poem seems to indicate that there is something wrong with this distrust, just as there is something wrong with the perception of beauty. Can we trust perceptions that only rely on surface impressions? The "knowledge ... gnaws at us" because, according to the speaker, we know that beneath the surface the "misshaped cells remain." A typical response of even the most beautiful women is to see themselves as flawed, because the expectations, the standards of beauty, have been created throughout history by the visions of others. Besides a reference to Levertov's own illness, the misshaped cells could be the cancer of false visions of beauty, imposed upon women to the extent that they no longer trust their own perceptions.

What are these flaws, these misshapen cells? Are they real or imagined? On the surface, they appear to be the actual pollution of the earth. The lake's sign says: "'Swim at your own risk. The lake is polluted.'" Our "earthly paradise" is flawed, and we are hurt when we ignore this fact. It gnaws at our spirit and distorts our vision of reality. Is there a cancer gnawing at our spirit? Are *we* the cancer that is threatening the earth's existence? The still small voice "of the spirit" gnaws at us to take moral responsibility for what is happening to the earth. Our conscience tells us to open our eyes and see beneath the surface, deep within ourselves. To ignore the warning signs is a spiritual malady that puts us at risk.

The discussion of the complex nature of how we interpret visual signs in this poem, while emphasizing the pollution of the earth, questions the pollution of perception both on a cultural level and a spiritual level. It is this blending of issues of gender, nature, and spirit that gives Levertov's poetry such wonderful depth. Nature is in the foreground in this poem, but what lies beneath the surface is what is important. We are asked to question the very nature of perception—the perception of beauty, of the feminine beauty of the natural scene. The theme is still one of complexity, of much beneath the surface that is not at first perceived, or is perhaps denied.

On first inspection "Tragic Error" (*ET* 69)—like "The Reminder"—does not seem to belong in a discussion of gender, nature, and spirit at all. One might say that it better belongs with Levertov's more overtly religious poems. But closer examination shows that its religious dimension is only one part of the poem's complex perspective and that it does, indeed, belong in a discussion of spirit, nature *and* gender. The poem presents a commentary on the Biblical injunction to "subdue the earth." Like a number of the poems we are discussing, it is premised on a dialogue—and therefore a tension—between the speaker and the subject of the poem. Entering into a conversation with Scripture, the poem dramatizes the tension between the speaker and the scriptural text. The issues raised in this dialogue become the subject of the poem. Insofar as Scripture is assumed to be "Revelation" given to human beings, this poem emphasizes "spirit" in a way that the earlier poems do not, while nature and gender assume important but secondary roles.

The poem's opening sets up the dialogue, allowing the scriptural text to speak first. But then the speaker undermines the Biblical resonances of *"The earth is the Lord's"* by qualifying that clause with "we gabbled." A similar tactic recurs in the first stanza's other "comments" on the scriptural texts. The connotations of "looted and pillaged" are implicitly male, while "gabbled" and "preened" imply a feminine perspective. That the criticism embraces both genders is further underlined when the speaker does not hesitate to include herself in the condemnation.

The second stanza gives greater place to the speaker's commentary. Asserting that writers and readers of Scripture have "Miswritten, misread" the divine "charge" [to care for the world], the speaker suggests that it is human beings' task "to have been / earth's mind, mirror, reflective source." Further implying a feminine perspective in the nurturing attitude expressed and the tone suggested by "Surely," she adds that "Surely our task / was to have been / to love the earth." The final detail, "to *dress and keep it* like Eden's garden," also implies a feminine—not to mention ecological—attitude.

Conceiving of the earth as a body and human beings as "cells" of that body (recalling the "cell" metaphor in "The Reminder"), the final stanza proposes that human perception and imagination have a "respons-ability" far different, and more subtle, than mere *"dominion."* Only human beings can "perceive and imagine" the earth. Only human beings "could bring the planet / into the haven it is to be known." Dimly echoing a passage in St. John on "knowing as we are known," the poem's conclusion suggests both peace and blessedness. The final analogy, suggesting that human beings would bless the earth as the eye blesses the hand, also obliquely recalls the Pauline theology of the Mystical Body.

"Tragic Error" resembles some of the earlier poems discussed in that it too involves a dialogue between the speaker and the subject of the poem. One partner in the conversation is putatively male and dominating; the other partner is feminine, reciprocal, and—if you will—more mystical. Despite its many contrasts, however, the poem achieves a tenuous synthesis as ecological and spiritual insights merge. The speaker of the poem urges a more participatory relationship between the environment and those who hold it in trust. Permeated, as it were, with a gendered perspective on the world, the poem figures the complex response with which a woman poet feels it necessary to address the impending destruction of the natural world.

In "Salvator Mundi: Via Crucis" (*ET* 114) spirit remains the dominant focus, but nature and gender are thoroughly integrated. The poem seeks to understand "from the inside" the experience of Christ's Incarnation. Evoking "the burden of humanness" which Christ felt, the poem explores the dynamics of betrayal, passivity, and acceptance. Ultimately, the poem is about the difficulty of conceiving, let alone expressing, the depth of Christ's suffering humanity. Implicit in this effort is the struggle to overcome the "otherness" that Christ's life and experience represent. Once again, the poem seems premised on a series of tensions whose most obvious sign is the self-other opposition, as the poet seeks to understand the mystery of divine personhood.

Like "In Memory" (and numerous other Levertov poems), "Salvator Mundi" is inspired by a work of art—or, here, a series of works—by Rembrandt. The poem imagines the young, "unjudging" "gaze" of the "very intelligent face" depicted in a series of "small heads" that the artist painted. The poet seems to dwell on these faces, finding in them "a soul-mirror gaze of deep understanding." This dwelling upon the faces suggests a first, intimate interaction between the speaker and the subject spoken about. The speaker then imagines Christ's face, as it were, years later, "in extemis"—that is, how it might look in its suffering. The speaker can at best imagine the grimace, since no artistic rendering of the crucifixion could portray its reality. "The burden of humanness" is the theme, along with "dread" and the "wanting to let the whole thing go."

On the colloquial note in "let the whole thing go," the poem becomes strikingly personal—and radical—as it proposes that Christ's situation resembles that of "any mortal human hero out of his depth." But the speaker closes this analogy with an even more potent one: "like anyone who has taken a step too far / and wants herself back." What accounts for this transformation of gender? Did "the soul-mirror gaze" that the speaker saw in those earlier, artistic renderings contain a feminine aspect? In what is probably the climax of the poem, the speaker acknowledges a blending with the subject that involves moving from the male to the female "register." Like Keats' merging with the identity of the nightingale in the famous ode, the speaker's identifying herself with Christ is sudden, and disruptive.

Reaffirming art's inability to convey "the human longing / to simply cease, to not be," the second half of the poem nevertheless successfully imparts (via a series of negative statements) a sense of what Christ—as human—endured. Art is incapable of rendering the longing "to not be." It can only manifest an attitude of reserve and—as some theologians argue—suggest the divine nature by means of negation. Not torture, not betrayals, not weakness, and not anticipation of death can stop him. What could have stopped him, the poem suggests, is "this sickened desire to renege, / to step back from what He, Who was God,/ had promised Himself." Like the speaker of "The Dragonfly-Mother," the speaker of "Salvator Mundi" imagines the possibility of a broken promise, this time Jesus' breaking "what He, Who was God, / had promised Himself." The poem is fraught with complex tensions. These include both obvious contradictions and larger paradoxes concerning the attitude of "reserve." The poem achieves a degree of integration inasmuch as "Salvator Mundi" imagines the figure of Christ in the concrete natural surroundings of "the midnight Garden / or staggering uphill." It also transcends gender limitations to understand the Incarnation. In fact, nature—both human and non-human—seems to be literally raised to a spiritual level. It is as if in seeking to understand Jesus' complex humanity, the woman poet transcends nature *and* gender as she intuits something of the tremendous tension between the human and the divine.

As in so many of her poems, Levertov challenges us to see in new ways, yet manages to combine issues of nature, spirit, and gender that echo what has come before in her poetry. Spirit is foregrounded in "Ascension" (*ET* 115–16) in the very fact of its being a meditation on Christ's Ascension, an idea that can only be understood from the perspective of the Christian faith. Yet the images she uses to discuss it, the very concrete images of biological existence, only emphasize all the more the mystery of the event.

The central image of the poem is the metaphor of birth as an arduous journey. It begins with the picture of a plant struggling to emerge from the earth "through downpress of dust / upward, soil giving way / to thread of white, that reaches / for daylight, to open as green / leaf that it is...." Yet this is not really happening because it is "as if again" Christ is emerging into life. This birthing process is "arduous" and a paradox because it is both "Expulsion" and "liberation," both "torture and bliss." Levertov imagines that "Matter reanimate," even down to the level of the "human cells" and "molecules," must relinquish themselves by a process that could only be as painful "as the return / from Sheol, and / back through the tomb / into breath." This switching back and forth from one state of existence to another, from human existence to spiritual existence, is one that the poet tries to envisage. This attempt to understand a complex mystery of faith through the metaphor of the birthing process brings the gender issue to the forefront. Here is the ultimate fusion of images of nature, spiritual mystery, and gender, blending the male and female:

> He again
> Fathering Himself.
> Seed-case
> splitting.
> He again
> Mothering His birth:
> torture and bliss.

These lines sum up the paradox of Christ's being, both human and spirit, male and female, a Christ experiencing a spiritual ecstasy that is compared to an actual physical process, one which only a woman who has given birth can fully comprehend.

From this brief and selective survey, it should be clear that even Denise Levertov's most recent poems are strategies to assimilate, appropriate, and integrate a variety of experiences—of gender, nature, and spirit—to which she sought to remain open. Gender, nature, and spirit continue to make a potent mix in her effort to understand her place in the world. These poems ultimately record a transformation that most often affects the poet-speaker as much as the poem itself achieves a poetic transformation of the person, object, or experience about which the poem speaks. Although Levertov's poetry continues to test the relations that pertain among gender, nature, and spirit, the astute reader never forgets that Levertov sees from a woman's perspective, and what her poetry reveals is the complex nature of perception—down to the very cells and atoms of our being—and the complexities of the spiritual issues which such tensions imply.

Works Cited

Bowering, George. "Denise Levertov." *Denise Levertov: Selected Criticism.* Ed. Albert Gelpi. Ann Arbor: U of Michigan P, 1993. 243–54.

DuPlessis, Rachel Blau. "The Critique of Consciousness and Myth in Levertov, Rich, and Rukeyser." *Denise Levertov: Selected Criticism.* Ed. Albert Gelpi. Ann Arbor: U of Michigan P, 1993. 218–42.

Gelpi, Albert. *Denise Levertov: Selected Criticism.* Ann Arbor: U of Michigan P, 1993.

Gilbert, Sandra M. "Revolutionary Love: Denise Levertov and the Poetics of Politics." *Denise Levertov: Selected Criticism.* Ed. Albert Gelpi. Ann Arbor: U of Michigan P, 1993. 201–17.

Juhasz, Suzanne. *Naked and Fiery Forms: Modern American Poetry by Women, A New Tradition.* New York: Harper and Row, 1976.

Levertov, Denise. *Breathing the Water.* New York: New Directions, 1987.

———. *Candles in Babylon.* New York: New Directions, 1982.

———. *Collected Earlier Poems 1940–1960.* New York: New Directions, 1979.

———. *Evening Train.* New York: New Directions, 1992.

———. *New and Selected Essays.* New York: New Directions, 1992.

2

what they know, what
perplexities and wisdoms they exchange,
unknown to me as were the thoughts
of grownups when in infancy I wandered
into a roofed clearing amidst
human feet and legs and the massive
carved legs of the table,

from "From Below" (by Denise Levertov
from *This Great Unknowing*)

Winter Solstice, 1997

by Sam Green

My wife takes every candle in the cabin,
puts them on top the piano, the desk,
in all the corners, the counter
in the kitchen, lights every lamp
we own and turns the wicks up high.

The Christmas tree shines with burning
wax, the stove is undamped,
its fireproof glass door
a fixed and brilliant eye.

On this, the day of longest dark,
she celebrates the turn, the growing
strength of light to come.

We step out on the porch and gaze
back through the window which blazes
in brilliant glory from dozens of flames.

We didn't know she was one day
gone, the poet whose life was spent
"doing to things / what light does to them."
Not to dazzle, as with lesser poets,
but to cast out shadows as demons
to *illumine* in the old sense.

How do we subtract her from the world
and keep the sum of ourselves?

Light links us to light.
We move into the winter of mourning,
to days lengthening with grief
and only the bright rooms of her books
to sustain us, those sparks struck
from the vast dark flint
that catch in us as tinder
till we, too, glow and glow as the sender.

Remembering Denise[1]

Robert Creeley

Hard to believe we met about fifty years ago in New York, when she and Mitch had first married and she had returned from Europe with him in the classic manner to start her own life over again. Certainly as a poet she had to. The distance between her first book *The Double Image*, and the second, *Here and Now*, published by City Lights in its Pocket Poets series ten years later, is a veritable quantum leap. Kenneth Rexroth, editing *The New British Poets* for New Directions, thought her most able and, when he saw her, declared her Dante's Beatrice incarnate. W.C. Williams, writing of "Mrs. Cobweb" in *Here and Now*, said that one can't really tell if she's utterly virginal or if she has been on the town for years and years. Everyone was intrigued!

Was it Denise's long training as a dancer, when she was a child, that gave her such particularity of movement—her phrase and line shifting with the fact of her emotion, the rhythms locating each word? In a sense she was a wide-awake dreamer; a practical visionary with an indomitable will; a passionate, whimsical heart committed to an adamantly determined mind. It wasn't simply that Denise was right. It was that her steadfast commitments could accommodate no error.

I remember, when we were neighbors in France, riding our bicycles in Aix from the villages we lived in just to the north. There was a week-long celebration of Mozart. Denise's bike lost its brakes at the top of the three-mile hill into the city and down she came, full tilt, careening through early evening traffic, to come to rest finally at the far side near the railroad station. Was she terri-

---

[1]This essay was used at Stanford University's memorial service for Denise Levertov and then included in the tributes to her in the Poetry Society of America's online *Journal*. Used by permission of the author.

fied? I recall our going to the concert—so seemingly she soon recovered. Balance, quick purchase, passional measure rather than didactic, mind an antenna, not a quantifier merely. Her voice was lovely. Her laughter, particularly her helpless, loud giggles, were what finally must define "humanness." Her whole body took over. We used to sit out at the edge of the orchard near her house in Puyricard, rehearsing endlessly what it was Williams was doing with the line. We were fascinated by how the pace was managed, how the insistent breaking into of the grammatically ordered line made a tension and a means more deft than any we had known. That bond of recognition, shared between us, never lessened.

Back in the States, then to Mexico, as I also shifted about to Black Mountain—then to New Mexico, Guatemala, and Canada—Mitch's and Denise's son Nick grew and grew, as our own children did. Thanks to Donald Allen's *The New American Poetry* (with Denise ostensibly the one woman of Black Mountain's company, despite the fact that she never went there, even to look), we began to have a public condition, as they say. The Vancouver Poetry Festival of 1963 and the Berkeley Poetry Conference of 1965 were the greatest collective demonstrations.

Necessarily the Vietnam War and its politics bitterly changed our world. Insofar as that determinant in Denise's life is a solid fact of the period's history, there's no need now to rehearse it. I was closest to the poems of *The Jacob's Ladder* and *O Taste and See.* Repeatedly she found voices for our common lives.

Years passed, of course. We saw one another all too rarely and yet her presence, her stalwart integrity, were always a given. Work to offset the world's real ills became an increasing occupation, forcing a more generalized community, on one hand, and also an increased singularity as her son moved into his own life and she and his father separated. She has written poignantly, healingly, of this time.

Now and then we would intersect on our show biz travels, once in Cincinnati, then a few days later in New York. Finally we were together at a Poetry Society of America awards dinner—we'd been judges—after she moved to Seattle. Nick was with her; they were both solid and happy. There was always much I wanted to talk to her about—[Robert] Duncan, for example; my own confusions; the life I now lived with my family; the increased rigors of teaching. But we no longer seemed to find time or occasion to write. Last fall at Stanford, I got the news from friends that her cancer treatment seemed to have gone well. She had visited just a short time before and appeared much better.

Then bleakly, irrevocably, she was dead. No more chance to talk except in the way one finally always had—in what she wrote, what one had hoped to say, what one remembered.

Interview with Denise Levertov

Gary Pacernick

Questions and answers were submitted in writing.

G.P. What have you found the hardest thing about being a poet?

D.L. I can't say I've found *anything* hard about it!

G.P. What is the most enjoyable thing about being a poet for you?

D.L. I consider myself extremely lucky to have the gift. And I'm also lucky in having received a lot of positive response, all my life, for simply doing what it is natural for me to do. I've also been criticized, of course, but some negative criticism is salutary and the positive responses have outnumbered the negative.

G.P. Are we at the end of the long journey of poetry? What can a late twentieth-century poet hope to accomplish?

D.L. We may, if we continue destroying our environment, be at the end of our journey as a *species*!—but as long as the human species exists so will poetry, I believe, because it is a human characteristic. I don't have an answer to the second part of the question; or perhaps I do: poems can serve to remind people of many things they don't notice, and to reveal the extraordinary within the ordinary, and to stimulate imagination and intuitive knowledge, and by being beautiful, moving, powerful—just as poems have always done.

At this tail-end of the 20th century one of the things about which poetry can nudge people is about matters of ecological consciousness and conscience. Because poetry has traditionally dealt with "Nature" anyway (especially poetry in English), it is well placed to do so. "Consciousness raising" is certainly part of poetry's range, and is what links it to prophecy (though poetry and prophecy are not identical).

G.P. What does a poet need to know about craft? Are rhyme and meter still important enough to be part of the young poet's training? What is free verse? Can it be taught?

D.L. Of course, a poet needs to develop craft (although it is of little use without inborn ability). A poet needs to perceive and recognize the craft elements in other poets' work—though not necessarily to adopt them. The function of rhyme and meter, along with other technical devices, can be (and need to be) learned, but can be absorbed through attentive *reading*—they don't *have* to be taught in school. What *does* have to be taught (today, in America, anyway) is reading. And attention. "Free verse" (a name loosely applied to various "nonce" or non-traditional forms as well as to loose *vers libres*) is no different in this from any other mode, though it demands yet closer attention.

G.P. What do you think inspired you to be a poet?

D.L. I started to write as a young child. The ur-impulse is a native special relation to language (as, for a musician, to musical sounds or for a visual artist to color, form, paint) and *not* to subject matter. (For a writer of fiction the ur-impulse is probably more related to storytelling than to language as such.)

G.P. How did William Carlos Williams influence you as a young poet? And do you still feel his influence?

D.L. William Carlos Williams became an influence in my mid-20s by which time I had published my first book. His influence helped me to free my diction and rhythms from received habits, and to survive undiagnosed culture-shock at the same time! I think I *absorbed* his influence a long time ago, so I don't actively feel it today—but I know I would not be who I am without it (even if I'm not sure if he would have approved my work of later decades).

G.P. How did you meet Creeley, Duncan, and Olson? Have they and you learned from each other? Do you believe in the breath unit, projective verse?

D.L. I met Creeley through my husband (they had both been at Harvard). Duncan introduced himself to me with a poem-letter. I only met Olson a couple of times and did not correspond with him. NO, I don't believe in the "breath unit." To me, "projective verse" meant the possibility of a much more inclusive kind of poem ("composition by field") than the discrete focus of a more "bijou-like" poem prevalent in the 50's; and also the necessity for a good poem to follow its trajectory without stopping to "load the rifts with ore" (as Keats had said) because it would have no rifts. This may well not have been exactly what Olson meant. In any case, it was good advice as I understood it—though not particularly original.

G.P. In "Illustrious Ancestors" (*CEP* 77–78), you write of your dual ancestry and how it has influenced your poetic aspirations: "Well, I would like to make, / thinking some line still taut between me and them...." Do you suggest that your religious vision comes from the Rav and his people? Can you address your father's impact upon you as a writer?

D.L. I don't imply that it came to me more from the Rav than from Angell Jones of Mold—I was claiming them both as ancestors, equally.

G.P. "In "The Third Dimension" (*CEP* 46–47), you say "a simple honesty is / nothing but a lie." Is the third dimension something hidden in nature that only language can capture? Is this a mystical notion?

D.L. "The Third Dimension" was a poem about falling in love with someone although I still loved my husband, and about the inexplicableness of this. It wasn't "mystical." It was just about how complicated life is. (Incidentally, as is well known, I stayed married for many years after that and wrote love poems clearly addressed to my husband, as well as some to other people.)

G.P. In "Stepping Westward" (*SD* 15), were you conscious of the pregnant pauses and rich sounds of the lines, "There is no savor / more sweet, more salt // than to be glad to be / what, woman ..."? Or did the sounds flow spontaneously in the writing? Do you think of the poem as a feminist poem? Is there a controlling metaphor for you in the poem?

D.L. I was both conscious *and* spontaneous. No, it's not feminist in any ideological way, nor have I ever been an active feminist. I'm not sure what a "controlling" metaphor is.

G.P. You refer many times to the Jacob's ladder (Gen. 28:15) as well as Jacob's wrestling with the stranger (Gen. 32:28), after which he is known as Israel ("For you have striven with God and with men, and have prevailed"). Your epigraph re the ladder quotes Buber: "even the ascent and descent of the angels depends on my deed." How do you interpret your fascination with Jacob? Is this not evidence of your Jewishness?

D.L. Many non-Jewish people have been fascinated by the story of Jacob and the Angel! So I don't think my interest constitutes "evidence of Jewishness" at all! I do think arguing with God (or "God wrestling") is a (delightful) Jewish characteristic—but though I have poems expressive of doubt or the sense of disconnection I'm not, I think, particularly apt to argue with God. My friend David Shaddock wrote a wonderful series of "God-wrestling" poems a few years back, for which Arthur Waskow wrote an introduction (unfortunately the book was only published in a *very* limited edition …).

G.P. Have you been aware of the impact of the Song of Songs and other Biblical poetry on such poems as "Song for a Dark Voice" (*JL* 23), "The Ache of Marriage" (*OTS* 5) and other love poems by you?

D.L. Yes, of course I perceived the Biblical influence on the poems you mention, and others. I was brought up hearing the King James Bible.

G.P. In "In Memory of Boris Pasternak" (*JL* 32–33), you write of the great Russian poet's profound effect on you, as if you aspire to "fulfill / what he had written." Have you been drawn to the Russia of your father and to Pasternak in particular because of his and your Jewish-Christian roots? Did you ever meet him? You show this Jewish/Christian interplay as well in "A Letter to William Kinter of Muhlenberg" (*JL* 44–45).

D.L. Yes, I'm sure my love of Russian literature was not altogether unconnected with certain proprietal feeling. But not because of the Jewish-Christian roots. Russian (not Hebrew or Yiddish) was my father's first language, and despite his perfect German and virtually-perfect English it remained the language in which he dreamed. I did not meet Pasternak, but I did have that one wonderful letter in which he wrote, "I feel that we shall be friends." He died not long after, though. The letter is now in Stanford's Special Collections. I called William Kinter "Zaddik" because he stood in that relation, I felt, to his students—and at that moment, to me too. (Later on he sadly seemed to become more and more eccentric and got involved with flying saucers I believe. I don't know if he's still alive.) I was reading *The Tales of the Hasidim* a lot at that time, too.

G.P. Can you speak of the impact of the Holocaust on you? Do you remember what prompted you to write "During the Eichmann Trial" (*JL* 61–67)? Have your reactions to the Holocaust changed since you wrote that poem?

D.L. My parents and my sister (9 years my senior) were heavily involved in helping refugees get out of Germany and Austria and so before I was 10 I knew a bit about the persecution of the Jews by the Nazis. By the time the camps were liberated I knew a *lot* more than the average English person. *The New York Times* coverage of the Eichmann trial, with the many bizarre things he said, prompted me to write that poem. I don't think my attitudes about the Holocaust have changed since then—however, I don't have the poem with me here in Beloit and don't remember it very clearly. I know I later felt the peachtree part was not well written—all that Mr. Death stuff—slack language.

G.P. What's the religious impulse if any behind "O Taste and See" (*OTS* 53)? Do you suggest a belief in an earthly paradise?

D.L. I was pretty much an agnostic at the time of *O Taste and See*. It doesn't imply an earthly paradise but that (as an earlier poem said) "If we're here let's be here now"—a sentiment reechoed in many a later poem. See for example "A South Wind" in *Sands of the Well*.

G.P. This leads me to your Psalms. Are they part of an evolving series or are they separate poems to you? You seem to want to affirm earthly experience as holy. To "worship *mortal* ... without hope of heaven" (*OTS* 80). To affirm "somber beauty in what is mortal" (*OTS* 80). Is there a Jewish influence here from the Hebrew Psalms, etc.? In "A Psalm Praising the Hair of Man" (*OTS* 82), you affirm the body, sexuality, earthly love as holy. Again, this strikes me as Biblical, but you may think of it differently than I.

D.L. Some poems have just felt like Psalms to me. They are separate poems. I agree with you about their expressing a sense of the sacred in the earthly (the ones you mention).

G.P. "The Psalm Concerning the Castle" (*SD* 67) is more elusive than the other Psalms. Why a castle? Kafka? Can the castle be within the speaker?

D.L. The poem was inspired by a Han dynasty Pottery Watch Tower in the Boston Museum of Fine Arts. These were funerary objects. The poem describes it and also articulates what I felt to be its symbolic significance. (Not perhaps its intended significance but what it meant to *me*.)

G.P. There's a paradox in "City Psalm" (*SD* 72): "*I saw Paradise in the dust of the street*." How does bliss emanate from the violence of the streets?

D.L. It doesn't say "emanates from" and it says "dust" not violence—though it does speak of violence too I expect; of ugliness anyway. It is testifying to the paradox of bliss, the sacred, the ecstatic, being present ineffably *every*where....

G.P. When in "A Cloak" (*RA* 44) you speak of "breathing in / my life, / breathing out / poems," you make me think of Muriel Rukeyser. Did you know her well? Did she change your poetry, your life, in any way? She has a great sonnet ("To be a Jew in the 20th century / Is to be offered a gift ..."). The poem is included in an anthology of Jewish-American Literature edited by Abraham Chapman, which includes a selection of your poems as well.

D.L. I knew Muriel quite well (and as you probably know we went to Hanoi together—with Jane Hart, wife of the late Senator Philip Hart of Michigan, in 1972). She was a great human being but no, her poetry did not have any influence on mine. Nor did she "change my life" except in the degree that every single person one knows has *some* effect on one's life, unmeasured and indeed immeasurable. I've read the poem you mention but am not familiar with the anthology.

G.P. What madness do you write of in "Mad Song" (*RA* 49)? How is the madness dear to the speaker?

D.L. I was (again) madly in love. I knew that was a hopeless and stupid infatuation but—as one does at such times—continued to cherish it.

G.P. Can you speak of your involvement in the anti-Vietnam war movement? Has the Jewish prophetic impulse toward social and political action had an impact on your political poetry? If not, what did inspire you to write these poems?

D.L. Again, my social conscience, which caused me to become active in the anti-war movement, was stimulated even in childhood by that of *both* my parents and my sister. Since my active involvement was a condition of my daily life, I naturally wrote poems that arose from my concerns and experiences. I have always tended to reflect in my poems the places and the experiences of my life.

G.P. Is "Prayer for Revolutionary Love" (*FD* 97) a feminist prayer for you?

D.L. A former student, who was also a political comrade of mine, and his girl-friend were going to have to live in 2 separate cities, he because of his commitment to a local printing collective, she in order to take a nursing training course which was *also* a political commitment, like his. The poem was written for them. It's not specifically feminist—it addresses their *equal* rights.

G.P. Were you raised to be conscious of Judaism as a religion? And has the New York Jewish culture that you experienced had an impact on you as a poet?

D.L. Of *course* I understood that Judaism was a religion! And that it was the religion of all the first Christians, and that Jesus was a Jew. (Also that there were lots of Jews who did not believe or practice any religion, as well as those who, like my father, were Jews by inheritance but Christians in belief.) I never attended a Jewish worship service, however.

I don't think "New York Jewish culture" had *any* impact on me that I can think of, except to learn a few terms like "meshugganeh," "schickse," "oy veh" and the very useful word "kvetch"; also to eat lox and bagels and cream cheese. The usual superficial New York jargon for which, as the ryebread ads used to say, "You don't have to be Jewish." Many of our artist friends were Jewish, but entirely secular, and as you know, painters and poets form their *own* subculture. My in-laws were pretty typical Brooklyn working-class or petit bourgeois. They were loveable people, but I didn't spend much time with them and felt stifled when I did.

G.P. Do you consider yourself a Jewish poet? If not, why not and if not, how do you see yourself as a poet re your essential beliefs and influences?

D.L. As you already know, I *don't* consider myself a Jewish poet. Nor do I consider myself a Welsh, English, American, New York, Massachusetts, Californian, or Seattle poet, nor a Catholic poet. I cannot be categorized except as a mish-mash.

G.P. Does maturity give you a fresh, new perspective?

D.L. Age increases or decreases certain preoccupations and opinions and modifies certain convictions—as does the passage of time at *any* stage of one's life, in fact—but it doesn't (in my experience so far, some weeks before my 73rd birthday) suddenly introduce entirely new perspectives. Of course, new ideas and experiences continue to be encountered, but one's basic way of meeting them is long-established.

G.P. How does one face death? Can poetry help?

D.L. With awe. With hope that one's faith is not illusory. With the desire to be spiritually ready for it when it comes. Yes, I think poetry probably can help in that preparation.

G.P. What has poetry taught you about language?

D.L. I really can't think of a response to that one. It's almost like asking, what has breathing taught you about air.

G.P. What do you wish to still accomplish?

D.L. I hope to continue to write well and to surprise myself in each poem. I also hope to deepen my spiritual life and to manifest this in my dealings with others.

G.P. Do you have hope for the world's future, for America?

D.L. I don't have much reasonable hope, but I also have trust in the unpredictable—the possible as distinct from the probable.

G.P. What place do you most identify with?

D.L. England has so changed in the Thatcher (and now Major) years that I no longer feel the same attachment to it that I used to— nevertheless there are certain things about rural England and even dear old London that have not changed and which I have a special emotional response to. But I have never really "belonged" anywhere, and therefore in some degree am at home anywhere. Perhaps among well-filled bookshelves and galleries full of great paintings as much as anywhere.

G.P. If you could live your life again, what would you do differently?

D.L. I wouldn't want radical differences in events, I think—not the major settings and events of my history. But I'd like to have been kinder and wiser—doesn't everybody?

G.P. What is the most amazing thing about life?

D.L. That anything exists at all, rather than a void.

G.P. What is the most amazing thing about your life?

D.L. I'm so grateful for *all* the amazing good things in my history (not that it has not had its dark times) that I can't possibly specify a single one. Though I suppose I could say, Well, I've never led a boring existence, have wonderful friends, etc., etc.—not ever forgetting that I was born with a definite gift—but you see how it immediately becomes a *list*.

The Question of Denise Levertov's Gift

Gary Pacernick

When I asked Denise Levertov in our interview what she found the hardest thing about being a poet, she answered "I can't say I've found *anything* hard about it!" She reiterated several times that she was lucky to have "the gift." Because our interview was conducted through the U.S. mail, I did not get to ask a quick follow-up question. Although we had a brief correspondence before she died, we never discussed the implications of her answers to my questions. For the purpose of this essay, I would like to attempt an answer to my question regarding Denise Levertov's poetic gift.

In her "Statement on Poetics" in the anthology *The New American Poetry* (1960), Levertov's opening sentence reminds me of her answer in our interview 36 years later. "I believe poets are instruments on which the power of poetry plays" (*NAP* 411). This eloquent statement emphasizes one of the two enduring definitions of the poet: someone (prophet, seer, shaman) who is given the gift of poetry through magic, divine inspiration, madness, etc. The poet is dependent in some way on an uncontrollable and/or unpredictable force.

This romantic definition of the poet has been with us for centuries along with the other key definition: the poet as maker, craftsman, carefully ordering and controlling the writing of the poem as it evolves through the act of composition. Levertov alludes to the poet as maker and craftsman in the sentence following her reference to the poet as receiver of poetic power: "But they [poets] are also makers, craftsmen. It is given to the seer to see, but it is then his responsibility to communicate what he sees (*NAP* 412).

Since Levertov is often aligned with the Black Mountain poets (Olson, Creeley, and Duncan), it is not surprising that she advocates an organic, open approach to form. After all, Charles Olson quoted Robert Creeley's words in bold-face in his essay "Projective Verse": "FORM IS NEVER MORE THAN AN EXTENSION OF CONTENT" (*NAP* 38). The page is an open field that the poet must approach with spontaneity. "ONE PERCEPTION MUST IMME-DIATELY AND DIRECTLY LEAD TO A FURTHER PERCEPTION." Allen Ginsberg took this advice along with inspiration from Blake, Whitman, Kerouac, etc. to a wild crescendo in "Howl." And a new Beat generation of poets was born.

Neither the poet nor the poet's reader, however, is bound by a definition. The test of Levertov's gift, as that of any poet, is in her poems. The reader must decide whether or not to receive the gift, and having done so, how to interpret it and whether or not to keep it. While Levertov was a prolific poet over a long career, her talent was chiefly for the brief lyric poem in which she envisions the ineffable in the everyday and the mystical in the quotidian. In a number of her psalms and psalm-like poems and most memorably in "Stepping Westward," she writes directly from her experience with a visionary depth and intensity of meaning.

The poems in which I most convincingly find Levertov's gift are concentrated in the volumes *O Taste and See* (1964) and *The Sorrow Dance* (1967). They come between her early romantic poems and her slightly later anti-war poems. They spring from her interest in Jewish and Christian mysticism as well as her own experience. As I read them, they suggest a vision of the earth that may be enunciated through a poetry that acknowledges inconstancy and death and engages earthly experience without the intervention of traditional religion.

In "Earth Psalm" (*OTS* 80), Levertov writes that she is prepared to relinquish "hope of heaven" and God "to worship *mortal*." She invokes a god of sensuous experience who can be experienced through speech and music:

> god who has speech, who has wit
> to wreathe all words, who laughs
> wrapped in sad pelt and without hope of heaven,
> who makes a music turns the heads
> of all beasts
> as mine turns, dream-hill grass
> standing on end at echo even.

This god resembles the imaginative power that plays upon the poet. One could argue that Levertov is conjuring up not a god but the muse of poetry.

While the diction, rhythm, and line structure of "Earth Psalm" show the influence of Williams and Olson, the content of Levertov's brief lyric celebrating the poetry of mortal life recalls Wallace Stevens' "Sunday Morning." Stevens' poem dramatizes a philosophical debate between the Christian and secular-romantic points of view. The poem is composed as a series of scenes containing a wealth of imagery and figurative language as well as dialogue and/or interior monologue.

Levertov's "Earth Psalm" is much more concentrated and straightforward than "Sunday Morning." It is the poet's personal statement of her belief in mortality. She has found the language and form to compose a lyric that in an eloquent, clear way creates a deep and challenging meaning. It is one of a small number of poems that she wrote individually and chose to call psalms. In this and several other psalms, she celebrates earthly life experienced outside of a belief in God or an afterlife.

"A Psalm Praising the Hair of Man's Body" (*OTS* 82) sings the praises of sexual love. The wonderful refrain *"My great brother / Lord of the Song / wears the ruff of / forest bear"* begs to be sung or at least recited. As in "Earth Psalm," the poet affirms experience as an imaginative force that plays upon the poet and inspires song. Like the Biblical Song of Songs there is at least an implicit connection between the experience of sexual love and religious ecstasy: "Husband, thy fleece of silk is black, / a black adornment; / lies so close to the turns of the flesh, / burns my palm-stroke." Even without an allegorical interpretation, it is as if Levertov is saying, as Stevens does in "Sunday Morning," that if one lives as passionately and imaginatively as possible, the earth may indeed be the closest thing to paradise that one shall know.

In "City Psalm (*SD* 72), the poet continues to express her belief in the here and now. While many of the poem's details describe the "horror," "killings," and "despair" of earthly existence as symbolized by the secular city, she sees through the bleak surface to arrive at a blessed vision:

> Nothing was changed, all was revealed otherwise;
> not that horror was not, not that the killings did not continue,
> not that I thought there was to be no more despair,
> but that as if transparent all disclosed
> an otherness that was blesséd, that was bliss.
> *I saw Paradise in the dust of the street.*

It is as if the poet-narrator is chosen to imagine a paradoxical vision of paradise within the earth's dust and death. Although she does not describe this vision fully, she does suggest that in the visionary process "all was revealed otherwise." While the Hebrew Psalms express the voice of an exiled, marginalized people longing for the holy city of Jerusalem, Levertov's psalms express her belief that the poetic imagination can envision an earthly city where redemption is possible.

In "Psalm Concerning the Castle" (*SD* 67) Levertov writes in a series of lines beginning with "Let" that culminates in a long verse paragraph. In our interview, she said that she was describing a Han dynasty Pottery Watch Tower in the Boston Museum of Fine Arts. While the description of the castle is concentrated and specific, the meaning is mysterious.

> Let the young queen sit above, in the cool air, her child in
>   her arms; let her look with joy at the great circle, the
>   pilgrim shadows, the work of the sun and the play of
>   the wind. Let her walk to and fro. Let the columns
>   uphold the roof, let the storeys uphold the columns,
>   let there be dark space below the lowest floor, let the
>   castle rise foursquare out of the moat, let the moat be a
>   ring and the water deep, let the guardians guard it....

The poem ends with a personal statement by the poet-narrator: "Let there be wide lands around it, let that country where it / stands be within me, let me be where it is." The poem presents an architectural image that symbolizes an ancient culture, an integrated way of life that is rendered and ordered by art. As in her other psalms, Levertov envisions the possibility of an earthly paradise within herself, created by her poetic imagination.

In the volume *Candles in Babylon* (1982), there is "Psalm: People Power at the Die-in" (*CB* 84–85). Although this psalm comes considerably later than "City Psalm," it too speaks of trying to transform the corrupt city, but the vision is extended into the action of organized political protest. There is a religious aura to the experience symbolized by "the roses / of our communion." The protesters walk as if from their Biblical "tents by night" to instigate revolutionary change.

Of the many poems that I have read by Denise Levertov, "Stepping Westward" (*SD* 15–16) is my favorite. It is the poem that I will remember her by. In this poem, the two definitions of the poet (prophet and maker) merge. Like Levertov's psalms, it imagines the possibility of an earthly paradise; however, it is even more memorable because it suggests so much meaning so succinctly and dynamically.

The poem consists of two-line stanzas that sometimes run-on into the next. The music is fluid and graceful despite the short lines, because of the rich combination of the syllables but also the pauses both within and at the end of lines. Although the poem constantly starts and stops and starts, it never ceases to flow.

> What is green in me
> darkens, muscadine.
>
> If woman is inconstant,
> good. I am faithful to
>
> ebb and flow, I fall
> in season and now
>
> is a time of ripening.

Levertov renders a vision of life that is simple, earthy, part of nature's constant cycles and seasons, yet "true" as "a north star," as if the narrator's womanly experience also reflects an otherworldly constancy and grandeur.

Throughout the poem, there is tension between opposites: life/death; light/dark; ebb/flow; movement/stillness; burdens/gifts; ripe/spoiled. These conflicts can be resolved only through the imagination, which allows the narrator to accept that the only constant is change. Acceptance of change permits the narrator to experience and be "faithful to" the ripeness, energy, and wonder of life.

Levertov's confirmation of "inconstancy" recalls Whitman's lines from section 51 of "Song of Myself":

> Do I contradict myself?
> Very well then I contradict myself,
> (I am large, I contain multitudes.)

The poet has found the perfect organic form (merging her Whitmanian affirmation of earthly experience with a mastery of free verse craft that she learned chiefly from Williams) as she speaks to her reader, affirming how great it is to be a woman moving toward middle age and death, savoring life:

> There is no savor
> more sweet, more salt
>
> than to be glad to be
> what, woman...

Her sense of imaginative joy breaks through the clash of opposites so fully that "burdens" are "remembered / as gifts, good, a basket

// of bread...." In "Stepping Westward" Levertov's gift, as I receive it, comes to fruition: to suggest so much meaning so well and with so few and such simple words. It is a gift that I deeply cherish.

Works Cited

Levertov, Denise. *Candles in Babylon*. New York: New Directions, 1982.

———. *Collected Earlier Poems 1940–1960*. New York: New Directions, 1979.

———. *The Sorrow Dance*. New York: New Directions, 1966.

———. *O Taste and See*. New York: New Directions, 1964.

———. In *The New American Poetry*. Ed. Donald M. Allen. New York: Grove Press, 1960.

Whitman, Walt. *Leaves of Grass*. New York: Norton, 1973.

"I take up / so much space": Denise Levertov as Teacher

Anne-Marie Cusac

One morning, a coworker came up to me casually and asked, "Did you hear that Denise Levertov died?" It was a bright grey December day. The light reflected off the street, draining the room of subtlety and shadow. I said "no," and she left while I stared at the magazine page that had absorbed me a minute earlier—now muddled color and print. My friend thought I'd be interested because of Levertov's place as a leading poet and political activist. She didn't know that Denise Levertov had also been my teacher at the Stanford University Creative Writing Department seven years before.

This accidental news of her death made it seem not real— unreliable gossip. During the next few days, an image came to me each time I started to remember her. It was of a single piece of paper. (Someone had cut out a doll, which was missing.) There was just the white page, with a human-shaped hole in the middle.

Then the phone calls started. "I want to commiserate about Denise," said one. "I am looking at a photograph of her that I have above my desk," said another. "I feel like I owe her for my career," said a third.

Together, we did our best to put her back into place, to give her definition, to see her again. We may have tried too hard. During one of these conversations, I received a detailed third-hand account of her death. It appeared in a memoir I published in *The Progressive* magazine:

> Many of Levertov's friends knew of her lymphoma, though she rarely talked about it. She went through treatments about two years before her death, then repeatedly said she was fine. The day she went to the hospital for the last time, she went not for cancer treatments, but for an operation on an ulcer. That day,

the story goes, she was herself—not a tired woman or a woman in pain (though she might well have been both), but a woman with a loud laugh.

When the surgeons opened her body, they found lymphoma everywhere. They closed her up without carrying out the operation, woke her, and asked if she wanted life-support. She refused it, and died later that day.

A few weeks after the piece appeared, I learned from Marlene Muller, Levertov's personal secretary and her friend, that this version of the death was not accurate.

"Levertov entered the hospital very seriously ill," Muller wrote in a letter to the editor, "and despite a transitory improvement, continued to worsen over a ten-day period. She did not awaken from surgery, and at the end had no opportunity to make a statement about life support. She had made that decision, as well as all those governing her care in a serious illness, years before."

Why had my friends and I collaborated, however unintentionally, in rewriting the last days of a teacher who had nurtured and aggravated us? Were we simply making Levertov into a myth (something she would not have tolerated while alive)? Or did our creation say something about the woman we had known, her dogged, fighting nature, the laughter that took possession of her entire body? Dissatisfied with what seemed like our absolute distance from her, perhaps we had composed a death that made her seem familiar and obstinate—imaginable, rather than silenced. The Levertov we knew would have taken on death like she had taken on life, with vigor and, yes, joy. She would have been sure of herself until the instant she died. The woman had a will.

I came to Levertov with admiration and ambivalence. She was notorious as a fierce and dogmatic teacher, a "crusader" for her own brand of poetry, said one college professor. "Denise Levertov teaches rhythm by pounding on the floor," said another.

Levertov was not always imposing. She had a disarming cackle, rode an old bicycle around campus, and wore skirts and practical shoes. But the warnings weren't unfounded. Though I never saw her pound on the floor, she did not lose arguments, even when she was probably wrong. Students who showed her poems in rhyme and meter (which she called "anachronisms") or prose poetry (which she said didn't exist) suffered her wrath.

Her categorical pronouncements and her inability to let go of a fight once it had started led to infuriated mutterings outside the building after class. Once in a while, during workshop, a student erupted in anger. Levertov would respond with hurt wonderment. She did not understand how someone could take an argument about poetry personally.

It was Levertov's bravery as a poet that led to her didacticism in the classroom. She believed fervently in pushing poetry to be and do more, to carry new subject matter. Poetry was the realm of possibility. It should be able to handle all of life. And if she feared literary critics, she hid it well.

Levertov wrote her first overtly political poetry during the Vietnam War, a time when the U.S. poetry establishment was deeply anti-political. To her critics, the presence of such writing alongside poems in her well-known lyric voice seemed disruptive; most reviews either made small mention of the political poems or panned them as a group.

Those reviewers should have been more painstaking. Take, for instance, "Modes of Being":

> *Near Saigon,*
> *in a tiger-cage, a woman*
> *tries to straighten her*
> > *cramped spine*
> *and cannot.*
>
> *   *   *
>
> > Joy
> is real, torture
> is real, we strain to hold
> a bridge between them open,
> and fail,
> or all but fail.
>
> (FD 98–99)

Or take "A Note to Olga," Levertov's expression of grief both for the war and for her dead sister:

> Your high soprano
> sings out from just
> in back of me—
>
> *We shall*—I turn,
> you're, I very well know,
> not there,
>
> and your voice, they say
> grew hoarse
> from shouting at crowds …

yet *overcome*
sounds then hoarsely
from somewhere in front,

the paddywagon
gapes.—It seems
you that is lifted

limp and ardent
off the dark snow
and shoved in, and driven away.
                              (*SD* 88–89)

Levertov was careful about "the social responsibility" of writers. "If they are inspired to write about their political concerns, that is good," she said in a 1983 radio interview. "If they are not inspired to do so, they have exactly the same responsibility as any other citizen, any other conscious adult with a moral conscience—and that is to participate in any way they can.... Because you can't make a good poem out of 'ought to.' You cannot. And you can't make good poems out of opinion and good intentions."

Levertov managed to develop an aesthetic large enough for politics. She also created a supple poetic line, which she used to evoke hesitations, momentary questions, an intake of breath during an instant of wonder:

Everywhere among the marigolds
the rainblown roses and the hedges
of tamarisk are white
butterflies this morning, in constant
tremulous movement, only those
that lie dead revealing
their rockgreen color and the bold
cut of the wings.

                              (*EBH* 14)

Levertov's poems are also remarkable for their overt celebrations of female sexual appetite. Thanks in part to Levertov, erotic joy is now an available subject for women writers:

quiet and slow in the midst of
the quick of the
sounding river

our hands were
flames
stealing upon quickened flesh until

no part of us but was
sleek and
on fire

(*OTS* 55)

In line, subject matter, and aesthetic, Levertov broadened po-etry in English. Having done so, she seemed intent on passing her contributions to her students, whether they accepted them or not. One day, dismayed with a student's awkward use of line breaks, she sternly informed the class that she had already written her thoughts on this subject and was not going to waste time telling them to us.

"Don't lilt," she commanded another student, who had read his poem aloud in a popular style. Such a mannerism made every line sound the same, she said. If he read this way, he was not re-specting the poem and the demands it made of him.

One day, she stopped the class. "I just had a chill thinking about all the poetry that has gone through this room," she said. We stared at her, at each other, and at the walls and furniture satu-rated with poems.

Having witnessed her outbursts, I remained wary of Levertov for about a year, until the buildup to the Gulf War. Then things changed. One day in workshop, a friend of mine admitted he was having trouble concentrating because he was so upset. "What are we going to do about this?" asked Levertov. Her question implied responsibility, and a task.

It was uplifting to be organized by a woman with nearly thirty years' experience in the anti-war movement. Every Saturday, a dozen or so of her students and friends met in front of the Stanford Quad with homemade signs that read, "Poets for Peace." We took the train together to San Francisco and marched with the church groups, anarchists, stiltwalkers in black and white makeup, and thousands of other citizens.

On campus during the week, we organized read-ins against the war. They started small—we read to ourselves the first night. But as word spread, the library where we held them filled up. Our read-ins became a regular announcement at campus rallies.

Levertov was a committed protester, but not a dominating one. Once she had set us in motion, she let us go. At the rallies in her trench coat and sunglasses, she stood back from the crowds, an interested smile on her face. At the read-ins, she would sit at the far side of the room, silent and listening.

I last saw Levertov at a poetry reading in Berkeley. It was spring, the season I will always associate with her, since she taught our workshop in January and February, the months when Northern California breaks into flamboyant greenery and blossom. She read for an hour in her carefully modulating voice, with only a silent pause between most of the poems. Then, before reading from her libretto on El Salvador, she began to tell the audience about the human-rights situation in that country. Her listeners stirred in their seats. After several minutes, people began to leave, alone or in pairs. Her voice didn't change.

A favorite phrase of Levertov's, from the poet Rainer Maria Rilke, concerned the "unlived life, of which one can die" (*LUC* 98). Denise Levertov did not die of an unlived life.

I have never before grieved for someone who has left behind so much of herself. There are the thirty books of poetry, translations, and essays from sixty years of almost daily work.

Then there are the video recordings, and the peculiar experience of relief at seeing her whole again, with her gap-toothed smile, the high cheekbones, the controlled ringlets, a blue knit dress, and two necklaces (one a cross) draped from her neck.

Rereading her books, I am reminded of one of the oddities of good poetry. It imitates human breath. A line is the intersection of breath and thought—thought broken by a quick intake, the pause that brings with it meanings not communicated in language. This fusion of word and physical body has everything to do with the centuries of claims that poetry is magical, that it gives the poet immortality.

> I take up
> so much space
> *   *   *
> When I leave, I leave
> alone, as I came.
>   (*CB* 6)

Here is the mind and breath of Denise Levertov. Here, on a white page, are words that once vibrated in speech from her body. How can they not lead to that flirtatious, principled woman, with her loud laugh, and her will?

In her essay on her mentor Muriel Rukeyser, which appears in her collection *Light Up the Cave*, Levertov remarks, "It would be inappropriate to memorialize her, however briefly, without mentioning her humor" (*LUC* 190). The same is true of Denise Levertov.

During a radio interview, the questioner asked Levertov what her epitaph would be. "I have sometimes thought of having an epitaph which would say my name and dates of birth and death," Levertov answered. "And then it would say, 'She knew how to cure the hiccups.'"

Levertov's cure is this: "You hold your ears very tightly closed while gently sipping water."

Works Cited

Cusac, Anne-Marie. "Remembering Denise Levertov." *The Progressive* March 1998, 17–18.

Denise Levertov. Dir. Dan Griggs. Lannan Literary Series. The Lannan Foundation, 1994.

Levertov, Denise. *Candles in Babylon*. New York: New Directions, 1982.

———. *The Freeing of the Dust*. New York: New Directions, 1975.

———. Interview with Rebekah Presson. *New Letters on the Air*. Kansas City: New Letters. April 1983.

———. *Light Up the Cave*. New York: New Directions, 1981.

———. *O Taste and See*. New York: New Directions, 1964.

———. *The Sorrow Dance*. New York: New Directions, 1966.

———. *With Eyes at the Back of Our Heads*. New York: New Directions, 1959.

Muller, Marlene. Letter. *The Progressive* May 1998: 7.

"To Take Active Responsibility":
On Teaching
Denise Levertov's Poems

Harry Marten

Autumn is college-hunting season, and when I come back from my morning class, I find a prospective student and her parents waiting outside my office door. The Admissions Office has sent them over to talk about the Humanities offerings at the select liberal arts college where I've taught English for more than two decades. All three have been eyeing the gallery of cartoons and quotations that are taped to my door. They range from Snoopy proclaiming "I like a book where there's only one character and nothing happens to him," to a portrait of a large man collapsed on the floor behind a row of men and women who are listening to a lecture; the caption reads, "Sid Baldwin continues to be nagged by a short attention span." Above the lot, in a size 22 bold italic font, a quote from William Blake's October 19, 1801, letter to John Flaxman sits like a crown: "Blessed are those who are found studious of literature and human and polite accomplishments. Such have their lamps burning and such shall shine as the stars." I believe Blake, and I want those who stand before my door to accept his blessing, but the gentle cynicism of Snoopy and Co. offers a balance that is there to protect us all from seeming naïve or portentous as we go about the business of learning.

As I try to explain to the visiting family the virtues of an educational experience that's intimate and attentive but also homogeneous and sheltered, I realize with surprising clarity just what it is that so challenges me about the juggling act of my job, where for years I have been affirming the privileged status of my students, and at the same time trying to diminish it. To an extent my school sells a protected environment, and to a degree I've come to value it as what a college *should* provide, for the predictable routines of college life offer students and faculty alike the immense luxury of undisrupted time to play with ideas that matter and words that shape them. But the experience isolates us, encouraging fear of risk and discouraging active participation in the human issues that our readings and conversations clarify. I've often wondered how I can affirm the comforts that make learning a pleasure and at the same time hope to bring my students to an energetic and engaged imaginative comprehension of the world beyond the campus walls. One of the best solutions I have found over the years lies in the example of Denise Levertov's work, which I teach regularly in classes ranging from freshman and sophomore surveys to senior seminars.

Speaking as "The Poet in the World," Levertov instructs the instructor and his students:

> The obligation of the writer is: *to take personal and active responsibility for his words, whatever they are, and to acknowledge their potential influence on the lives of others.* The obligation of teachers and critics is: *not to block the dynamic consequences of the words they try to bring close to students and readers.* And the obligation of the readers is: *not to indulge in the hypocrisy of merely vicarious experience, thereby reducing literature to the concept of "just words," ultimately a frivolity, an irrelevance when the chips are down....* When words penetrate deep into us they change the chemistry of the soul, of the imagination. (*PW* 114)

Words are the crux, Levertov contends, affirming that "language, as Robert Duncan had declared, is not a set of counters to be manipulated, but a Power" (*PW* 54), which can keep us from falling victim to what Rilke has called "the unlived life, of which one can die" (in *LUC* 98). Consider what may happen if words are used carelessly, I tell my students, turning to the "Prologue: An Interim" of "Staying Alive." Though we've been talking about Vietnam in this survey of modern and contemporary American literature, this poem has not been assigned ahead of the class meeting so that we can experience it immediately, without studied preconceptions.

"While the war drags on, always worse," Levertov begins, "the soul dwindles sometimes to an ant / rapid upon a cracked surface" (*SA* 21):

> lightly, grimly, incessantly
> it skims the unfathomed clefts where despair
> seethes hot and black. (21)

The image of the war-damaged spirit as a scurrying insect is arresting, felt by the class in the nervous rhythmic contrasts of long lines set beside short, in the jarring mix of adverbial repetition and variation ("lightly, grimly, incessantly"), in the disconcerting juxtapositions of prosy declarative sentences with intense imagistic compressions ("it skims the unfathomed clefts where despair / seethes hot and black"). But after the ugly shocks of Larry Heinemann's *Paco's Story*, which we've just finished reading, the class finds the opening of the poem pale. Though vaguely unsettled, they are not now emotionally engaged by the poem's first stanza. The reaction is what I've expected. For this lesson is not simply to be about the horrifying happenings of war one more time, but about other related degradations and destructions that are part of the shape of our lives.

Rather than being swept up in the horror of it, the class is led by the poet away from what she has elsewhere described as the terror of "Life at War": "transformation of witnessing eyes to pulp-fragments, / implosion of skinned penises into carcass-gulleys" (*SD* 80). Instead, these students, who have never been at war, probably never even seen it much on CNN, find themselves witness to commonplace habits and recurrences, with "Children in the laundromat / waiting while their mothers fold sheets" (*SA* 21). Unexpectedly relieved after the initial edgy expectancies of the opening stanza, they remember their younger selves, and smile knowingly while observing the way "A five-year-old boy addresses / a four-year-old girl":

> ... 'When I say,
> *Do you want some gum*? say *yes*.'
> 'Yes ...' 'Wait!—Now:
> Do you want some gum?'
> 'Yes!' 'Well yes means no,
> so you can't have any.'
> He chews. He pops a big, delicate bubble at her.
> (*SA* 21)

My class loves the delicacy of that bubble, delights in the sassiness of that sibling pop. Absorbed as they are in the ease of comfortable childhood memory, the tone of lamentation in Levertov's next stanza strikes them uniformly as postured and pretentious. The poet's sad, exclamatory "O language, virtue / of man, touchstone / worn down by what / gross friction" (*SA* 21) has them straining to let me know their opinion of writers who, losing sight of "the real world," make much out of little. But the class in its complacency has lost sight of the opening subject of war, and though they don't recognize it yet, the poet has caught them fast in her web of words.

Ironically juxtaposing serious adult communication with the child's talk, Levertov shakes us from our comfort zones as the poem unfolds, compelling us to recognize our own complacency and the breakdown of language that has come to define our public conversations. Quoting a news story of a military communiqué that has all the illogic of the five year old in the Laundromat, now suddenly turned dangerous, the poet explains:

> And,
> '"It became necessary
> to destroy the town to save it,"
> a United States major said today….'
> (*SA* 21)

In Levertov's next stanza, a second lament for language combined here with lingering echoes of her first now resonates with a disturbing urgency:

> O language, mother of thought,
> are you rejecting us as we reject you?
>
> Language, coral island
> accrued from human comprehensions,
> human dreams,
>
> you are eroded as war erodes us.
> (*SA* 22)

Our words and our acts reflect each other, Levertov seems to say; corruption of one invariably suggests corruption of the other faculty. And in discovering the poem stanza by stanza, my students have come to recognize that when the words of our public discourse are made childish, trivialized, unhinged from honest meaning, we are a society in danger of dissolution. They are surprised by the difference of this view of language from the one they accept as normal—a notion that most communication has a commercial purpose, typically offering what Levertov has described as the sound of "the buying and selling / [that] buzzes at our heads" (*SA* 17). It's the beginning of insight, but acceptance of the idea that words are not just manipulations or entertainments comes slowly, reluctantly, to these kids who have simply assumed that language is for lies, and that words have no real consequences in the TV drama of life.

Because this American literature survey class is expected to offer a final focus on Vietnam-era writing, we continue on through a dozen of Levertov's intense political poems of the late 1960s and early 1970s. The class is moved by the poet's steady portrait of human loss: "infant after infant, their names forgotten, / their sex unknown in the ashes, / set alight ... // moaning and stinking in hospitals three abed" (*SA* 16). They respond with empathy to the drama of her struggle to sustain her vision and her song in the face of so much destructiveness:

> ... my strong sight,
> my clear caressive sight, my poet's sight I was given
> that it might stir me to song,
> is blurred.
> There is a cataract filming over
> my inner eyes.
>
> (*SA* 16)

And they feel, throughout, the deep weight of her resonant language that reveals a knowledge of war's devastation ("our nerve filaments twitch with its presence / day and night"), but insists on hope: "nothing we do has the quickness, the sureness, / the deep intelligence living at peace would have" (*SA* 14).

At the same time, the poet's relentlessly serious didactic tone oppresses them, and before long some of these children of peace and comfort push back. "That was then, this is now," they say, as if conjuring Henry Ford's refrain that history "is more or less the bunk.... and the only history that is worth a tinker's dam is the history we make today." And, as if mistrusting their own responses even as they discover them, they make a categorical differentiation between writers and others, suggesting that while the Denise Levertovs of the world can find special poetic words to make temporary believers of them, it's something of a dead end of perception, not open to the rest who cannot express themselves as a poet can.

"Right, we're not poets, but we're readers," I say, unwilling to let them circle the wagons against the risk of insight. We experience language, *and* we use it; and once we've recognized that the words we use matter, we can't undo that perception, however much we may try to shrug it off. If Levertov has made us believe, made us feel, persuaded us not of the facts necessarily, but of the essential truths of her observations, if only for as long as it took to read through her verses, we've discovered that there is truth in words. And not just in the ones we choose, but in the ways we use them—in their combinations, in their rhythms, their emphases, their pace and pause. Our words may not have the genius of poetry, but they can shape meaning and so deserve the full care we can give them.

"Listen up," I say, in my best little-league-coach voice. "This is what I want you to think about: you've got the words, how are you going to put them together, and why?" I read to them from *Light Up the Cave*, as Levertov discusses "the *process* of thinking/feeling, feeling/thinking, rather than focusing more exclusively on its *results*" (*LUC* 62). Writing about "the slight (but meaningful) hesitations between word and word that are characteristic of the mind's dance among perceptions but which are not noted by grammatical punctuation"(*LUC* 62), she explains that often "the crucial precision tool for creating this exploratory mode is the linebreak"(*LUC* 62):

> If readers will think of their own speech, or their silent inner monologue, when describing thoughts, feelings, perceptions, scenes or events, they will, I think, recognize that they frequently hesitate—albeit very briefly—as if with an unspoken question,— a 'what?' or a 'who?' or a 'how?'—before nouns, adjectives, verbs, adverbs, none of which require to be preceded by a comma or other regular punctuation in the course of syntactic logic. To incorporate these pauses in the rhythmic structure of the poem … allows the reader to share more intimately the experience that is being articulated. (*LUC* 62)

As Levertov does in her essay, I write out lines from "Four Embroideries: (III) Red Snow." I want my class to see that though we've left the emotionally charged subject of war behind, meanings are still shaped by the ways language is used by the writer and perceived by the reader:

> Crippled with desire, he questioned it.
> Evening upon the heights, juice of the pomegranate:
> who could connect it with sunlight?
>
>   (*RA* 37; *LUC* 64)

Levertov offers us two variations of these stanzas, shifting in each the points at which words hang over the visual and semantic precipice that forms at the end of a line. I write out bits of the first, ask several students to read it out loud, ask for comments on how meanings have shifted with the shifting words. The opening now looks like this:

> Crippled with desire, he
> questioned it. Evening
> upon the heights....
> 　　　　(*LUC* 64)

With "he" displaced to the end of the line now, and poised against a large expanse of black space on the board, the students who are selected to read make a longer pause before tumbling down into the second line to complete the thought. They notice the stretched hesitation, recognize that the visual and aural cues now associate "he" with "Crippled with desire" more than with "questioned it." Similarly, they observe that the immediate juxtaposition in line two of "it" and "Evening"—coupled with the longer hesitation after "Evening" at what is now the last word of the line—has changed meaning as well. The lines now suggest something like this: the poet announces that "He is crippled with desire" ("Crippled with desire, he"); the poet suggests that "He questions Evening" ("he / questioned it. Evening"). At the same time, of course, the meaning is also that he questioned "desire." But "it" and "desire" now inhabit different lines, different spaces, different units of sound and sight perception, and we don't simply fall into the meaning that was obvious in the original version ("Crippled with desire, he questioned it"). It's not that the meanings have changed substantively, but that in rearranging the lines we have been able to perceive how meaning forms and reforms in the arrangements of spoken or read words.

Levertov's second variation shifts emphases again:

> Crippled
> with desire, he questioned
> it. Evening
> upon the heights....
> 　　　　(*LUC* 64)

My students perceive immediately the sonic thump of the single-word first line; and they recognize that their initial response has changed from attention to "desire" as an emotional handicap, to a consideration of what seems to be a physical handicap. They notice that "questioned" is now linked most immediately with "desire" because of the physical juxtaposition, suggesting for a moment that he is questioning with desire rather than crippled with it. "It" now seems linked to "Evening" by physical proximity—an association that is intensified, however briefly, by the recognition that "Evening" again requires an aural and visual pause in its position at the end of the line before the reader/listener continues-on to reassemble meanings. The shifting and shape-shifting logic runs something like this: He is crippled; he questions with desire; he is crippled with desire; he questions "it"—"evening"; he questions "it"—"desire." Attending to grammar and punctuation marks alone, of course, gives us less flexible significations. But even if the lines were written as prose sentences, our newly discovered awareness of the ways words combine, conflict with one another, energize one another, suggests that language is a fluid source of meaning rather than an assemblage of "proper" rules of meaning to be parsed. Expressive language is not only a matter of a poet's genius for metaphor and image; it's a matter of sensitivity to the dynamics of sentence and line structure and length. Simple words may reveal rich textures when embroidered into a complex tapestry of sound and meaning.

We play with the lines for a while, offering rhythmic changes as lines lengthen and contract, vowels flow and consonants clatter together in nearby associations, or soften when separated by new linebreaks. The words don't change, but their emphases and meanings do, fractured into shards that appear as short lines, or gathered in waves of sound that wash over us in long lines. For the rest of the class my students build and undo linguistic combinations, approving some, making fun of the strained quality of others, but always learning from seeing language afresh.

"The awakening is / to transformation, / word after word" (*SD* 28), Levertov wrote in a poem for her friend Muriel Rukeyser. And for two weeks more, my students range through Levertov's work, discovering their own awakenings and transformations, not just in the moving intensity of the poet's meditations on war—our ostensible point of focus in the survey—but in the force of her empathy for the frustrations and diminishments of old age ("The 90th Year," "A Daughter [I]," "A Daughter [II]," "Death in Mexico," *LF*); in her sensual delight in the pleasures of love and the body ("Eros at Temple Stream," *OTS*); in the joy of her celebrations of friendship, people, and places ("In Memory of Muriel Rukeyser," *CB*; "Missing Beatrice," *BW*; "A Map of the Western Part of the County of Essex in England," *JL*; "A Mystery, [Oaxaca, Mexico]," *LF*); and in the honesty of her direct observations about marriage ("The Ache of Marriage," "About Marriage," *OTS*), gender roles and identity ("Hypocrite Women," *OTS*), family relationships ("Olga Poems," *SA*). Our tour of the poet's world steadily enlarges our own with recognitions of what it means to discover "**a mystery, // a person, an / other, an I**" (*JL* 61).

We end our Levertov reading, and the course itself, with reminders of the nature of human history and the power of the imagination to clarify it. Turning to her observation and meditation on the nature of evil, "During the Eichmann Trial," we discover what happens "When we look up" from our self-absorbed, self-protected, individual lives. Surprisingly, the class has no idea who Eichmann was. Some have seen *Schindler's List*, read Eli Wiesel's *Night*, even visited the Holocaust Memorial. But the dark facts of modern history remain elusive. For context, I talk briefly about Eichmann's central role in the history of the Holocaust, about his life, about his capture and trial. But Levertov's work is not about facts, it's about imagination and memory, and we quickly turn to the poem to tell us what we need to know and why we need to know it.

The class is moved and confused by each of the poem's sections. Expecting a monster, they encounter a man; comfortable with condemnations, they find themselves involved with the war criminal in a more complex way. Without offering forgiveness, Levertov nonetheless insists upon the reader's recognition of Eichmann's place in the human community of which we are all members. "... No recognition of others is possible without the imagination" (*PW* 53), Levertov writes in an essay that I read to the class at the outset:

> The imagination of what it is to *be* those other forms of life that want to live is the only way to recognition; and it is that imaginative recognition that brings compassion to birth. Man's capacity for evil, then, is less a positive capacity, for all its horrendous activity, than a failure to develop man's most human function, the imagination, to its fullness, and consequently a failure to develop compassion. (*PW* 53)

My students—pragmatic engineers, pre-meds, economics majors, as well as budding Humanists—are justifiably uncomfortable with the literariness of the formulation. But the poem is persuasive, not just holding up for our contemplation a view of the Nazi on trial behind bullet-proof plate glass—a "pitiful man whom none // pity" (*JL* 61), but in the same motion raising a mirror to our own humanness, caught in the face of this man "whom all / must pity if they look // into their own face" (*JL* 61).

Eichmann's excuses are predictable, banal, sickening:

> 'I was used from the nursery
> to obedience

all my life …
Corpselike

obedience.'
. . . .
'And what would disobedience
have brought me? And

whom would it have served?'
'I did not let my thoughts

dwell on this....'
                                                    (*JL* 61–63)

But though words quickly "'slur into a harsh babble'" (*JL* 63), revealing the madness at the core, still the poet insists that we recognize that the face of evil is not simply "other." "Pity this man who
saw it," the poet writes, "whose obedience continued—// he, you,
I, which shall I say?" (*JL* 63):

He stands

isolate in a bulletproof
witness-stand of glass,

a cage, where we may view
ourselves, an apparition

telling us something he
does not know: we are members

one of another.
                                                    (*JL* 63)

The class recoils from the identification, as I do; but we have all
felt the force of the poet's urgent lesson: we must not separate ourselves from imaginative comprehension of the full range of acts of
which human beings are capable; or in our failure to know them—
in distancing ourselves from them—we will lose our full potential
for empathy, action, and reaction. And whatever degree of identification we carry with us through the rest of the poem, Levertov's
image of us linked with the man inside the cage goes a good way
toward shattering our complacency, as her vivid recreation later in
the poem of Crystal Night in November 1938—the night of breaking glass, when synagogues were destroyed and Jews were
rounded up all over Germany for trips to death camps—shatters
the notion that we can simply be non-participatory observers of
the dark and troubling events of our time:

The scream!
The awaited scream rises,
the shattering
of glass and the cracking
 of bone
. . . .
terror has a white sound
every scream
of fear is a white needle freezing the eyes
the floodlights of their trucks throw
jets of white, their shouts
cleave the wholeness of darkness into
sectors of transparent white-clouded pantomime
where all that was awaited
is happening, it is Crystal Night
. . . .
smashing the windows of sleep and dream
smashing the windows of history
a whiteness scattering
in hailstones
each a mirror
for man's eyes.

(*JL* 66, 67)

Ten years ago, at one of our college's general faculty meetings, someone presented a plan to take down the ancient iron fences that ring our campus, separating our green fields from the industrial gray of the rust-belt city beyond. As the fence has always seemed more symbolic than practical, keeping no one out or in, literally, this too was to have been a symbolic gesture, declaring that our privilege did not isolate us from the world. In the fuss that followed, the plan was withdrawn and, for the most part, we have continued to be "in," but not "of," the world "out there." And yet when I put before my classes poems by Denise Levertov that sing of the interpenetration of private and public actions, of the inevitable intertwining of art and reality, of the responsibility of the writer, teacher, reader to respond to aesthetic form as a way of remaining anchored "in the world," the walls come down.

As I direct my visitors toward their next appointment, my eye catches one last cartoon stuck up on my door. It's a small one on a postcard I received from a recently graduated student gone off to work in Manhattan. In it, a woman sits at the wheel of a jaunty sports car that has been jacked up on a platform and can only be reached by climbing up a small ladder; the tires hang in the air, a floor fan in front of the car blows the woman's hair back behind

her; the car radio blares. Behind the car, there is a coin meter attached to a sign that reads "**Escape From Reality Only $1.00.**" On
the card, my student, quoting Levertov (*RA* 85), has written simply
"'what we have lived / comes back to us. / We see more. / … /
our agony and the way we danced. / The Music!' There *is* no escaping it. Thanks."

Works Cited

Levertov, Denise. *Breathing the Water*. New York: New Directions, 1987.

———. *Candles in Babylon*. New York: New Directions, 1982.

———. *The Jacob's Ladder*. New York: New Directions, 1965.

———. *Life in the Forest*. New York: New Directions, 1978.

———. *Light Up the Cave*. New York: New Directions, 1981.

———. *O Taste and See*. New York: New Directions, 1964.

———. *The Poet in the World*. New York: New Directions, 1973.

———. *Relearning the Alphabet*. New York: New Directions, 1970.

———. *The Sorrow Dance*. New York: New Directions, 1967.

———. *To Stay Alive*. New York: New Directions, 1971.

The Dark Wing of Mourning:
Grief, Elegy and Time
in the Poetry of Denise Levertov

Dorothy Nielsen

I

Denise Levertov has been called a poet of love, of the here and now, of mysticism, incarnation, politics, myth. All of these labels are, of course, appropriate. She is also a poet of grief, having written both elegies for specific people and poems that meditate more generally on the process of mourning. This poetic openness to grief is closely related to her apperceptive, or process, poetics. When during the 1950s she developed a form that could capture her own "thinking/feeling, feeling/thinking" experience (*LUC* 62), she committed herself (inadvertently perhaps) to a poetry that would be full of lament, because it would bear witness to what she has recently called "the tragic and fearful character of our times," which "we are *in* … as fish are in the sea" (*NSE* 4).

Levertov wrote some of her finest elegies at the very juncture in her career that causes so much critical consternation. Many critics have complained that the apperceptive techniques she had developed in the 1950s were more appropriate for celebration than for the anguished testimony of an anti-war activist.[1] "Olga Poems" and "A Note for Olga" first appear in the volume that marks this fall from critical grace, *The Sorrow Dance*. They then reappear in *To*

---

[1]For example, Charles Altieri, James Mersmann and Lorrie Smith have contended that Levertov's objectivist poetics, known for celebrating the *here and now*, was inadequate for poetry about political crisis. Sandra Gilbert, Marie Borroff and Cary Nelson have focused on Levertov's early celebratory lyricism and have concluded that it was disrupted when she began to write about the Vietnam War.

Stay Alive, one of the volumes in which Levertov strives to come to terms with the new issues and emotions that took hold of her life and poetry once she began to protest U.S. involvement in Vietnam. These elegies for Levertov's sister help to show that her protest poetry was the natural outgrowth of her apperceptive style and therefore that the move from mystical celebration to anguished engagement does not constitute a break. They also instruct the reader in a lesson already inherent in the earlier poetry: the importance of dark emotions as a vital source of political and private power.[2] By bearing witness to the transformative power of grief, these two poems for Olga imply the message that the opening poem in *The Sorrow Dance*—"The Wings"—asserts when it turns the image of a hump on the back swirling with rage into a dark wing which, along with its paired light wing, allows flight.

In these two elegies, Levertov's unconventional treatment of time further underlines the continuity between her pre-war and her political writing. By tracking the thinking/feeling experience of the poet-speaker,[3] apperceptive poetics automatically takes up the subject of time—of process. Beginning in the 1950s, Levertov uses her line endings as a temporal marker. She instructs readers to interpret them as a pause equal to a half comma (*LUC* 64). This way, she argues, her page becomes a score that records the rhythm of the poet's thought process (62).

Levertov's apperceptive elegies contrast markedly with conventional elegies in their attitude toward time. Traditionally, poems of mourning do battle with the temporal realm, often employing as weapons self-reflexive reminders of the endurance of the poem itself (as in titles such as Jonson's "Epitaph on Elizabeth, L.H.") or reminders of the permanence of the art of the lost one (as in Auden's elegy for Yeats or Milton's "Lycidas"). Even more of-

---

[2]Anne Colclough Little also explores the combination of joy and sadness in Levertov's poetry. Little sees it as a unity "that comes from [Levertov's] attempt to define the temporal and eternal questions in the dialogue she has with herself and her heart" (34), and she demonstrates Levertov's belief that "the strongest poetry, the most powerful song, is that which comes from an awareness of joy and suffering" (39).

[3]I use the terms "poet-speaker" and "speaker" interchangeably throughout, in order to indicate the autobiographical source of most of Levertov's poetry. Two exceptions are my analyses of "What Were They Like?" and "El Salvador: Requiem and Invocation," neither of which is autobiographical.

ten, time is resisted with references to ontological transcendence; take for example the triumphant resurrection images in "Lycidas" or the Platonic idealism of Shelley's "Adonais," or the image of the Heavens struggling against Earth for the boy's life in Jonson's "An Epitaph on Solomon Pavy." In contrast, in these poems following her sister's death, Levertov does not cast time as the destroyer of life, to be resisted. Instead, the process of life—like the process of the poet-speaker's perception—must be embraced. In fact, in the longer of the two elegies, "Olga Poems," Olga makes what to the mourner is the tragic mistake of refusing to submit to time.

The date that follows "Olga Poems," *May–August 1964,* reminds us that the poet is tracing a thinking/feeling process over a period of several months. Perhaps initially it seems as if Levertov casts time as the destroyer of physical life when between the first and second sections of the poem the loving memory of a teenage Olga "raking / her nails over olive sides" transmutes into a picture of the price that the adult Olga has paid for an enraged activism: "the skin around [her] nails / nibbled sore" (*SD* 53). Furthermore, the poet-speaker remembers that in childhood she associated Olga's aphorism *"Everything flows"* with a line from a hymnbook that links time with death: *"Time / like an ever-rolling stream / bears all its sons away"* (55). However, Olga's aphorism itself is ambiguous. It might be read as conveying the poet-speaker's belief that time is the material of—not the enemy of—life. As the poem unfolds the process of grief, the mourner recalls over and over again examples of Olga ignoring her own youthful wisdom about "everything flowing" as she tries to work against the course of the inevitable. So in iii–ii, Olga's "dread" leads her to "raise bulwarks" unsuccessfully "against the rolling dark / oncoming river" (55). She tries to label her desk's disorder and she attempts to control her verses by basing them on the Christian calendar. To Levertov's eyes, this "rage for order" causes Olga "to manipulate lives to disaster" (55). Her activist's love causes her to attempt too much; she tries "[t]o change, / to change the course of the river!" (55). Ironically, Olga's "rage for order / disordered her pilgrimage" (55). Throughout Olga's lifetime, and even after her death, her desire to control the uncontrollable increases the distance between the sisters, which had begun to open up in early childhood when Denise mocked Olga's precocious revolutionary rage, as recalled early in the elegy (section ii). The gap between the two grows wider as the poem progresses. In iii–iii, the mourner remembers Olga haunting her dreams like an incubus. "Sisters" becomes a simile for dissension in iv, when the poet-speaker describes Olga's first hospital stay: "while pain and drugs / quarreled like sisters in you" (57).

A counterpointing of distance and closeness complicates the process of grief. The mourner draws close to her sister in moments of reverence for the revolutionary love she believes drove Olga to her premature death. In v–i, Olga's life seems to wind through the poet-speaker, who remembers that they used to fantasize about escaping into lands below the earth and into medieval romance. But section vi ends with reminders of a lack of understanding between the two; the "brown gold" (59) of stones the poet-speaker glimpses in brooks calls up memories of Olga's "unknowable gaze" (60). This final section of the elegy reintroduces the metaphor of a river for time with images of the mourner crossing over brooks and streams as she moves through the months following her sister's death. These images of crossing over water contrast starkly with the picture of Olga trying to change the course of the river, and therefore compound the sense of estrangement between the sisters, who have been shown to inhabit time in such different ways.

With the earlier reference to Olga's desire to order her verses (iii–ii), the poet makes the form itself a site of contrast between herself and her sister. Unlike Olga's purposefully ordered verses, this elegiac series has a style that reflects the poet-speaker's complementary beliefs that one cannot change the course of the river and that the form of poetry should be taken from the form of experience. In an essay published just two years before *The Sorrow Dance*, Levertov expresses her version of the theory of organic form in the axiom, "Form is never more than the *revelation* of content" (*PW* 13).[4] In this "exploratory" poetry (7), "content and form are in a state of dynamic interaction" (9) in which the poet traces her unfolding experience. Therefore, rather than celebrate its own solidity in the face of destructive time, this elegy draws attention to its own fluid process of memory and emotion, as the speaker's feelings shift between intimacy and estrangement. Throughout the

---

[4]Robert Creeley's formula, quoted by Olson in his manifesto on projective verse, is that "form is never more than an extension of content" (Allen 410). Levertov changed "extension" to "revelation," perhaps to indicate an even closer connection (an identity between form and content) and perhaps to emphasize process. Her version of organic form distinguishes itself from the New Criticism's, with its emphasis on organic unity, because she is more interested in embodying a process of thinking/feeling than in constructing a closed, self-contained structure.

poem, the alternation between short and long lines gives the effect of mood shifts, from calm memory to less-controlled lamentation. If one reads the poem orally according to Levertov's theory that line endings serve as half-comma pauses, the transition from sections ii to iii creates a striking change of mood. With the phrase "everything flows" in iii–i, the verse begins to open up because its longer lines require the reader to take larger breaths. Even read silently, the form denotes these mood shifts. Paul Christensen, writing on Charles Olson (one of the chief influences on Levertov's apperceptive poetics, especially on her theory of the line), argues that "[t]he projective poem has visual impact on the reader: one can glance at the overall shape of the poem to be read and know with some accuracy whether the thinking is turbulent and difficult or meditative and evenly paced" (84).

"Olga Poems" ends with an ellipsis, suggesting that the process of relationship will continue "outside" the poem and into the future, long beyond the separation caused by Olga's death. The final ellipsis also erodes the boundary between this poem and the next, suggesting that the subjective grief of "Olga Poems" and the public action of many other poems in *The Sorrow Dance* and in *To Stay Alive* do not belong in separate spheres. While "Olga Poems" embraces *time* because it celebrates process, it is rarely explicit in its political context, that is, in its reference to *the times*. The poet-speaker does mention politics explicitly in part ii's description of Olga's reaction to seeing slums and indirectly in several other places, but it is primarily this elegy's context in *To Stay Alive* that makes it clear that "Olga Poems" alludes often to the problems of an activist's life. In *The Sorrow Dance*, Levertov had placed "Olga Poems" in a separate section from the poems about Vietnam, but she chose this elegy to open her completely political volume, *To Stay Alive.*

In the later volume the placement of "Olga Poems" just prior to another reprinted elegy, "A Note to Olga," makes its political allusions especially clear. "A Note to Olga" concerns the poet-speaker's lamentation for and inspiration from her dead sister. The mourner imagines carrying a reliquary for Olga that gives her pain by rubbing against "the knob of [her] spine" (*SA* 11). It also, however, gives her power because the memory of Olga fires her up. As she puts it in an apostrophe: "Though I forget you / a red coal from your fire / burns in that box" (11). The second section of this brief, two-part poem reveals that this energy provides political motivation. During an anti-war protest, the speaker imagines Ol-

ga's presence. The poem is filled with ironic uses of political slo-
gans that refer to both Olga and the protest. The marchers' cry,
"We shall ... overcome" (11–12), with its final word split off from the
rest and placed in a separate stanza, reminds us that Olga was
overcome by her own political ardor. Yet this line is, at the same
time, inspiring to the protestors. Levertov creates the same kind of
irony with the final image of stiff bodies being carried off to jail in
the paddy wagon. The act of non-violent resistance gives hope, but
it also echoes Olga's helpless death. Irony of word and image both
turn on the stark contrast between the protestors' united defiance
as they are "driven away" (12) in the police van and the speaker's
individual grief and pity for the sister who, in the previous elegy,
is driven away by her political intensity from all those who love
her.

In many lyric poems the text, in one way or another, parallels
a monument, so that lyric's characteristic suppression of both its
temporal progressions and its relation to historical time allows the
text to symbolize permanence. In brief lyrical elegies, this permanence acts as a substitute for the actual presence of the absent
loved one.[5] However, in "A Note to Olga," the dated title and the
1960s protest jargon disrupt the introspective self-containment that
is typical of so many traditional lyrics. These reminders of the
historical context of the poem make it impossible to see the text as
an analogy for the solid and permanent reliquary worn by the
speaker. Once again, then, Levertov fashions an elegy to Olga that
does not conquer time. Even so, there is hope in this poem, with
the apotheosis in which Olga inspires political activism. Despite
the mournful associations of terms like "driven away" and
"overcome," the image of protestors being carried off gives the
poet-speaker a renewed sense of contact with her sister. Yet even
these hopeful elements of "A Note to Olga" provide no triumph
over time, for they are part of the process of grief, which here, as in
"Olga Poems," includes complex, ever-growing reactions to the
dead one. The ambivalence of these references to Olga—at once
pitying and yet respectful, sad and yet comforting—turns what

---

[5]This happens in both elegy and other lyrics not only when the work
alludes explicitly to the permanence of poetry (Shakespeare's Sonnet #18),
but also when the text refers to itself as a monument (Jonson's epitaphs or
Keats's "Ode to Psyche"), and even when, as Sharon Cameron has shown,
lyrics about absence and presence mask their temporality by substituting
immortality for progression.

might seem at first like static snapshots of a moment of grief into a shifting struggle with the death of someone who was both sister and stranger to Levertov. Both elegies imply that even after death relationships are in flux, as they are in life, filled with unresolved contradictory impulses. Perhaps, then, we cannot apply the term apotheosis to "A Note to Olga," despite the similarity of her role to, say, the part played by a figure such as Lycidas when he rises as a star that will guide and inspire poets after him. Unlike the static stellar figure imagined by Milton, the figure imagined by the mourner in "A Note to Olga" shifts, sometimes inspiring activism, but sometimes evoking pity or even regret.

If Levertov's attitude toward time is not typical of elegy or conventional lyric, it is consistent with the apperceptive poetics she had already developed by the late 1950s, well before she wrote the darker poems of *The Sorrow Dance* and *To Stay Alive*. Both "Olga Poems" and "A Note to Olga" demonstrate that apperceptive poetry, because it presents both time and the times, is capable of embracing the political realm even as it records intensely subjective meditations. In fact, then, the main change in Levertov's poetry between the volumes *O Taste and See* (1964) and *The Sorrow Dance* (1967) is a shift in tone rather than the disruption of form about which, as I have noted, so many critics have complained. From the late 1960s through the early 1990s, her poems address anguished topics as often as—or more often than—the purely peaceful or happy ones that had dominated her early career. Apperceptive poetics always concern themselves with a poet-speaker's *here and now*, which is one reason that Levertov chose that title for her 1957 book. Once Levertov became intensely involved in political issues, then her *here and now* involved anguish alongside celebration. Public and private spheres became intertwined. As she put it in an interview with Lorrie Smith,

> So how did I come to start writing more specifically political poems? As a natural process of becoming more politically involved … once I became able to [write out of my daily life] my poetry has always sprung from my experiences, so if my experience was a political one, it was bound to happen that I would write poems out of that. (596–97)

When she says "more politically involved," she alludes to her earlier anti-nuclear activism, which began in the late 1950s. Her poetry of the 1950s also made some political allusions—to the Eichmann trial, for example. However, even more than her early political poems, her early grief poetry presages the change in tone that will happen in the 1960s, because it reveals the commitment to be open to all shades of feeling. It reveals, in other words, Levertov's Hasidic attitude toward an inclusive ecstasy.

Levertov traces the influence of Hasidism on her thought back to her reading of Martin Buber, as well as to her Jewish father, and to the "illustrious ancestors" on her father's side of the family. Since one well-known tenet of Hasidic thought proclaims that "joy alone is the true service of God" (Buber, *Tales* 15), many readers have had difficulty detecting Levertov's Hasidic heritage in her bleak issues-oriented poetry. Yet when in the mid-1960s Levertov adopted the image of the sorrow dance, she was exploring Hasidic ecstasy, which includes "negative" emotions. Despite its emphasis on joy, Hasidism ignores neither the social here and now, nor the "negative" emotions that result from engagement with worldly problems. Buber believed that Hasidic tradition exemplifies what he claimed is a Jewish tendency for one extreme to stir up another. It shows that there can be "a vibration of one's pain from which ecstasy can break forth" (*Tales* 5). He explicates this idea of ecstasy (*hitlahavut*) as an appreciation of all moments of life, citing the tale of a "grandfather" who could do a holy dance that caused his watchers to experience "both weeping and rapture in one" (*Legend* 21). This definition of inclusive ecstasy might have influenced Levertov's definition of the poetry of ecstasy: a "supernatural" poetry that, by looking closely at what is, reveals "the heavens and hells that lie about us" (*PW* 98). Etymologically, the term "in ecstasy" refers not exclusively to a state of joy, but rather to the state of being outside oneself; the O.E.D. says, "thrown into a frenzy or stupor with anxiety, astonishment, fear or passion." During the late 1950s and early 1960s, Levertov's poetry recorded moments of this ecstasy, brought on by the speaker looking closely at what is, in order to reveal the heavens about her. Then, as the Smith interview cited above reveals, when the poet's everyday experience began to include detailed knowledge of war and protests, her poetic attention shifted automatically. By the mid-1960s she could not avoid revealing the hells about her, as well. Obviously, the poetry of the late 1960s was, like that of a decade earlier, still based on attention to the poet-speaker's thinking/feeling experience. Perhaps less obviously, it was still a poetry of ecstasy. Inclusive ecstasy becomes a theme that Levertov returns to periodically throughout her career. The title *The Sorrow Dance* refers to the Hasidic tradition of performing a dance on the occasion of a death. It also alludes to the poem "A Lamentation" (*SD* 52), which refers to the robe "my sister wore / to dance *Sorrow*," as well as to the dance Levertov's father got up from his own deathbed to perform, which Olga mentions in the piece Levertov chose to close the volume. In all these allusions, the poet returns to the theme of one of her poems from the 1950s, "In Obedience" (*OI*). In this earlier poem, the speaker describes the dance she performed in honor of her dying father and tells of learning afterwards that he had gotten up the same day to perform his sorrow dance. She begins by interpreting her ritual, in obedience to a letter from her mother, as an act of happiness that cancels sorrow; however, by the end of the poem, she comes to accept an inclusive ecstasy that fuses celebration and mourning.

We might also read the title *The Sorrow Dance* as a description of the volume as a whole, which finds patterns and energies emerging from this kind of paradoxically affirmative lamentation for death and for war. This volume instructs the reader to interpret the dark poetry of the next thirty years—poetry about divorce, war, U.S. foreign policy, genocide, personal loss and environmental degradation—as a testament to the same reverence for life that inspired Levertov's more obviously ecstatic pre-Vietnam writings. Levertov argues that this poetry is "affirmative" because it "creates autonomous structures that are imbued with life and which stir the life of those who experience them" (*LUC* 60). It as a poetry of both the "joy" and the "woe" that Levertov discovers at the etymological roots of the word "'Jubilation'" (*SD* 35).

II

If apperceptive poetry can include the dark times and yet still be intrinsically affirmative, then grief can become a tool for protest. So from the 1960s through the 1990s, Levertov wrote not only elegies for specific people (such as "In Memory: After a Friend's Sudden Death" or "Missing Beatrice" [*BW* 23, 24]) and poems about grief in general (such as "Grief" [*FD* 68]), but she also wrote many poems that show even more clearly than "A Note to Olga" the ways that lamentation can combine with protest. These same poems demonstrate that affirmation can grow out of observation of dark times, and that personal mourning and political consciousness can inform one another.

Grief and protest interconnect right from the title of "El Salvador: Requiem and Invocation" (*DH* 15–39). Levertov wrote this libretto to accompany an oratorio by composer Newell Hendricks as a memorial for Salvadoran dissidents Archbishop Oscar Romero, three U.S. nuns, and one lay sister, all of whom were murdered for their protests against the government of El Salvador. The requiem weaves together the voices of a chorus, a narrator, a questioner, as well as excerpts from letters and sermons by the five martyrs, including Romero's litany intoning the names of those who died for opposing government policy. This poem both mourns the dead and invokes their spirit as an aid for living protestors.

With its conceit of perpetual silencing to represent a possible loss, the poem "What Were They Like?" (*SD* 84), written thirty years before the El Salvador libretto, serves as another prime example of lamentation as protest. It begins not as an elegy, but as a catalogue of inquiries about the people of Vietnam. Nevertheless, there are from the beginning hints of the sorrow to come. The past tense signals that the poem is set in an imaginary post-genocidal Vietnamese future—or non-future, to be more accurate. During the 1960s and 1970s, anti-War activists were concerned that U.S. military tactics, including napalm spraying, saturation bombing, and defoliation by means of giant bulldozers and agent orange, would annihilate the Vietnamese people if the war went on for too long.[6] One of their goals, therefore, was to prevent the genocide that would lead to a perpetual silencing of Vietnamese culture. The poem "What Were They Like?" imagines this silence. In the first half, some vaguely authoritative questioner poses questions about Vietnam's past. Since the six questions are posed in a group before the second voice responds, expectation builds. The reader awaits reverent responses, presaged by the delicate wording of the questions, with their curiosity about the beauty of Vietnamese life. The queries lead us to expect to learn whether "the people of Viet Nam / [used] lanterns of stone"; whether they held "ceremonies to reverence / the opening of buds"; whether they were "inclined to quiet laughter"; what their ornaments, poetry, and speech or singing were like. The initial answer, despite its respectful tone (the answerer addresses the questioner as "Sir"), and despite its controlled emotion, completely extinguishes the reader's expectations for information: "Sir, their light hearts turned to stone. / It is

---

[6]For an account of anti-war activists' charges of genocide and an examination of the validity of these charges, see Guenter Lewy's *America in Vietnam*, 299–304.

not remembered whether in gardens / stone lanterns illumined pleasant ways." All the answers include phrases that imply loss of this people's history: "it is not remembered," or "who can say," or simply "perhaps." The poem ends: "It is silent now." This polite, unemotional answering voice contrasts with the tragic message it reveals of genocide and the death of a culture, thereby burying poignant lamentation beneath an apparently distanced tone.

Something in the answerer's deference as well as in his (or her) very role suggests Vietnamese descent. Levertov has not escaped the charge of poetic colonialism, or appropriation of voice, for occasionally creating a Vietnamese speaker. However, this poem implies its own defense against such a charge. Its topic, the perpetual silencing of an "enemy's" people, indicates that she borrows another voice in order to demonstrate the horrific implications of casting the North Vietnamese in the role of subhuman enemy. Critics such as Marlene Nourbese Philip and Linda Alcoff argue that sometimes appropriation of voice serves a worthwhile purpose. The danger that advocacy will undermine the other's authority by purporting to speak for her/him might be cancelled by a worse danger: the other's complete silencing in death.[7] Poet Carolyn Forché tells of requests she received from Salvadorans, such as Archbishop Oscar Romero, that she go back to the United States and tell the story of oppression by the Salvadoran government before it was too late for the dissidents. Levertov's poem serves a similar purpose, and it illustrates Nourbese Philip's and Alcoff's contention that while advocacy risks perpetuating the image that the oppressed cannot speak for themselves, it is sometimes necessary to take that risk. In the case of "What Were They Like?" Levertov's advocacy takes the form of a catalogue of loss that invites her audience to lament the possible outcome of the U.S. military policy in Vietnam.

Lamentation set in a possible future is implied in all dystopic literature, and also in much apocalyptic writing. Since environmental protest poetry so often employs dystopic settings or apocalyptic imagery, it is no surprise to find that during the 1980s grief shows up often in Levertov's ecological poetry. The piece "Silent Spring" (*OP* 29–30), a poem protesting the over-use of pesticides, again uses images of silence to lament not only a horrific future,

---

[7]See Linda Alcoff's "The Problem of Speaking for Others" and Elizabeth Harvey's "Ventriloquizing Sappho" for examinations of the risks involved in advocacy.

but also the frightening present. The speaker laments absent sounds ("no crisp susurration of crickets") as she watches a pesticide truck driving by. The title refers to Rachel Carson's famous book, which led to the banning of DDT spraying in the United States, in which the scientist predicted the eventual end of human life if current (1962) rates of pesticide use continued. Levertov mixes Carson's futuristic title with the speaker's current sorrow to create the chilling sense that we are already standing at the threshold of the silent future the scientist described. Levertov emphasizes this sense of apocalypse by spending the first half of the poem celebrating in visual imagery the sky, the land, the ocean, the rain and the sunlight, before she begins the lamentation and warning of the second half. The speaker interrupts her own celebration of visual beauty with a reference to the frightening silences: "But listen...// no crisp susurration of crickets. / One lone frog. One lone / faraway whippoorwill. Absence. / No hum, no whirr" (29). Levertov uses line endings ("lone") and distance ("faraway") to emphasize the sense of loss the speaker states in these lines (29). She implies the ecological message that pesticides enter the food-chain by suggesting that her own fields, though unsprayed, are affected ("Drop the wild lettuce!" [29]). She also alludes to damage to species dependent on the sprayed insects, with her reference to a single frog and single bird. The poem has moved from its initial joyous celebration of plentitude to a mournful sense of loss, and then to a more intense grief tinged with ecological warning with the line "Try not to breathe!" which alludes to Carson's predictions that even unsprayed parts of the world will be affected by pesticides (29). As does "What Were They Like?" this poem ends with the image of silence, this time in an oxymoron: "Hear your own steps / in violent silence" (30). It ends not with the peaceful silence of its opening, but with an apocalyptic silence that laments the loss of the insects and the possible extinction of animals dependent on them.

A Door in the Hive, published at the end of the 1980s, includes "Two Threnodies and a Psalm" (45–48), another ecological poem that warns that we have arrived at the crisis. The first threnody (i.e., song of lamentation) begins: "It is not approaching. / It has arrived. / We are not circumventing it" (45). The second song of lamentation compares the degraded earth to a "body being savaged," then points out the ecological fact that as we destroy our environment we slowly kill ourselves: "The body being savaged / is alive. / It is our own" (45). In this poem, the speaker grieves for

both human and non-human life. Therefore, in the third section of
the poem, protest extends beyond purely environmental details to
include more broadly political categories of oppression:

> Our unbroken skin
> one with the ripped skin of the tortured
> > the shot-down, bombed, napalmed,
> > the burned alive.
> One with the sore and filthy skin of the destitute. (46)

Levertov makes the point that while the wealthy and the comfortable can still buy environmental luxuries like clean air, water and
protection from weapons, in the long run those who poison the
destitute will end up poisoning themselves, since all human beings
are, ecologically speaking, interconnected with one another.

A poem from earlier in the 1980s, "Gathered at the River" (*OP*
40–42), also uses lamentation for both human and non-human life,
this time to protest the arms race. The poem is an elegy for human
beings who died in World War II and also for the other, non-
human beings (trees) that would die in future nuclear wars.
Reflecting on a combined protest and memorial service for those
who were bombed at Hiroshima and Nagasaki, the speaker imagines the trees around her listening in, since they "are not indifferent" to nuclear war (40). It is, she says, "as if" they are "well aware
that if we fail, / we fail also for them" (41). The speaker mourns
for the devastation that would follow a general nuclear war. The
poem ends with an apocalyptic scenario, a non-landscape in which
"there will be nothing left of [the trees'] slow and innocent wisdom, / … no memory / of shade, / of leaf, / no pollen" (41–42).
The reference to memory in the fourth-last line reminds the reader
that this non-landscape is also void of human life, and so brings
the poem back to its earlier lamentation for human victims of the
first nuclear war, thereby suggesting the poem's central point: that
this kind of war destroys all kinds of life. The memorial service described mid-poem is a protest because it mourns the past in order
to change the future. The speaker believes that as "we stand in a
circle / …remembering the dead / of Hiroshima, / of Nagasaki
//…we are invoking … the heroes and heroines" of the peace
movement "to help us / stop the torment of our evil dreams" (41).

The evil dreams of "Gathered at the River" are metaphors for
the diabolically brilliant technological imaginations that have allowed us to create such weapons. In a poem from her next volume,
Levertov uses dreams more literally in another protest against the

arms race. The apocalyptic "Age of Terror" (*CB* 98–99) spends
most of its lines describing the speaker's horrific dream of surviving a nuclear war alongside four family members. It begins,
though, outside the dream, with a lamentation for this age of terror, this age in which we are caught between dread of global annihilation and, ironically, the fear that we might possibly survive a
nuclear war. Surviving such a war presents terrifying scenarios,
and the idea of no one surviving presents the dread of an impossible-to-imagine post-human future. So the poem begins: "Between
the fear / of the horror of Afterwards / and the despair / in the
thought of no Afterwards, / we move abraded, / each gesture
scraping us / on the millstones" (98). In her description of a
nightmare about survival, the speaker refers back to this sensation
of being scraped, thus linking our general nuclear dread with the
nightmare. In its opening, specifically in its fourth line, the poem
plays with a paradox embedded in much late twentieth-century
apocalyptic writing, that the future state we grieve, the future in
which global nuclear war has destroyed our species, is one that
cannot actually be narrated from a human point of view.[8]

Levertov again contrasts the impossible-to-imagine obliteration of our species with the "desolation / of survival" in the poem
"During a Son's Dangerous Illness" (*BW* 34–35). This time, however, the fear of survival refers to the speaker's dread that she will
face the "unnatural" fate of outliving her own child. This piece
emphasizes the connection between personal grief and political
consciousness:

> Grief for the menaced world—lost rivers,
> poisoned lakes—all creatures, perhaps,
> to be fireblasted
>   off the
> whirling cinder we
> loved, but not enough...
> The grief I'd know if I
> lived into
> your unthinkable death
> is a splinter
> of that selfsame grief,
> infinitely smaller but
> the same in kind.... (35)

---

[8]See also W.S. Merwin's *The Rain in the Trees* and *The Lice* for apocalyptic poems implying the end of the human voice.

While "During a Son's Dangerous Illness" names the connection between the personal and the political, most of the other poems I have been examining imply that same relationship. As is expected of a poet who seeks to record her own thinking/feeling experience, Levertov does not make arbitrary divisions between the kinds of grief she comes across. In poem after poem published between 1967 and 1989, including the elegies for Olga and the ecological poems I have discussed, the sorrows that tear at her when she pays attention to tragedies concerning family and friends reverberate with the griefs to which an activist opens herself.

III

The urgency of Levertov's ecological poetry of the 1980s matches in intensity the bitter irony of her anti-war work in the 1960s, 1970s and 1980s. Then, in the 1990s, in *Evening Train, Sands of the Well*, and *This Great Unknowing*, her tone changes. Edward Zlotkowski presents an insightful analysis of the "new and distinctive turn," a "new-found calm" (150), in some of Levertov's latest poetry, which he locates in the spiritual focus of the 1996 volume *Sands of the Well*. He defines her new spirituality as an ability to "lose track" of her "obsessions" (*SW* 49; quoted in Zlotkowski 142) in order to pay attention to the "art of being" (142). I would add that in the final volume that Levertov arranged, *Sands of the Well*, this new, or newly rediscovered, calm treats grief in a distinctively open way. It does not cancel grief, but instead includes faithful attention to mourning as an aspect of being.[9] Attention to dark emotions, as I have argued, has long been a feature of Levertov's poetry. What is striking about *Sands of the Well*, however, is the fullness of the poet-speakers' acceptance of lamentation. The startling grief-filled protests of the Vietnam years and of the 1980s ecological and other political poetry have given way to a gentler sense of grief as a daily companion. It is as if the poet has reached a goal set out almost twenty years earlier in the poem

---

[9]One might argue that in the posthumously published *This Great Unknowing*, the calm seems to override grief. Although *This Great Unknowing* includes a few poems that address the political and environmental issues that have crystallized grief in earlier volumes, the tone is more nostalgic than mournful. See, for example, "A Hundred a Day" (13), "Fugitives" (32), and "Alienation in Silicon Valley" (58–59).

"Talking to Grief" from *Life in the Forest* (43). In this poem, the speaker charges herself with the need to domesticize and trust mourning. In an extended metaphor, she compares grief to a pet who has been a stray, but who needs a proper home. The poem begins:

> Ah, grief, I should not treat you
> like a homeless dog
> who comes to the back door
> for a crust, for a meatless bone.
> I should trust you.

The speaker tells the animal that she knows it has been living like a stray under her porch, waiting for its "real place to be readied." She confesses: I know you need "to consider / my house your own." Never realized in the poem, always cast in the future tense or conditional mood, is the goal of letting grief become a part of daily life, as acceptable as joy or laughter. That very acceptance, that very end of denial, the poem implies, would—ironically— tame the emotion.

As a whole, the volume *Sands of the Well* illustrates this accep- tance that tames grief. To switch to one of Levertov's other metaphors, to which I have already alluded, the speakers of this late volume do not interrupt their daily activities in order to "dance sorrow" so much as they simply walk beside it. So there are no elegies *per se* in *Sands of the Well*, nor is there any of the paradoxically startling silence found in earlier protest poetry. In- stead, grief appears for brief moments both in poems of political protest and in poems tracing the poet-speaker's growing sense of individual frailty and mortality. This volume, as does every work since *The Sorrow Dance*, still blends darkness with affirmation, and it still employs an apperceptive poetics, which traces the think- ing/feeling process, but it is distinctive in its calm domesticization of mourning. In "Wondering" (9), for example, the poet-speaker briefly laments the effort it now takes to pray hopefully. Similarly, in the poem "In Question" (6), the speaker momentarily regrets the chances for pleasure that will never recur because her time is run- ning out. Despite this traditional image of time in tension with life, which contrasts with Levertov's unconventional use of time in "Olga Poems," these later poems do repeat the earlier elegy's commitment to process. In poem after poem from *Sands of the Well*, Levertov traces the shifting tensions between one moment of con- sciousness and the next. So in "As the Moon Was Waning" (15), the speaker's mournful sense of a "mortal weariness that it's not yet time for" distracts her from contemplating "[s]mall intimations of destiny." Similarly, the speaker of "Empty Hands" (11) records the physical pains that at vulnerable moments draw her attention away from the beauties of nature. In all four of these poems, the speakers hold in consciousness both the desired meditations and the distracting attention to pain.

As often as these flashes of grief appear in relation to purely individual concerns, they also integrate personal and political lamentation. In "The Danger Moments" (10), the speaker feels "some moments / shiver in extreme fragility." This is not, she asserts, an "apprehension / of mortality," but rather a more universal fear, that all of life seems to have stopped breathing, "as if" God has "turned away." The poem "The News and a Green Moon, July 1994" (54–55) catalogues global crises, until the speaker laments "the earth's cries of anguish" that are "almost audible" (55). Much as this poet would like a respite from the dark times that cause her so much sorrow, she is committed to a poetry of attention, which includes attention to "the tragic and fearful character of our times," which "we are in … as fish are in the sea" (*NSE* 4). In "Hymns to Darkness" (*SW* 102–3), the speaker would like to spend a night just observing somber beauties such as shadows, alders around a dark pool, or black swans. She would like to be for a time "without thought of history," especially of the "Contemporary" history recorded in "the shameful news each day" (103). Yet the conditional verbs ("How good it *would* be to spend such a night" [emphasis mine]) remind the reader that this poet has written for nearly four decades a poetry of attention to the *here and now*, whether heavenly or hellish. In this volume, the heavens of friendship, natural beauty, and prayer are integrated more fully than ever before with the hells of violent times and personal illness and death. The piece "In the Woods" (57) captures this poetic taming of grief, which allows it to coexist peacefully with celebration in Levertov's most recent poetry. It begins with a lamenting reference to these dark times of the arms race, environmental degradation and global unrest, and then it moves on immediately to affirm life in the face of contemporary troubles: "Everything is threatened, but meanwhile / everything presents itself." Protest, affirmation and grief merge for the speaker when she perceives that "Everything answers the roll call / and even / … speaks for those that are gone." These five lines might be a description of Levertov's achievement over the final three decades of her life, during which dark wing and light wing together made possible her poetic flight.

Works Cited

Alcoff, Linda. "The Problem of Speaking for Others." *Cultural Critique* 20 (1991–92): 5–32.

Allen, Donald M., ed. *The New American Poetry*. New York: Grove, 1960.

Altieri, Charles. *Enlarging the Temple*. Lewisburg, PA : Bucknell UP, 1979.

Borroff, Marie. "To Stay Alive." In *Denise Levertov: In Her Own Province*. Ed. Linda Welshimer Wagner. New York: New Directions, 1979. 129–30.

Buber, Martin. *The Legend of the Baal-Shem*. Trans. Maurice Friedman. New York: Schocken, 1969.

———. *The Tales of Rabbi Nachman*. Trans. and ed. Maurice Friedman. Indianapolis: Indiana UP, 1962.

Cameron, Sharon. *Lyric Time: Dickinson and the Limits of Genre*. Baltimore: Johns Hopkins UP, 1979.

Carson, Rachel. *Silent Spring*. Boston: Houghton Mifflin, 1962.

Christensen, Paul. *Charles Olson: Call Him Ishmael*. Austin: U of Texas P, 1975.

Forché, Carolyn. "Honoring the Particulars: An Interview with Carolyn Forché." *Sojourners* 19.9 (Nov. 1990): 18–22.

Gilbert, Sandra M. "Revolutionary Love: Denise Levertov and the Poetics of Politics." *Parnassus* 12.2–13.1 (Spring–Winter 1985): 335–51.

Harvey, Elizabeth D. "Ventriloquizing Sappho: Ovid, Donne, and the Erotics of the Feminine Voice." *Criticism* 1.2 (Spring 1989): 115–38.

Levertov, Denise. *Breathing the Water*. New York: New Directions, 1987.

———. *Candles in Babylon*. New York: New Directions, 1981.

———. *A Door in the Hive*. New York: New Directions, 1989.

———. *The Freeing of the Dust*. New York: New Directions, 1975.

———. *Here and Now*. San Francisco: City Lights, 1957.

———. "An Interview with Denise Levertov." With Lorrie Smith. *Michigan Quarterly Review* 24.4 (Fall 1985): 596–604.

———. *Life in the Forest*. New York: New Directions, 1978.

———. *Light Up the Cave*. New York: New Directions, 1981.

———. *New & Selected Essays*. New York: New Directions, 1992.

———. *Oblique Prayers*. New York: New Directions, 1984.

———. *O Taste and See*. New York: New Directions, 1964.

———. *Overland to the Islands*. Highlands, NC: Jargon, 1958.

———. *The Poet in the World*. New York: New Directions, 1973.

———. *Sands of the Well*. New York: New Directions, 1973.

———. *The Sorrow Dance*. New York: New Directions, 1967.

———. *This Great Unknowing: Last Poems*. New York: New Directions, 1999.

———. *To Stay Alive*. New York: New Directions, 1971.

Lewy, Guenter. *America in Vietnam*. Oxford: Oxford UP, 1978.

Little, Anne Colclough. "Old Impulses, New Expressions: Duality and Unity in the Poetry of Denise Levertov." *Renascence* 50.1–2 (Fall 1997/Winter 1998): 33–48.

Mersmann, James. *Out of the Vietnam Vortex: A Study of Poets and Poetry Against the War*. Lawrence: UP of Kansas, 1974.

Merwin, W.S. *The Lice*. New York: Atheneum, 1971.

———. *The Rain in the Trees*. New York: Knopf, 1989.

Nelson, Cary. "Levertov's Political Poetry." In *Denise Levertov: In Her Own Province*. Ed. Linda Welshimer Wagner. New York: New Directions, 1979. 131–35.

Nourbese Philip, Marlene. "The Disappearing Debate: Racism and Censorship." In *Language in Her Eye: Views on Writing and Gender; Voices by Canadian Women Writing in English*. Ed. Libby Scheier, et al. Toronto: Coach House, 1990. 171–77.

Smith, Lorrie. "Songs of Experience: Denise Levertov's Political Poetry." *Contemporary Literature* (Summer 1986): 213–32.

Zlotkowski, Edward. "Presence and Transparency: A Reading of Denise Levertov's *Sands of the Well*." *Renascence* 50.1–2 (Fall 1997/Winter 1998): 135–51.

The Eye as Mirror of Humanity:
Social Responsibility and the Nature of Evil in Denise Levertov's
"During the Eichmann Trial"

Eric Sterling

"All There is to Know About Adolph [sic] Eichmann"
—Leonard Cohen

EYES..	Medium
HAIR..	Medium
WEIGHT...	Medium
HEIGHT...	Medium
DISTINGUISHING FEATURES...........................	None
NUMBER OF FINGERS.......................................	Ten
NUMBER OF TOES...	Ten
INTELLIGENCE...	Medium

What did you expect?
Talons?
Oversize incisors?
Green Saliva?
Madness?

(194)

Denise Levertov's poem "During the Eichmann Trial" (*The Jacob's Ladder*) passionately criticizes the abnegation of social responsibility during the Holocaust. The poem also is an integral work in Levertov studies because it signifies her "newly sharpened and intense concern with social issues" (Rodgers 71). Levertov admits that it is her first political poem and the beginning of her "sense of the social role that the poet, specifically, can play ..." (Estess 90). In her poem, Levertov employs the metaphors of the eye (and the I, as in one's self) to illustrate her feeling that the Holocaust represents a universal breakdown in human conscience and social responsibility—not only among the perpetrators but also among the bystanders and humanity as a whole. The poet's thoughts foreshadow the belief expressed by renowned Holocaust scholar David S. Wyman in his book *The Abandonment of the Jews*:

> The Holocaust was certainly a Jewish tragedy. But it was not *only* a Jewish tragedy. It was also a Christian tragedy, a tragedy for Western civilization, and a tragedy for all mankind. The killing was done by people, to other people, while other people stood by. The perpetrators, where they were not actually Christians, arose from a Christian culture. The bystanders most capable of helping were Christians. The point should have been obvious. Yet comparatively few [European and] American non-Jews recognized that the plight of the European Jews was their plight too. (xvi)

Levertov, like Wyman, observes that this immense tragedy occurred in part because people failed to recognize the interconnected nature of humanity and instead acted (or failed to act) because they adhered to arbitrary and superficial distinctions between human beings. Levertov's tripartite poem portrays not only the villainy of Nazis such as Adolf Eichmann but also the refusal of bystanders to care for and aid "the other" (in this case, Jews), which constitutes a violation of collective responsibility. Although Sophie B. Blaydes claims that "Levertov turns to Eichmann's trial to validate man" (211), actually the reverse is true. The poet implies in "During the Eichmann Trial" that because "we are members / one of another" (63), human beings must share the guilt for the atrocities committed during the Holocaust. Nobel Peace Prize Winner Elie Wiesel, a victim of Eichmann who attended the trial, remarked that a woman refused his offer of a ticket to the trial: "She did not want his eye to focus on her. She did not want to have anything in common with that man. Then I understood that perhaps during the Holocaust the cosmic eye was focused on mankind, taking in everybody, making us all guilty" (III, 214). Levertov's use of the word "we" indicates that all are responsible, even Jews such as herself. Levertov's poem suggests that we must look objectively at ourselves from without, blurring superficial demarcations between various categories within our species and seeing others as we do ourselves, in order to empathize with others.

Levertov begins her poem with the section entitled "When We Look Up," which concerns the 1961 trial of Adolf Eichmann in Jerusalem. This segment opens with an epigraph from the poetry of Robert Duncan: "When we look up / each from his being" (61). Duncan's epigraph suggests that readers should scrutinize themselves from without so that they may objectively examine their consciences and their souls. Harry Marten believes that Levertov begins with these two lines to suggest that such self-scrutiny "is something not often done" (82), perhaps because many people are not sufficiently introspective (they fail to look at themselves from without) and are too egotistical, caring only about themselves and their loved ones.

Similarly, Eichmann "stands // isolate ..." (*JL* 63) in the Jerusalem courtroom because he also distinguishes himself from "the other," considering Jews a different and inferior species from himself; this dehumanization allows him to kill without remorse. Robert E. Conot notes, for instance, that Eichmann's dealing with French Jews "revealed the inhuman banality of the perpetrators of the Final Solution—Eichmann had not thought in terms of human beings, of despair and agony, terror and torture, but of *Judenmateriel*: So and so many Jewish carcasses that he had contracted to deliver" (259). He distinguishes himself intellectually and emotionally from the Jewish people just as the glass booth in which he sits separates him physically from Jews during the trial. Levertov thus suggests that when people believe that the fate of others does not affect their own lives, they refuse to see and to concern themselves with the suffering of others. It is a failure of the imagination because they fail to imagine themselves in the predicament others face. It is also easy to excuse the indifference of bystanders—both governments and ordinary citizens—by blaming solely the Nazis for the atrocities perpetrated during the Holocaust. The narrator claims, however, that although none pity Eichmann,

> all
> must pity if they look
>
> into their own face.... (61)

Here Levertov implies that many people (not a mere few such as Eichmann, Hitler, Himmler, and Goering) must share responsibility for the tragedy, that perpetrators and bystanders must share the blame; Eichmann is, as the poem by Leonard Cohen that serves as an epigraph for this paper indicates, simply a human being, not the grotesque monster that some onlookers during the trial expected to see in the glass booth. Marten concurs that "Levertov refuses to reduce the man, Eichmann, to monster" (82). Wiesel observes:

> The most fascinating thing about Eichmann is that he is human.
> If he were inhuman, he would be easy to understand. If he could
> not sleep nights, that too would be understandable. But he can
> sleep, he does care for his wife, he does love his children. And if
> it were not Eichmann, it would have been any number of other
> Germans in his place. (II, 47)

In this passage, Wiesel humanizes and demystifies Eichmann's character, indicating that the war criminal is similar to many other ordinary human beings.

The realization that Eichmann was perhaps a mere human being like himself proved too traumatic for one witness during the trial, writer Yehiel Dinur (also known as K. Zetnik, which means concentration camp inmate; he changed his name because he felt that his experiences at Auschwitz had altered him into a mere number and object, and thus he was no longer a human being). Dinur began to speak of his horrific experiences at Auschwitz—where Eichmann had sent him and countless others—claiming that the Nazis had transformed him into a subspecies: "They [Jews] breathed according to different laws of nature. They did not live nor did they die according to the laws of this world. Their name was 'Number … Katzetnik'" (Hausner 171). Dinur thus began his testimony about Eichmann's abominable cruelty, but shortly into his deposition he fainted on the witness stand. His trauma arose partly because of the terror of recounting his hardships but also because he found himself in the same room with a man who engineered the destruction of his life and whom he always had regarded as a monster. Dinur was hospitalized for two weeks because of shock. Subsequently, he committed suicide.

Eichmann, like many of his Nazi cohorts, destroyed countless human lives yet remained a devoted family man, thus rigidly demarcating his evil job from his familial life. Furthermore, many Nazis did indeed long for Eichmann's authority, wishing that they could have attained the powerful bureaucratic position that enabled him to avoid the front while sending millions of Jews to their deaths.

In her poem's middle segment, entitled "The Peachtree," Levertov focuses on Eichmann's alleged murder of an innocent young Jewish boy whom he finds in his orchard. Israeli Attorney General Gideon Hausner, the main prosecutor in the Eichmann trial, issued a fifteen-count indictment against the Nazi war criminal concerning Eichmann's atrocities during the Holocaust—horrific actions that covered a myriad of crimes against the Jewish people, such as "caus[ing] the killing of millions of Jews, in his capacity as the person responsible for the execution of the Nazi plan for the physical extermination of the Jews, known as the 'final solution of the Jewish problem'" (Papadatos 111). The reader of "During the Eichmann Trial" might ponder why the poet, knowing full well of Eichmann's heinous orders that sent millions of innocent Jews to their deaths, decides instead to focus on the murder of one Jewish boy.[1] Although Marten believes that "the crime is so unspecial" (85), the murder is actually quite unique for Eichmann: it is the one in which the victim is not merely a faceless statistic, one of millions sent to their deaths, but rather an individual. The answer also lies, perhaps, in the personal nature of this particular killing Levertov chooses to portray. In all the crimes described in Hausner's indictments, Eichmann arranged for millions of Jews to be sent to concentration camps, where they were starved to death or gassed; this murder, however, captures Levertov's attention because it is unique, for, unlike the events that led to the massacre of millions of others, in this case Eichmann murdered the boy himself and personally watched the child die. Because Eichmann actually committed the murder himself and witnessed the boy's death, Levertov finds chilling Eichmann's lack of remorse and emotion.

Levertov suggests this lack of emotion through her use of metonomy. Because of his role in the murder of millions of Jews, she refers to him in "The Peachtree" as "mister death" and the "Devil" (64). These words briefly describe Eichmann as if he is not a murderer but rather death itself. The poet labels the place of the murder of the innocent boy as the Devil's garden—an inversion of the Garden of Eden. Death, not God, controls this garden. Instead of being a place of innocence, Eichmann's garden symbolizes his evil nature. That is why Eichmann's fruit (the peach) tempts and beckons the boy, as the serpent does in the Book of Genesis, into eating from it; Levertov writes:

> and of its fruit one peach
> calls to him

---

[1]Ironically, Eichmann was found not guilty of this crime but was convicted of crimes against humanity for sending millions of Jews to their deaths.

> he sees it yellow and ripe
> the vivid blood
> bright in its round cheek
>
> Next day he knows
> he cannot withstand desire
> it is no common fruit
>
> it holds some secret
> it speaks to the yellow star within him. (64)

When the boy, like Adam and Eve, succumbs to temptation by eating from the fruit of the tree, he knows death. But Levertov's conjectural description of the aftermath of Eichmann's murder of the boy demonstrates that the killer is indeed human, albeit one without conscience; she suggests that Eichmann will now act as apathetically as he does after all his heinous deeds:

> mister death who signs papers
> then eats
>
> telegraphs simply: **Shoot them**
> then eats
> mister death who orders
> more transports
> then eats
>
> he would have enjoyed
> the sweetest of all the peaches on his tree
> with sour-cream
> with brandy (64–65)

The villain murders and then resumes his routine; death, in fact, has become an integral part of his routine. Eichmann, ironically, fails to distinguish between the Jewish boy's need to eat, possibly for survival, and his own decadent desire for a pleasant dessert. Furthermore, Levertov's vision of Eichmann's reaction suggests a gross moral indifference, not only because the Nazi murders the boy in response to the theft of a mere peach, but also since he regrets the loss of the fruit, but not the loss of the boy. Immediately after the murder, the killer exhibits no remorse—only indifference.

The reader could contrast Eichmann's lack of emotion regarding the murder to the strong feelings Levertov herself displays when she describes the boy's unfortunate death. She empathizes with, and pities, him. She characterizes him as a child who is so hungry for the yellow peach that he climbs into Eichmann's orchard and eats it; she wants to make the reader also empathize with the boy—an innocent and harmless human being. The poet says that the boy "scales the wall" (64) to enter Eichmann's garden; in the poem Levertov creates the wall, for historically it did not exist—the boy was already working inside the orchard. The poet's insertion of the wall is telling, implying that a figurative wall exists between Eichmann and the boy, between Aryan and Jew. Wiesel remarks that during "the first years of the Nazi occupation a curtain of steel isolated European Jewry. To them the ghetto has cosmic significance. Its walls separated them not only from their surroundings, but from the rest of humanity" (II, 180). It is not surprising, then, that during his trial, as well as during the Nuremberg Trials, Eichmann was quoted as saying that after the war, he "would leap laughing into the grave because the feeling that he had 5 million people on his conscience would be for him a source of extraordinary satisfaction" (Taylor 248). Eichmann may remorselessly murder this boy because of the arbitrary and superficial yet impenetrable barrier Eichmann uses to demarcate himself from "the other."

Levertov, furthermore, employs metonomy so that the reader may view the child through Eichmann's perspective; to him the boy is not a human being but rather a yellow star. The metonomy reduces the boy to an inanimate and insignificant object, dehumanizing him and making it easy for the Nazi to commit murder to punish the theft of a peach and then not give the killing another thought. Levertov employs the image of the yellow star to manifest Eichmann's dehumanization of Jews. He loves yellow: "Yellow / calmed him later," such as the images of yellow autumn leaves in Wienerwald and the yellow sun (62). But during the Holocaust, he began to hate yellow stars (Jews):

> It was the yellow
> of the stars too,
>
> stars that marked
> those in whose faces
>
> you had not
> looked. 'They were cast out
>
> as if they were
> some animals, some beasts.' (62)

Yellow was an image that he had shared with Jews, yet he represses this correlation. The color yellow was formerly a positive image to Eichmann, yet he transformed the image into a despicable one in order to separate himself mentally from the group of people who were scapegoated. Eichmann's dehumanization prevents him from empathizing with, and acting compassionately towards, the boy because if he does not consider Jews to be human beings, he cannot *envision* what it would be like to be a Jew himself, to be "the other." His lack of imagination derives from his refusal to look at himself objectively.

In *The Poet in the World*, Levertov states:

> The imagination of what it is to *be* those other forms of life that want to live is the only way to recognition; and it is that imaginative recognition that brings compassion to birth. Man's capacity for evil, then, is less a positive capacity, for all its horrendous activity, than a failure to develop man's most human function, the imagination, to its fullness, and consequently a failure to develop compassion. (53)

Eichmann's failure to develop compassion signifies his apathy and prejudice, which, again, derives from his lack of imagination and introspection; it explains why he casually gives the order to "**Shoot them** / then eats" (65). Dr. Edith Kramer, an inmate at Theresienstadt, encountered Eichmann during a visit: the Nazi "asked me eagerly about their number [in a transport], and when I replied so and so many dead, he would acknowledge it with the simple word, 'Good'" (Ritvo and Plotkin 144).

Levertov cannot totally fathom Eichmann's lack of feeling during the trial and during the Holocaust, partly because the atrocities that come to light during the trial leave her rather fervent. Consequently, her poem exhibits great emotion and intensity, partly because she composed it during the trial. Perhaps the key word in Levertov's title is "*During* the Eichmann Trial" because her emotions provide a sense of immediacy that would have been lost had she penned the poem years or even months later. Marten, furthermore, believes that in the peachtree section, Levertov employs "color to stir emotion ..." (84). Levertov decided not to correct her two factual errors in the work, perhaps because she realized that her emotions at the time she wrote the poem are a significant attribute of the piece.[2] The poem claims that the boy steals a peach (actually it was cherries) and that the boy climbed secretly into the orchard (actually he was already working there). Levertov perhaps

---

[2]In a footnote to the poem, Levertov admits that the poem is based on the initial mentioning of the incident during the trial and is factually incorrect regarding the peach and the wall: "The poem therefore is not to be taken as a report of what happened but of what I envisioned" (n. 65).

decided that correcting minor details was not as significant as the emotional intensity she wished to convey, and as mentioned previously, the peach and the wall are significant metaphors in the work.

Levertov indicates that Eichmann attributes his chilling lack of emotion to his defense mechanism—that he was simply following orders from his Nazi superiors. Ironically, this feeble excuse is the same one Hermann Goering and other Nazi officers employed during the Nuremberg Trials in 1945—that when they arranged for the murder of countless Jewish victims, they were merely carrying out orders of another Nazi administrator—Adolf Eichmann. According to their claims, therefore, Eichmann gave orders to kill rather than meekly following them. Furthermore, Eichmann's former assistant, Dieter Wisliceny, wrote that Eichmann

> was personally a cowardly man who went to great pains to protect himself from responsibility. He never made a move without approval from higher authority, and was extremely careful to keep files and records establishing the responsibility of Himmler, Hedyrich and, later, Kaltenbrunner.... Eichmann was very cynical in his attitude toward the Jewish question. He gave no indication of any human feeling toward these people. (Pearlman 199)

Levertov quotes Eichmann as saying that he is not a murderer but rather an obedient civil servant:

> 'I was used from the nursery
> to obedience
>
> all my life …
> Corpselike
>
> obedience.'
>   (61–62; Levertov's ellipsis)

In this passage, Eichmann justifies his participation in an unprecedented genocide, implying that legal positivism and military law supersede moral law, that any atrocity, no matter how heinous, is acceptable if the government sanctions it. Blaydes believes that Levertov "is struggling to identify the individual in Eichmann, the 'I' that could destroy obediently and mindlessly" (211).

Eichmann's adherence to authority renders him mindless and thus, in his eyes, blameless. The word "Corpselike" is ironic because Eichmann's obedience led to the deaths of millions of people.[3] In his play *Auschwitz*, Peter Barnes characterizes several Germans who, like Eichmann, act and excuse their moral indifference; they shield their culpability from themselves as well as from others by refusing to discern the ramifications of their actions. These civil servants in Barnes's play help to construct the concentration camp Auschwitz and send the Zyklon B poison to the death camp yet consider themselves innocent because they work in a bureaucratic office in Berlin and thus never see the deaths to which they contribute. Similarly, Eichmann arranges for transports that send millions of Jews to their deaths, yet he denies his guilt because he remains in the sanctuary of his office and almost never witnesses the gruesome results of his transports with his own eyes. This, perhaps, is what Levertov means when she says of Eichmann, "He had not looked" (l.1). Eichmann could kill easily because he never saw (with the exception of the Jewish boy murdered in the orchard) the grief and suffering he caused. Not seeing the pain and the death of his victims allows him, Levertov suggests, to transform his victims from human beings into abstractions, with Jews turning into mere objects (yellow stars). In "The Peachtree," Levertov implies that Eichmann has so dehumanized his victims that he possesses the ability to make this transformation in person as well as in absentia.

In addition, the word "corpselike" refers to his mindlessness because he says that he followed orders without thinking or knowing. This assertion resembles the controversial ideas that philosopher Hannah Arendt presented in her book *Eichmann in Jerusalem*. Arendt, who covered the trial for *The New Yorker*, reported that Eichmann did not fully understand his own actions because the Nazis relied heavily upon the employment of euphemisms. She argued that Eichmann's actions signified apathy—an indifference resulting from the dehumanization of his victims that desensitized him to the genocide; in fact, "banality of evil" is

---

[3]It is noteworthy that near the end of World War II, Eichmann disobeyed orders from his superiors to stop sending Jews to their deaths. This fact is especially true in regard to the murder of Hungarian Jews; thousands were murdered after Eichmann disregarded orders he received; Eichmann, furthermore, ignored Heinrich Himmler's orders in September 1944 to stop sending Jews to Auschwitz (Reitlinger 455).

the subtitle of her book.[4] This "banality of evil" arises partly because the murder of Jews became commonplace: when murder (such as during a war) becomes a frequent occurrence, along with the fact that the victims are stripped of their citizenship and labeled subhuman, killers can become desensitized to the atrocities they commit and may even justify their crimes. Arendt asserts, furthermore, that the reduction of language to symbols allowed the Nazis to slaughter countless human beings without being affected by the deaths emotionally: The communication regarding genocide

> was subject to rigid "language rules," and, except in the reports from the *Einsatzgruppen*, it is rare to find documents in which such bald words as "extermination," "liquidation," or "killing" occur. The prescribed code names for killing were "final solution," "evacuation" (*Aussiedlung*), and "special treatment" (*Sonderbehandlung*).... For whatever other reasons the language rules may have been devised, they proved of enormous help in the maintenance of order and sanity in the various widely diversified services whose cooperation was essential in this matter. Moreover, the very term "language rules" (*Sprachregelung*) was itself a code name; it meant what in ordinary language would be called a lie. (85)

It was easier for Eichmann to send thousands at a time on transports to concentration camps when he could label it "special treatment." Such euphemisms desensitize the user and the audience to the inhumanity of the acts and numb their consciences. The poet describes Eichmann's words as "harsh babble" because they, too, were full of such euphemisms. Furthermore, "babble" may be Levertov's pun on "Babel" because the Nazis, like those who attempted to build a tower to Heaven (Genesis 11:1–9), swelled with pride and consequently perceived themselves as gods and sinned. "The Final Solution," like the Tower of Babel, depicts the outrageous hubris exhibited by man when he fails to understand his place in the universe because he refuses to "look up / each from his being." Levertov, like Arendt, believed that people employ language to fool others as well as themselves—especially during turbulent times, such as in war. In "Staying Alive," Levertov writes that a major in the United States army defends the decision

---

[4]It should be mentioned that Arendt's book on Eichmann, especially in regard to her theory about the banality of evil, has been challenged by several scholars.

to bomb a town, ignoring the inevitable civilian deaths, because "'[i]t became necessary / to destroy the town to save it'" (21). The major tells not only the media but also his own soldiers that they are acting virtuously, regardless of the many innocent people they kill, because they are saving the town; this idea, firmly implanted within the minds of impressionable soldiers, allows them to feel that they may kill with impunity. The poet continues:

> O language, mother of thought,
> are you rejecting us as we reject you?
>
> Language, coral island
> accrued from human comprehensions,
> human dreams,
>
> you are eroded as war erodes us. (22)

This segment of the poem suggests Levertov's belief in the power (and the potential abuse) of language to control behavior. This passage from Levertov's poem manifests her belief that language can be used as a tool during war to disguise the atrocities; it is thus conceivable that Levertov would concur with Arendt's theory.

The final segment of Levertov's poem ("Crystal Night") refers, of course, to Kristallnacht (the Night of Broken Glass), a terrifying pogrom that occurred on November 8–10, 1938. It is noteworthy that the father of Herschel Grynzpan, whose murder of a Nazi official triggered Kristallnacht, testified against Eichmann at his trial. Unlike "The Peachtree," which employs vivid color imagery, "Crystal Night" contains black and white images exclusively. Levertov thereby creates a newsreel, documentary effect. Furthermore, the images possess cold, heartless connotations, emphasizing words such as "brick," "stone," "glass," "ice," and "knives" (66), which allude, perhaps, to the cold and heartless reign of terror inflicted by the Nazis, who could shamelessly destroy innocent people's lives through murder, transportation to concentration camps, desecration of synagogues, and looting of stores. Shattered glass lay everywhere in the streets, signifying to those Jews who had remained in Germany the precarious nature of their existence. The broken glass of Jewish homes, stores, and synagogues proved fragile—quite unlike the strong glass that protected Adolf Eichmann as he witnessed his trial. Hertha Nathorff, writing in her diary on November 8 as she observed the terror inflicted on others and suffered the pain of the atrocities (the Nazis had just taken away her husband), illustrated the sense of terror that Levertov wanted her poem to convey:

Deep, deep night. With a trembling hand I will try to write down the events of today, events that have engraved themselves in my heart in a script of flames. I want to write them for my child so that one day he will be able to read how [the Nazis] have reduced us to nothing, driven us into the ground. I want to record everything the way I experienced it. At midnight, alone and trembling at my desk, groaning like a wounded animal, I need to write to keep myself from screaming into the silent night. (69)

Levertov describes a similar version of the terror that the Nazis inflicted:

> the jackboots
> are running in spurts of
> sudden blood-light through the
> broken temples...
> (*JL* 66)

The passage refers, on a literal level, to the desecration of almost 200 synagogues in Germany by soldiers, but the poet perhaps alludes also to the destruction of Jews' lives and faith by using the phrase "broken temples." The transformation from silence to noise suggests the suddenness and the horror of the pogrom, as well as the ultimate destruction of the belief by many Jews that it was still possible to live in peace in Nazi Germany. Levertov indicates that this violence, this atrocity, will forever alter history:

> smashing the windows of sleep and dream
> smashing the windows of history
> a whiteness scattering
> in hailstones
> each a mirror
> for man's eyes. (67)

This horror will also forever alter humankind because people must thereafter force themselves to see the truth about the evil capacity of human nature: "the veils / are rent in twain" (66). In these two lines, Levertov alludes to Mark 15:38, which relates the story of Jesus Christ's death and the concomitant breaking in two of the veil of the temple. Thus, Levertov alludes to the Crucifixion and the consequent distancing of God from humankind in her poem about Kristallnacht. Just as Pontius Pilate washes his hands of guilt, people refused to help—or worse yet, like Eichmann, contributed to the genocide because they lacked the imagination and introspection necessary to empathize and identify with the innocent and guiltless victims. Rodgers ponders whether Levertov might be asking, "'Are these the veils that have screened us from the horror of events?'" (71). Without the veils with which people shade themselves from the truth, people would have to scrutinize themselves closely in this metaphorical mirror and discern their roles in the tragedy and their place in humanity. As Lorrie Smith states, "There is more in these poems than Eichmann's guilt—Levertov believes there is the shared guilt of all *civilized* mankind" (158).

Works Cited

Arendt, Hannah. *Eichmann in Jerusalem: A Report on the Banality of Evil.* 1963. New York: Penguin, 1994.

Blaydes, Sophie B. "Metaphors of Life and Death in the Poetry of Denise Levertov and Sylvia Plath." In *Critical Essays on Denise Levertov.* Ed. Linda Wagner-Martin. Boston: G.K. Hall, 1991. 204–15.

Cohen, Leonard. "All There Is to Know About Adolph [sic] Eichmann." In *Reading, Analysing and Teaching Literature.* Ed. Mick Short. London: Longman, 1989.

Conot, Robert E. *Justice at Nuremberg.* 1984. New York: Carroll & Graf, 1994.

Estess, Sybil. "Denise Levertov." In *Conversations with Denise Levertov.* Ed. Jewel Spears Brooker. Jackson: UP of Mississippi, 1998. 87–100.

Hausner, Gideon. *Justice in Jerusalem.* New York: Harper & Row, 1966.

Levertov, Denise. "During the Eichmann Trial." In *The Jacob's Ladder.* New York: New Directions, 1961. 61–67.

———. *The Poet in the World.* New York: New Directions, 1973.

———. "Staying Alive." In *To Stay Alive.* 1965. New York: New Directions, 1971. 21–84.

Marten, Harry. *Understanding Denise Levertov.* Columbia: U of South Carolina P, 1988.

Nathorff, Hertha. "A Doctor's View." In *Hitler's Exiles: Personal Stories of the Flight from Nazi Germany to America.* Ed. Mark A. Anderson. New York: The New Press, 1998. 69–77.

Papadatos, Peter. *The Eichmann Trial.* London: Stevens & Sons, 1964.

Pearlman, Moshe. *The Capture and Trial of Adolf Eichmann.* New York: Simon & Schuster, 1963.

Reitlinger, Gerald. *The Final Solution: The Attempt to Exterminate the Jews of Europe 1939–1945.* New York: Beechhurst Press, 1953.

Ritvo, Roger A., and Diane M. Plotkin, eds. *Sisters in Sorrow: Voices of Care in the Holocaust.* College Station, TX: Texas A & M UP, 1998.

Rodgers, Audrey T. *Denise Levertov: The Poetry of Engagement.* Rutherford, NJ: Fairleigh Dickinson P; London: Associated UPs, 1993.

Smith, Lorrie. "Songs of Experience: Denise Levertov's Political Poetry." In *Critical Essays on Denise Levertov.* Ed. Linda Wagner-Martin. Boston: G.K. Hall, 1991. 156–72.

Taylor, Telford. *The Anatomy of the Nuremberg Trials: A Personal Memoir.* Boston: Little, Brown, 1992.

Wiesel, Elie. *Against Silence: The Voice and Vision of Elie Wiesel.* Ed. Irving Abrahamson. 3 vols. New York: Holocaust Library, 1985.

Wyman, David S. *The Abandonment of the Jews: America and the Holocaust, 1941–1945.* New York: Pantheon Books, 1985.

Denise Levertov and Paul Cézanne
"in Continuance"

Emily Archer

I

One afternoon in 1951, Denise Levertov mounted her "ancient bicycle" in the simmering, cicada heat of Aix-en-Provence, and made her way to the studio of Paul Cézanne: "The air quivers, blue and green. I am a human ant, moving across the painted landscape over which le Mont Ste. Victoire presides—aloof judge, ever-changing unchangeable belovéd, massive geometry of rock" (*T* 103). When she arrived at the house on Chemin des Lauves, she found neither a tourist attraction nor a museum. "Everything in it was so unguarded, so simply *there*," she recalls about the small, slightly dusty room (*T* 105). The objects she recognized from Cézanne's *nature morte* paintings—clock, vase, statuette, woven cloth—seemed imbued with a sense of recent use, and the air, with "the intensity of his sensations" (*T* 106).

The title of this memoir, "Pilgrimage," suggests that her relationship to the painter and the excursion to his studio involved more than curiosity or artistic obligation. Denise Levertov considered "pilgrimage" to be the "plot behind the plot" of her life, and defined it as her recurring "myth" or theme, that "of a journey that would lead from one state of being to another" (*PW* 63). In a phrase from "Relearning the Alphabet," it is a lifetime of "faring / forth into the grace of transformed / continuance" (*P2* 91–92). Thus the title "Pilgrimage" bears a double image: of Levertov's journey to a sacred place, and of Cézanne's place as a *luminaire* on her larger journey, a life of making art.

The contributions of Rainer Maria Rilke, Robert Duncan, Anton Chekhov, and William Carlos Williams to Levertov's vocation are well-established and familiar, thanks largely (but not entirely)

to the essays in which she articulates their influence.[1] This memoir
["Pilgrimage"], along with many other provocative statements and
images in her work, suggests that Cézanne also deserves a place in
her constellation of mentors, and a closer look at his largesse. Levertov's assessment of Chekhov's gift to her reminds one of Cézanne's: "His influence was not on my work as a writer, directly....
it was Chekhov's vision of life that I received and cherished, and
which, however imperceptibly, affected my own vision and consequently the course of my life" (*LUC* 279). It was Cézanne's vision
of work that she received and transformed, forging her "own blue
link in the chain" (*T* 106) of artists and poets who have "cast ethereal intensity in bronze" and learned "to see again" (*CEP* 130).

The "sister arts" have never been decorative backdrops for
Levertov's poetics. A lifetime of reading, looking, and listening
yields poems the arts have clearly in-formed. One may take the title "The Life of Art" broadly to describe Levertov's practice, even
while the poem itself speaks quite particularly of the "exquisite
balance" between the making and the "fictive truth" of the made
thing. The poet's knowledge of art is no bookish abstraction. She
has stepped up close to many canvasses and can intimately, accu-
rately describe a painting's

> ... impasto surface, burnt sienna, thick,
> striate, gleaming—swathes and windrows
> of carnal paint—
> or, canvas barely stained,
> where warp and weft peer through....
> (*DH* 85)

And then she has stepped back to let the work reveal its "fictive
truth: a room, a vase, an open door / giving upon the clouds" (*DH*
85). She would like to live, the poem yearns, in that "borderland,"
that barely attainable edge between surface, palette, and brush and

---

[1]Levertov discusses Rilke's profound influence on her aesthetic in
"Rilke as Mentor," found both in *Light Up the Cave* (*LUC*) and *New and Selected Essays* (*NSE*). Those volumes also contain her memoir and tribute to
Robert Duncan in "Some Duncan Letters." Her essay, "On Chekhov," is
published in *LUC*. And four essays in *NSE* articulate Levertov's understanding, and defense, of Williams' aesthetic. The recently published *Letters of Denise Levertov and William Carlos Williams* (New Directions, 1998)
gives additional insight into the character of their influence on each other,
not just that of Williams on Levertov.

"what lies beyond the window, past the frame, beyond …" (*DH* 85).

Levertov's intimacy with music likewise informs a major tenet of her aesthetic, that "the *being* of things has inscape, has melody, which the poet picks up as one voice picks up, and sings, a song from another, and transmits, transposes it, into tones others can hear" (*PW* 17). In her lucid statements on craft, Levertov makes the analogy between poem and musical score, teaching the relationship between the linebreak and the *melos* or melodic element of the poem (*LUC* 63). But her response to hearing music also yields many poems, such as those in "Raga," the sixth grouping in *Sands of the Well*, with its variations and improvisations on a pilgrim's recurring themes: recollection, recognition, "and moving on." Along the pilgrim way, Haydn's "frank" intervals and rhythms become

> morning suns,
> roadside gold, each dandelion
> dipped in his elixir,
> the secret depths of candor.
> (*SW* 86)

A trio by Henze stirs in her the image of

> Moving
> along the brief path, charged
> with still unlit brands that will gild the dark.
> (*SW* 87)

And Bruckner's daimon is lodged in a poem brief and evocative as a haiku:

> Angel with heavy wings
> weathering the stormwracked air,
> listing heavenward.
> (*SW* 85)

Like the masters of *midrash* in her Jewish ancestry, Levertov often "spins off" of a text or work of art—story, painting, photograph, proverb, string trio, poem—neither to supplant nor appropriate it, but to serve it, by writing a poem that moves "at a tangent to, or parallel with, its inspiration" (*BW* 85–86). Her response to Cézanne is both particular, in her love for individual paintings, and quite vast, having taken shape as an incorporation of his "vision of art, the act of making paintings or poems, a life of doing that" (*T* 107) into her own acts and vision.

Levertov is not the only contemporary poet to "translate" Cézanne's work into her own. Charles Wright also pays homage to Paul Cézanne and his "sacramental desire" in the opening poem of *The World of Ten Thousand Things*.[2] Wallace Stevens, similarly, found a struggle parallel with his own to realize "essence" without relinquishing the ordinary stuff of existence.[3] William Carlos Williams was powerfully influenced by Cézanne's understanding of "origins,"[4] and its bearing on technique. In her essay on Chekhov, Levertov questions whether other art forms can have a "direct" influence on a poem's crafting (*LUC* 279). The answer, vis-à-vis Cézanne, is beyond the scope of this essay, but therein lies an aesthetic thread "still taut," and worth considering: the relationship between Cézanne's painterly attention to distance, color, and line[5] and Levertov's poetic one. It is not a thread ultimately sepa-

---

[2]See Bruce Bond, "Metaphysics of the Image in Charles Wright and Paul Cézanne," in *The Point Where All Things Meet: Essays on Charles Wright*, ed. Tom Andrews (Oberlin, OH: Oberlin College P, 1995), 264–73.

[3]See Betty Buchsbaum, "Contours of Desire: The Place of Cézanne in Wallace Stevens' Poetics and Late Practice," *Criticism* 30.3 (Summer 1988): 303–24.

[4]See Christopher J. Knight, "William Carlos Williams, Paul Cézanne and the 'Technique of Originality,'" *Mosaic* 20.2 (Spring 1987): 83–96. It is the craft which Williams calls Cézanne's "technique of originality," in the oldest sense of *original*. According to Knight, this technique became Williams' way to apprehend the distinction Cézanne rendered in painting between art which represents and art which imitates. Simply put, the former obscures nature; the latter reveals it. And revelation, Williams believed, was art's true function, achievable only at the poem's most primitive, concrete foundation, "in the words themselves and what you find to do with them" (MacGowan 65).

[5]Cézanne's radical aesthetic was born in his alternative to "modelling" external reality. Rather than a focus on light, shadow and perspective, he showed a way of "modulating" the play between color and form. Behind this technique lay the greater, more difficult adjustment between inner and outer, and a new focus on the process of perception itself. Cézanne's aesthetic required the painter to "Penetrate that which is before you, and persevere to express it as logically as possible" (qtd. in Bernard 43).

In Cézanne's way of perceiving, traditional hierarchies of background and foreground, light and shadow, near and far, are dissolved. The ground of being, or "background," is just as privileged in the painting, through Cézanne's careful adjustment of color and plane, as the objects themselves. The adjustment was always painstaking, for Cézanne

rable from the larger ground of his influence, and any exploration of its textures must finally rest on Cézanne as the model of an artist "faring forth in transformed continuance." He showed Denise Levertov a way of persisting in her work with courage, of reaching back to the "origins" of her own art for renewal, and of returning endlessly to the incarnate world to wait for its wondrous and certain revelations, the many faces of an "ever-changing, un-changeable belovéd."

II

Levertov awoke early to a love for Cézanne's art. The memoir records that the "extraordinary sense of having entered something of Cézanne's life" in the studio was a seed sown early in her adolescence. His vision "vibrates in me as it did when I first took Gerstle Mack's *Paul Cézanne* out of the Ilford Public Library when I was 13," she recalls, "already in love with the lilt of pineboughs over *Le Lac d'Annecy* in the National Gallery" (*T* 106–7). From the beginning, her image of the artist was that of continuance, of students "working away day by day and week by week" while some great teacher "utters the magic words, '*Continuez, mez enfants, continuez*'" (*T* 74). Levertov herself "drew and painted for hours every day" and believed that she would become an artist. The bohemian life of the painter with its "whiff of romance" was naturally attractive to her adolescent spirit and for a short while, she pursued teachers who might usher her into that world of "thrilling conversations and midnight oil" (*T* 82). The memoir "Meeting and Not

---

built his technique upon relation: "Painting is the art of combining effects, that is, of establishing relations among colors, contours, and planes" ("Maxims" 38). And prior to all is the "original" form of nature: "Everything in nature models itself on the cone, the cylinder and the sphere" (Smith 10).

In his paintings, shadows are neither simply the "blacks and soupy browns" of color *in absentia*, nor the Impressionists' colored "effects of reflected light" (Mack 305). "The sun here is so tremendous," says Cézanne of the landscape of Provence, "that it seems to me that the objects are defined in silhouette, not only in black, but in blue, in red, in brown, in violet" (Smith 10). Every contour of the "thing" has its own integrity, as well as a distinct relationship to the whole. Thus, the so-called shadows in a Cézannian object are instead a "different darkness," colors "poised" in the plastic form of the object, as if waiting to be seen.

Meeting Artists" documents her disappointments in that pursuit, and the gradual revelation that "all along, my pursuit of art—visual art, that is—had been half-hearted, not a true compulsion. My true vocation was and had always been, virtually from infancy, poetry" (*T* 81).

When she was nineteen, Levertov received a bilingual edition of Rainer Maria Rilke's poems as a gift from her father, thereby introducing her to the literary mentor, more than any other, to whom she would turn throughout her life for "his concept of the artist's task" (*NSE* 231). Despite the fact that other poet friends, such as Robert Creeley, held some contempt for Rilke, Levertov maintained that Rilke's work revealed "a depth and generosity in his perceptions that made them go on being relevant to [her] through the decades" (*NSE* 231). In his own great love for the "surly" Cézanne, Rilke played an important role in translating those perceptions into a language Levertov could absorb as she began to live into her "true vocation." Rilke was the example of a poet who could apprehend, with something beyond appreciation, the extra-literary arts, and his example strengthened her passion and respect for the labor of art in its many forms.

While Rilke's poems and his *Letters to a Young Poet* were certainly formative, it was the *Selected Letters*, Levertov claims, that year after year "yielded up so many layers of significance ... as if of a palimpsest" (*NSE* 234). Words from the *Selected Letters* became phrases and titles we recognize in her own poems: "*each step an arrival ... vowels of affliction ... open secret ...* " (*NSE* 234–35). But also important and enduring, as Levertov calls them, are those passages in which Rilke

> described and evoked the working life of Rodin and Cézanne— to increase my understanding of the vocation of art, the obstinate devotion to it which, though it may not lead to any ordinary happiness, is nevertheless at the opposite pole to the morbid self-absorption often mistakenly supposed to be typical of artists. The models Rilke presents as truly great ... even though he did not underestimate Cézanne's mistrustful and surly personality— were heroically and exhilaratingly impassioned about art itself, and unflagging in its alluring, demanding service. (*NSE* 235)

In one letter to Clara, Rilke expresses the kind of gratitude for Cézanne that gave Levertov continued reason to solicit the painter's presence on her own pilgrimage:

> From the many things Cézanne now gives me to do I realise how very different I have become. I am on the road to becoming a

worker, on a long road perhaps and probably only at the first milestone.... (*R Letters* 151)

The thing at hand, so "unguardedly there," whether apple, model, or mountain, was the sole object of Cézanne's attention and energy, and he returned to it day after day, indisposed to all other matters. When Cézanne failed to attend his mother's burial, Rilke explains that "he happened to be '*sur le motif*,'" for "in those days his work was so important for him and brooked no exception, not even one which his piety and simplicity must surely have recommended" (*R Letters* 147). This intensity "must have been agonizing to the unfortunate models who sat for him," offers Gerstle Mack, the biographer whose volume Levertov read as a young girl (306). Near the end of his portrait sittings in 1899, Ambroise Vollard[6] called Cézanne's attention to two small bare spots on the canvas, and the painter responded,

> "'Don't you see, Monsieur Vollard, that if I put something there by guesswork, I might have to paint the whole canvas over, starting from that point?'" "The prospect," adds Vollard, "made me tremble"—as well it might, considering that the portrait, even though the two bare spots of canvas were never covered, required a hundred and fifteen sittings. (Mack 306)

Human models apparently weren't the only ones that withered under the artist's prolonged study; flowers faded, and apples rotted before many *nature morte* compositions were complete (Mack 307).

Whatever allure Levertov found as a young girl in this dogged "continuance" was transformed over the years into her artistic credo, whose antithesis is clearly spelled out in the title essay for *Light Up the Cave*. There Levertov offers Anne Sexton and her popularity, especially among younger, more "vulnerable" poets, as an example of the confusion between "creativity and self-destruction" (*LUC* 80). Certain historical and political forces, Levertov explains, have helped blur that distinction and engender a kind of anguish-mongering in "a public greedy for emotion at second hand because starved of the experience of community" (*LUC* 83). Not surprisingly, she lists Cézanne among those whose lives stand in contrast. Those "greatest" artists, full of their own passion, suffering, and endurance, "seem not to attract us as models," she •

---

[6]Ambroise Vollard, also a biographer of Cézanne, was an art dealer and gallery owner who organized the 1895 exhibition that brought the painter's obscurity to an end (Mack 339).

laments, despite the "romance in their tenacity, their devotion" (*LUC* 81).

If Sexton and her poetry are the example of a subjectivity which sees nothing but its self *in extremis*, there is also the problem of its opposite, a likewise self-defeating cold objectivity which "shrivels what it sees" (*LUC* 97). Levertov's alternative to both is an aesthetic relationship that will preserve the integrity of the "thing" before the artist, not exploit or subdue it. It is part of the poet's task that Ibsen articulated for her, "to make clear to himself, and thereby to others, the temporal and eternal questions ..." (*PW* 44). Levertov insisted that such "making clear" not only assists the *making* of art; it "*is* art," and "engages both the subjective and objective" in the poet (*PW* 47). Rilke also clarifies this aesthetic necessity for her:

> If a thing is to speak to you, you must for a certain time regard it as the only thing that exists, the unique phenomenon that your diligent and exclusive love has placed at the center of the universe, something the angels serve that very day upon that matchless spot. (qtd. in *LUC* 97)

This persistent and loving regard of the world was the only way of approaching *la réalisation*, the term Rilke defined in a letter as Cézanne's "ultimate desideratum":

> The incarnation of the world *as a thing carrying conviction*, the portrayal of a reality become imperishable through his experiencing of the object—this appeared the purpose of his inmost labours. (*R Letters* 146)

Rilke believed Cézanne had achieved his purpose. "All of reality is on his side," he remarks after an encounter in the *Salon d'Automn* with the "lived life" of Cézanne's colors: " ... as you walked, there broke forth in this theatre a streak of reality through the cleft through which you went—green of real green, real sunshine, a real forest" (*R Letters* xvii).

Some of Denise Levertov's early struggles in approaching her own goal of *la réalisation* involved making poems with no hiatus between word and flesh, body and spirit. She confesses in an early poem that it is "easy" to remain in the language of lament, disembodied and self-circumscribed, but

> difficult to write
> of the real image, real hand, the
> heart of day or autumn beating steadily ...
> (*CEP* 10)

An important and decisive change for Levertov is her move to New York, away from the misty subjectivity of her British neo-romanticism and into the incarnational poetics for which Rilke had helped lay the ground. In the alchemical contact with American English and poets such as Duncan, Creeley, and especially Williams, Levertov became a vital member of that community of mid-century artists struggling with the "being of language" and the "language of being." Williams' exhortations to her to keep writing, even if some poems are merely "finger exercises," were fueled by his early recognition of her gift:

> I haven't even finished reading [*Here and Now*] and shall not finish reading it soon (maybe) keeping it to enjoy slowly, stretching it out to make it go slow to enjoy as I would a delicious dish of food. It is really a beautiful book. The fine points! I am really amazed and a little in awe of you. I didn't realize you were so good though I had an intimation of it on that day in our front room when you were reading to me and I saw that you were really a poet. (MacGowan 69)

From the mid-fifties on, Levertov began to answer her own charge in "O Taste and See"—"The world is / not with us enough"—with poems that see the "here and now" in all its mystery and candor (*CEP* 125).

The fine balance of subjective and objective in Levertov's aesthetic ethic preserves the integrity of both seer and seen. But this relationship also depends on the equipoise of near and far, a conviction Rilke expresses in a letter:

> … all things can work on us. And all work on us from out of the distance, the near as well as the far, not one of them touches us, all commune with us over and across great divides, and as little as the uttermost stars can pass into us, so little can the ring on my hand; only as though with their radiance can things reach us … so they, through their influence, create within us a new ordering. (*R Letters* 121)

As Levertov grew to understand it, this aesthetics of distance has an essential role in love: "To be. To love an other only for being" (*P2* 91) and

A wanting
to love: not
to lean over towards
an other, and fall....
(*LF* 115)

At some point Levertov would surely have read Rilke's comments about art and love in the letter of October 13, 1907. Having once again been in the presence of Cézanne's paintings and their ordering "radiance," Rilke finds in his own work

> ... how necessary it was to get beyond even love; it comes natu-
> rally to you to love each one of these things if you have made
> them yourself: but if you shew it, you make them less well; you
> judge them instead of *saying* them. You cease being impartial;
> and love, the best thing of all, remains outside your work, does
> not enter into it, is left over unresolved beside it: this is how the
> sentimentalist school of painting came into being (which is no
> better than the realist school). They painted "I love this" instead
> of painting "Here it is." ... This consuming of love in anonymous
> work, which gives rise to such pure things, probably no one has
> succeeded in doing so completely as old Cézanne.... he now
> turned to Nature and knew how to hide his love for each apple
> and lodge it in the painted apple for ever. (152)

The painter "names" what he loves with color and contour, stepping close to the canvas with the palette knife, and then back, to
assess the "fictive truth" of his stroke. Near and far, I and Thou are
also relations required of the poet in her primal work of naming:
"Linguistically, relation defines our capacity to name," Levertov
says (*NSE* 20). But to name is not to explain, she clarifies in the
poem "Artist to Intellectual." Naming begins in respect for a world
that presents itself as

> '... The lovely *evident*, revealing
> everything, more mysterious
> than any
> clueless inscription scraped in stone.
> The ever-present, constantly vanishing,
> carnal enigma!'
>
> (*LF* 103)

These words remind us of the way Levertov described Cézanne's mountain, the "ever-changing, unchangeable" Ste. Victoire. And they look ahead to the many poems that find her returning again and again to the "ever-present, constantly vanishing" Mount Rainier. But they also express a *motif* she speculates
may have been "imprinted ... on my sensibility early in life" and is
"integral to how I perceive" ("Genesis" 487, 498). It has to do with
"the possibility of 'entertaining angels unawares,'" of "the sense
that things or persons may be more than what they seem" ("Genesis" 497–98). Citing examples from Genesis and the Gospels,

Levertov discusses her life-long attraction to stories that contain moments of sudden recognition, or poems that contain "revelations of the wonderful in the apparently ordinary" ("Genesis" 499).

It isn't difficult to find some affinities with Cézanne in such poems as "Pleasures," where she recognizes that this "integral" perception is at work,

> I like to find
> what's not found
> at once, but lies
>
> within something of another nature,
> in repose, distinct.
>
>   (*CEP* 90)

Cézanne is similarly aware that his perception depends on patient waiting for revelation: "I progress very slowly," he says in a letter, "for nature reveals herself to me in very complex ways; and the progress is endless" (qtd. in Knight 86). Roger Fry interprets Cézanne's patient waiting for revelation as a spiritual quality: "Reality, no doubt, lay always behind this veil of colour, but it was different, more solid, more dense, in closer relation to the needs of the spirit"; thus Cézanne "gave himself up entirely to this desperate search for the reality hidden beneath the veil of appearance" (83). In this common way of perceiving may lie the numinous core of Levertov's attraction to Cézanne, for we hear his theme again in her sense that these "real miracles" of revelation are not "culminating solutions" but "beginnings, or gateways to continuance" ("Genesis" 493).

III

The good work that Cézanne and Rilke began in Levertov, William Carlos Williams encouraged and helped implement, sharpening her attention to language. In February of 1957, Williams writes to Levertov about his struggle to be objective before her work, and prevent his esteem for her from clouding his critic's search for the essential "thing" in her poems, the love she has "lodged in the painted apple":

> Even the alertest reader can miss it. The poet herself (himself) might miss it. and quit trying. And yet if it is important enough to her she will never quit trying to snare the "thing" among the words.... Even recently I fight against accepting you uncondi-

tionally. It must always be so with a person we love and admire.
It must be in the words themselves and what you find to do with
them and what you have the spirit and trust to rely on the reader
to find what you have put among them. (MacGowan 65)

In her preface to Nancy Willard's study of four *Ding*-poets,
Williams, Rilke, Ponge, and Neruda, Levertov explains that she
came to Williams

> already partly formed by Rilke; and where Rilke had given in-
> sight into what it was, essentially, to be a poet, Williams opened
> up the language in which to live those insights and made it clear
> to me ... that for the poet there was no vision without language,
> no reality without language, that the sound and rhythm of the
> poem are the poem, thing among things. ("Preface" x)

For Cézanne, there was no reality without the sensation of
color, for "sensations form the basis of everything," he said, and
through them, "we must render the image of what we see, forgetting everything that existed before us" (*C Letters* 336, 316). The result of diligently practicing his own imperative, observes the phe-
nomenologist Merleau-Ponty, is that Cézanne "speaks as the first
man spoke and paints as if no one had ever painted before ...
Cézanne's difficulties are those of the first word" (124). As Knight
makes clear, Cézanne's "originality," with its roots in "origin," at-
tracted and compelled Williams who, similarly, wanted words
freed from the burdens of connotations and distortions so that
they could reveal the world anew (93).

Their "descendant"[7] Denise Levertov reveals her own primor-
dial intuition of words, the "sensations" of their sound and
rhythm, as well as her practical sense of the hard work required in
rendering "first" words in the poem. "To hell with easy rhythms
... Only robust / works of the imagination live in eternity," proclaims an early poem-credo, "Art." In those lines, the artist is

---

[7]"Illustrious Ancestors," one of Levertov's most well-known and anthologized poems, speaks of the line "still taut" between the essential
spiritual gestures of her Hasidic and Christian forebears and her own
desires as poem-maker (*CEP* 77). "September 1961" laments the passing
of three "illustrious" poet-ancestors: Ezra Pound, H.D., and William
Carlos Williams. "We have the words in our pockets," the poem says of
their legacy, even though they are "obscure directions" (*P2* 81). Levertov's
sense of having inherited such gifts is part of her ethic of gratitude, accountability, and service: to transform, as one can, what has been received, and continue.

urged to look back to the ancients and their "hard, strong materials":

> Renew the power men had in Azerbaijan
> to cast ethereal intensity in bronze
> and give it
> force to endure any number of thousand years.
>
> (*CEP* 130)

And Cézanne's words (attributed in a footnote to the poem) become part of her imperative:

> Painter, let be the 'nervous scratches' the
> trick spontaneity; learn to see again,
> construct, break through
> to 'the thrill of continuance with the appearance of all its
> changes'....
>
> (*CEP* 130)

What Levertov "found to do with words" was built upon a foundation of reverence for language itself. She consistently approaches language as a constitutive, world-making power, a living thing, not abstract derivatives of experience. In Levertov's aesthetic, words do not merely follow or refer to insights or ideas, as a translation of something anterior. Instead, ideas cannot exist apart from the sensuous word that bears them like a body, a "thing among things." "The imagination does not reject its own sensory origins but illuminates them," she insists in a defense of Williams' aesthetic (*NSE* 45). Words are living things with their own origins, histories, vulnerabilities, communions, illnesses, deaths. And that means, says Levertov, that "the poet can discover the universal only in the local—in the concrete particulars both of the material world and of language itself." ("Preface" xi). In Levertov's aesthetic, the poet is the "instrument" of the word; the word is not the poet's tool. "One should speak words as if the heavens were opened in them," says the legendary Hasid Baal-Shem Tov, "and as if it were not so that you take the word in your mouth, but rather as if you entered into the word" (Buber 39).

In her poetry of the late 1960s and 1970s, Levertov laments the misuse, silencing, or erosion of language. In exchange for the creating word are "Those groans men use / passing a woman on the street....

> It's a word
> in grief-language, nothing to do with
> primitive, not an ur-language;

> language stricken, sickened, cast down....
> (*P1* 196)

Language appears to have become a system of random squeaks and grunts entirely emptied of meaning save its immediate appropriation. Unmoored from their "origin," words can be made to mean anything:

> '"It became necessary
> to destroy the town to save it,"
> a United States major said today.
> He was talking about the decision
> by allied commanders to bomb and shell the town
> regardless of civilian casualties
> to rout the Vietcong.'
>
> (*P2* 20)

In his essay "War and the Crisis of Language," Thomas Merton could easily have been speaking of Denise Levertov when he suggests that "poets are perhaps the ones who, at the present moment, are most sensitive to the sickness of language ..." (99). Emptied of its constitutive power, language becomes merely a tool, and the covenant between word and world is broken. It can only represent, can only be an abstraction or shadow of something else. A return to the first word is urgent. "If there's an Ur-language still among us, / hiding out like a pygmy pterodactyl," Levertov muses some twenty years later in "Primal Speech," it lives to pronounce all things good:

> ... it's the exclamation,
> universal whatever the sound, the triumphant,
> wondering, infant utterance, 'This! This!',
> showing and proffering the thing, anything,
> the affirmation even before the naming.
>
> (*SW* 95)

Unlike her "ancestor" Cézanne, Levertov was politically engaged throughout her life. During the heat of her activism in the late 1960s she wrote "Relearning the Alphabet," a sequence recalling Psalm 119's acrostic structure which begins with *aleph*, the first letter of the Hebrew alphabet. As though it had been inspired by the Jewish mystics, this sequence embodies "a theory of letters ... which dealt with [each letter] as with the elements of the world and with their intermixture as with the inwardness of reality" (Buber 39). A response, in part, to the rampant "word sickness" fueling the logic of war and racism, the poem seeks to return to an

Ur-language, and serve it in acts of renewal. The language Levertov seeks is not one she must create herself; she is re-learning an alphabet anterior to her acts of art. It will not be "original." This lack of "anxiety of influence" she learned in part from Cézanne and his deep, acknowledged reverence for the masters: "One does not substitute oneself for the past; one only adds a new link," he once wrote (qtd. in Murphy 8). In his memorial essay for Levertov, Wendell Berry pays tribute both to Levertov's language and to her sense of its proportion and place:

> Her English is robust, responsible, aware, and exact, at once principled and particular. She did not remake her language in pursuit of "originality," but only wonderfully extended its reach and power, from "Laying the Dust" in the 1950's to "The Physical Resurrection of Christ" forty years later. Finally she could gather the earthly and the heavenly into one breath." (7)

In this poem's economy, to relearn the alphabet is to revisit her calling to poetry. The poet's vocation requires "The seeing / that burns through, comes through to / the fire's core" (P2 91), in an endless returning to *caritas*, in spite of personal or political suffering. Because of the horrors she witnessed in Vietnam, suggests "Advent 1966,"

> because of this, my strong sight,
> my clear caressive sight, my poet's sight I was given
> that it might stir me to song,
> is blurred.
>
> (P2 124)

Some critics took this confession as an admission to poetic failure,[8] but in the *gestalt* of her corpus, it was yet another "gateway to continuance." She relearns the alphabet, "that the mind's fire may not fail" and that the "*vowels of affliction*" may once again be "transformed in utterance / to song" (P2 91).

"Relearning the Alphabet" takes "joy," a word with a history in both her text and in a larger context, as "a beginning." "A" beginning, not "*the*" beginning—the indefinite article is given strong semantic weight as the first word of the letter—**A**—in question. That indefinite quality is consonant with the spirit of *midrash*, to

---

[8]In his acerbic response to Levertov's poetry of this period, Alvin Rosenfeld implies that her art changed under the "battering of ideologies" and "in the change we witness the abandonment of poetry to politics" (549).

which so much of Levertov's aesthetic belongs: the unendingness of interpretation, of seeing, and in Cézanne's language, of "sensation." There is no definite beginning of the alphabet any more than there is a finality of the incarnate world, or of one's pilgrimage through it. Unlike the monologies she has been lamenting, these utterances declare nothing final; their destination is the "fire's core," an image Paul Lacey calls Levertov's "signature for the contrarieties of joy" (130). The word *is* the pilgrim path:

> All utterance
> takes me step by hesitant step towards
>
> **T**
> —yes, to continuance: into
> that life beyond the dead-end where
> … I was lost.
>
> (*P2* 98)

The poem becomes less a matter of calling upon the alphabet than of being "called forth" by the letters themselves, of being summoned by language to its own mysterious inscape. The pilgrim eye sees the world "only as / looked-up-into out of earth," its way of traveling open to the leading of the imagination. By the time the poet, whose path is language, reaches '**Z**', the blaze from the fire's core

> addresses
> a different darkness:
> absence has not become
> the transformed presence the will
> looked for,
> but other: the present,
> that which was poised already in the ah! of praise.
>
> (*P2* 100)

Levertov's lifelong conversation with language depends on the discovery, by indirections, of the *present* that lies hidden and poised within elusive *presence*, the "ever-changing, constantly vanishing / carnal enigma," to which she is "called forth" over and over, even as she calls it forth in acts of praise.

IV

Cézanne's artistic necessities spoke to Levertov's own need, again and again, as she looked at his paintings, read his biography, absorbed the letters of Rilke, or heeded his maxims: "It is necessary to be workmanlike in art. To get to know one's way of realisation early. To paint in accordance with the qualities of painting itself. To use materials crude and pure" (Bernard 42). The strength of Cézanne's connection with Levertov lies in their single-minded service to art. However, certain parallels in their lives are also difficult to ignore. And nowhere is the symmetry between the later work of both Cézanne and Levertov more evident than in their attention to a mountain.

During the last twenty years of his life, Cézanne returned again and again to Mont Ste. Victoire, to which he walked from his home in Aix, setting up his palette from several different angles, varying the canvas size and the medium, rendering in color and plane all the mountain's fluid inflections of presence. Cézanne's persistent, varied approach to the mountain-*motif* is an example of *periplum*, a term Levertov renames as "news that stays news":

> I see its applicability to the experiencing of numinous works of art from the mobile vantage point of one's own growth and change ... the experience of discovering, in a supposedly familiar work, fresh and unexpected meanings.... The newly seen aspect, fact, layer, was there all the time; it is our recognition of it that is new. (*LUC* 57–58)

Here, its applicability is to the poet's and the painter's experience of a numinous "thing" of nature, a mountain. Mont Ste. Victoire and Mount Rainier become "news that stays news" in the hands of the artist working "in continuance."

In her own last years living in Seattle, Levertov's poems return again and again to Mount Rainier to witness how clouds variously illumine the mountain, conceal it, transform it, and float it above the tree line, shaping her faith in the "vast presence, seen or unseen" (*ET* 3). Mists in turn rest, rise, veil, efface, and in one poem, transform the mountain, such that

> majestic presence become
> one cloud among others, humble vapor, barely discernible,
>
> like the archangel, walking
> with Tobias on dusty roads.
>
> (*ET* 7)

This mountain rings its changes upon one who has taken a post, like the heron of many poems in *Evening Train*, to wait for Being, "whatever hunger / sustains his watchfulness" (92). Within the mountain poems in *Evening Train* and *Sands of the Well*, one finds

that compassion toward nonhuman beings that Levertov learned
early, that subjectivity she grants to the lowly "disgusting" multipede who remains multipede even as it speaks to her of pilgrim
ways (*ET* 107–10), or to Sylvia, a Vermont-bred pet pig whose stories became the poems in *Pig Dreams*. In Levertov's "ecotheology"
the mountain is not merely symbolic of something else; it is a
mountain, a being-in-itself whose presence "comes and goes / on
the horizon" (*ET* 4). One day the mountain is "absent / a remote
folk-memory" (*ET* 5). The next day through the clouds "one perceives / the massive presence, obdurate, unconcerned / among
those filmy guardians" (*ET* 6). The language clearly recalls what
she saw forty years earlier, in Provence: "aloof judge, ever-changing unchangeable belovéd, massive geometry of rock" (*T* 103). The
poet is sure of the mountain's "steadfastness" beneath all its veils
of appearance, and such surety, in turn, tells something of Levertov's great capacity for faith in the unseen, and in a Creator who
"continues." In "Primary Wonder," the clouds of "clamor" recede
to reveal the presence of a "quiet mystery,"

> … the mystery
> that there is anything, anything at all,
> let alone cosmos, joy, memory, everything,
> rather than void: and that, O Lord,
> Creator, Hallowed One, You still,
> hour by hour sustain it.
>
> (*SW* 129)

Toward the end of Levertov's life, the two mountains begin to
share a spiritual and imaginal geography. "Le Motif" summons
Cézanne to the landscape of Levertov's home near Seward Park:

> Southwest the moon
> full and clear,
>
> eastward, the sky
> reddening, cloudless
> over fir trees, the dark hill.
>
> I remember, decades ago,
> 'day coming and the moon not gone,'
> the low ridge of the Luberon
> beyond the well
>
> and Ste. Victoire
> shifting its planes and angles
> yet again.
>
> (*SW* 74)

In the language of a painter, "Pentimento" recalls that earlier poem, "Pleasures," in which one's long attention to appearances is rewarded with a serendipitous *réalisation*,

> To be discerned
> > only by those
> > > alert to likelihood—
>
> the mountain's form
> > beneath the milky radiance
> > > which revokes it.
>
> It lingers—
> > a draft
> > > the artist may return to.
>
> > > > (*SW* 30)

The visual airiness of these lines and the spaciousness of the poem's scoring provides its own "likelihood" (a word implying both possibility and analogy) with Cézanne's later, more transparent paintings of Ste. Victoire, watercolors that incorporated the white of the canvas as part of his "palette." But always beyond the similarities in these "canvasses," lies the greater likelihood that, in his own way, Cézanne had encouraged Levertov to return to her "draft": "*Continuez ... continuez.*"

Without the "grace of transformed continuance" there can be no enduring art, no renewal of language, no redemptive imagination. Levertov knew this, both as a child on the verge of her vocation, and as an older poet remembering her mentors. In an interview at her home in Seattle, she said,

> I've seen how, when I wasn't thinking about myself but of the work of poets I love, like William Carlos Williams, for example, there are recurrent themes; and for everybody with a large output over a lifetime—it's appropriate that they have recurrent themes. The sort of Protean artists, as represented by Picasso, are not really what I admire. I'm not really very keen on Picasso. I'll see a Picasso and go "Oh, my god!" The man was fantastic. He could draw so well; whatever he did he did with a lot of panache. But I never felt that he was there. Who was Picasso?! So I don't really like that. My model of the great artist is Cézanne.... (October 1994)

And in her last years, in the midst of self-doubt, perhaps Levertov somehow recalls the way Cézanne often exhorted other artists, such as Emile Solari, to renew their "courage and hard work" (Mack 360). "Work gives one the courage to go on. He con-

tinued to preach that gospel all his life," wrote Cézanne's biographer, "and practised it as well" (359). It was a "gospel" for Denise
Levertov, who received it gratefully and thoroughly, transforming
it into her own way of praising the here and now. Thus, she returns to Cézanne again in her last years to keep supple and strong
for the task, especially in times of doubt:

> When you discover
> your new work travels the ground you had traversed
> decades ago, you wonder, panicked,
> 'Have I outlived my vocation? Said already
> all that was mine to say?'
>
> *(SW 96)*

The answer lies not in technique or originality, but in gratitude
and remembrance:

> There's a remedy—
> only one—for the paralysis seizing your throat to mute you,
> numbing your hands: Remember the great ones, remember
>   Cezanne
> doggedly *sur le motif*, his mountain
> a tireless noonday angel he grappled like Jacob,
> demanding reluctant blessing.
>
> *(SW 96)*

The shifting planes of Ste. Victoire and the elusive Rainier become
"things carrying conviction" once again:

> And then, look,
> some inflection of light, some wing of shadow
> is other, unvoiced. You can, you must
> proceed.
>
> *(SW 96)*

Works Cited

Bernard, Emile. "From 'Paul Cézanne' (1904)." *Cézanne in Perspective*. Ed.
    Judith Wechsler. Englewood Cliffs, NJ: Prentice-Hall, Inc., 1975. 39–
    47.

Berry, Wendell. "Memorial, Denise Levertov, 1923–1997." *American Poet:
    The Journal of the Academy of American Poets* (Summer 1998): 7.

Buber, Martin. *The Legend of the Baal-Shem*. Trans. Maurice Friedman. New
    York: Schocken Books, 1969.

Buchsbaum, Betty. "Contours of Desire: The Place of Cézanne in Wallace Stevens' Poetics and Late Practice." *Criticism* 30.3 (Summer 1988): 303–24.

Cézanne, Paul. *Cézanne: Letters.* Ed. John Reward. 4th ed., rev. Oxford: Bruno Cassirer, 1976.

———. "Cézanne's Maxims." Intro. Bob Kirsch. Trans. Joel Agee. *The New Criterion* 6.4 (Dec. 1987): 42–45.

Fry, Roger. "From *Cézanne: A Study of His Development* (1927)." In *Cézanne in Perspective.* Ed. Judith Wechsler. Englewood Cliffs, NJ: Prentice-Hall, Inc., 1975. 82–86.

Knight, Christopher J. "William Carlos Williams, Paul Cézanne, and the 'Technique of Originality.'" *Mosaic* 20.2 (Spring 1987): 83–96.

Lacey, Paul. "A Poetry of Exploration." *The Inner War: Forms and Themes in Recent American Poetry.* Philadelphia: Fortress Press, 1972. 110–31.

Levertov, Denise (in chronological order). "Preface." In *Testimony of the Invisible Man.* Ed. Nancy Willard. Columbia: U of Missouri P, 1970. ix–xi.

———. *The Poet in the World.* New York: New Directions, 1973.

———. *Life in the Forest.* New York: New Directions, 1978.

———. *Collected Earlier Poems 1940–1960.* New York: New Directions, 1979.

———. *Light Up the Cave.* New York: New Directions, 1981.

———. *Pig Dreams: Scenes from the Life of Sylvia.* Illus. Liebe Coolidge. Woodstock, VT: The Countryman Press, 1981. Also in *Candles in Babylon.* New York: New Directions, 1982. 25–40.

———. *Poems 1960–1967.* New York: New Directions, 1983.

———. *Breathing the Water.* New York: New Directions, 1987.

———. *Poems 1968–1972.* New York: New Directions, 1987.

———. *A Door in the Hive.* New York: New Directions, 1989.

———. *Evening Train.* New York: New Directions, 1992.

———. *New and Selected Essays.* New York: New Directions, 1992.

———. Unpublished interview (by the author). Seattle, WA. 8–9 Oct. 1994.

———. *Tesserae: Memories and Suppositions.* New York: New Directions, 1994.

———. "Genesis (Abraham) and Gospels." *Communion: Contemporary Writers Reveal the Bible in Their Lives.* Ed. David Rosenberg. New York: Anchor Books, 1996. 487–99.

———. *Sands of the Well.* New York: New Directions, 1996.

MacGowan, Christopher, ed. *The Letters of Denise Levertov and William Carlos Williams*. New York: New Directions, 1998.

Mack, Gerstle. *Paul Cézanne*. New York: Alfred A. Knopf, 1935.

Merton, Thomas. "War and the Crisis of Language." *The Critique of War: Contemporary Philosophical Explorations*. Ed. Robert Ginsberg. Chicago: Henry Regnery Co., 1969. 99–119.

Murphy, Richard W. *The World of Cezanne, 1839–1906*. New York: Time-Life Books, 1968.

Rilke, Rainer Maria. *Selected Letters of Rainer Maria Rilke: 1902–1926*. Trans. R.F.C. Hull. London: Macmillan, 1947.

Rosenfeld, Alvin H. "'The Being of Language and the Language of Being': Heidegger and Modern Poetics." *Boundary* 2 4 (1976): 535–53.

Smith, Paul. *Interpreting Cézanne*. New York: Steward, Tabori & Chang, 1996.

Denise Levertov's "Variations" on Rilke's Themes: A Brief Explication

Tammy Hearn and Susie Paul

"As we prayed for human help: angels soundlessly with single strides, climbed over our prostrate hearts."
(R.M. Rilke, *Uncollected Poems*, Venice, July 11, 1912)

Rilke writes of these silent angels at the beginning of what his biographer Ralph Freedman describes as "the harrowing decade from 1912 to 1922," in which *The Duino Elegies* "unfolded" (331), roughly a decade after he began *The Book of Hours*. Set out here are the parameters of the territory both he and Denise Levertov traversed in their poetry—"human," "heart," "angel." Levertov claimed him as her "mentor," though he died before she was born, and, though, when she came to America, Robert Creeley "cringed" when she acknowledged Rilke's influence on her work (*NSE* 231). Three poems from her 1987 collection, *Breathing the Water*, are each entitled "Variations" on "a Theme by Rilke"; the poems she "translates" come from his *The Book of Hours, Book I*—or *The Book of Monastic Life*. A comparison of these poems carries us to the heart of their kinship, their longing to move with the angels, stitching earth to heaven word by word.

Edward Zlotkowski, writing on "Levertov's apparent affinity with Rilke" (325), argues that Rilke "helped Levertov attain that very balance which has been fundamental to her achievement as poet—... between what she has called her 'sense of the pilgrim way' and her 'new, American, objectivist-influenced, pragmatic, and sensuous longing for the Here and Now' (*PW* 69)" (1–2). Levertov insists that it was Rilke's letters, not his poetry, that she knew best. "The edition [of his poems] I have is just choc-a-bloc with the things that are essential statements about the vocation of the artist" (Smith 83). She felt her German too rudimentary for "reading anybody without a crib, and a dictionary." "Certainly" it was "not adequate to reading Rilke without those helps" (83). Other direct statements Levertov makes about her "mentor" (*NSE* 231) in interviews and essays suggest she benefited from her study of him in two barely distinct ways. The first was his sense of the "concept of the artist's task—a serious, indeed a lofty concept, but not a sentimental or smug one" (231). In what becomes almost a refrain, and one closely related to vocation, Levertov reminds us of Rilke's "phrase," which by 1975 has already "been part of [her] thinking and feeling for thirty years," the "'unlived life, of which one can die'" (*LUC* 98).

Second, and closely bound to Rilke's insistence upon a life truly "lived," is Levertov's conviction that poetry is and should be intrinsically united with the immediacy of life in its every aspect, a credo repeatedly urged and reflected in her writing. In "The Poet in the World" she quotes then interprets Rilke as "saying … that though the work of art does not aim at effect but is a thing imbued with life, that *lives* that life for its own sake, it nevertheless *has* effect; and that effect is ultimately moral" (*PW* 113). While we see here Levertov defending her choice to take a political stand in her life and work, as in her poetry of the Vietnam War for example, she also emphasizes art as something "imbued with *life*, that *lives* for its own sake …" (113). That the poetry has a moral effect is undeniable, but is not the work's chief "aim" (113).

In "Origins of a Poem" Levertov writes, "The substance, the means, of an art, is an incarnation—not a reference but phenomenon. A poem is an indivisibility of 'spirit and matter' much more absolute than what most people seem to understand by its 'synthesis of form and content'" (113). This blending is evident in what Freedman finds in the work Rilke composed following an intense period of viewing and reviewing art and architecture the summer before his important first visit to Russia: "The repeated alternation of painting and sculpture with narrative time became for Rilke a form of religious and mythical history blurring boundaries between the visible and invisible" (101). Rilke himself describes the process—the poet's necessary labor—that achieves that synthesis:

> It is our task to imprint this temporary, perishable earth into ourselves so deeply, so painfully and passionately, that its essence

can rise again, "invisibly," inside us. We are the bees of the invisible. We wildly collect the honey of the visible, to store it in the great golden hive of the invisible. (qtd. in Mack 1652)

According to Zlotkowski, Rilke is for Levertov "perhaps the single most important spokesman for inner experience," for what produces "the transcendence of simple mimesis in favor of spiritual realization" (325). Levertov's three "Variations" assert that the earthly world and each part of it, including the human part, is not an object separate from the Divine, but, instead, is the Divine as lived. The "task" is the poet's artistic nature made manifest, self-recognized rather than self-appointed, thus, a consciously accepted way of life—"breath[ing] the water." In any case, both poets affirm, poetry *lives*.

Given Levertov's unique willingness readily to assume responsibility for her beliefs, her variations on Rilke's themes for three of the poems from his *Book of Monastic Life* intrigue the reader interested in the relationship between Levertov and her mentor. Given her reluctance to translate his poems from the German, her re-presentation of Rilke's monk's prayers suggests she had something she must risk saying in translation and that could, or must, be made living in a poem. Ordinary discourse would not do. When she wrote her "Variations," she was a mature poet and well into that period of her "development" that, as Albert Gelpi describes it, "begin[s] to test out, define, and affirm the transcendent third term that bridges the rupture between individual epiphany and public calamity." He continues, "Immersion in the immediate and divided world is still the way to an experience of immanence and so of transcendence, but now the centering mystery takes on a name, the Christian incarnation" (5). Rilke, on the other hand, wrote the poems comprising the *Book of Monastic Life* in a "white heat of creation" in 1899 (Freedman 104) when he was not quite 24.

In fact, the visit to Russia Rilke made earlier that year with his "maternal lover, teacher, and friend," Lou Salomé, was a "turning point," bringing about a "shift in sensibility" that "led to the creation of a poet of unquestioned range and power" (Freedman 92). H.F. Peters writes, "Rilke used to call *The Book of Hours*, *Duino Elegies*, and *Sonnets to Orpheus* his undatable books," books he felt had achieved a certain timelessness, but what the "three parts of *The Book of Hours* show" is, rather, a stage in Rilke's artistic development "less accomplished" than those that produced the other two works. In the first of *The Book*'s three parts, the monk who is its persona, has, according to Peters, "experienced God's vastness"

(68). Babette Deutsch, who translated poems from *The Book of Hours*, writes of Rilke in her preface,

> The poet felt Russia, which he had visited just prior to the writing of the first section, to be his spiritual home, and so the monk who is the imaginary author of the poems is represented as an adherent of the peculiar faith that Rilke ascribed to his spiritual kinsmen, a faith in a God remote from the august if benign Father of western Christianity, a God, rather, who was waiting to be born of the artist's alert and sensitive consciousness.

Neither Rilke's nor Levertov's religious views could be called orthodox Christian. Yet the relationship between their poems may be heard as a conversation between two similar but different theological viewpoints—if not between two religious poets. In the first poem, then, "Variation on a Theme by Rilke (Book I, Poem 1, Stanza 1)" (*BW* 3), Levertov takes from Rilke both his idea and image of a mystical experience in his first poem in *The Book of Monastic Life* (*First Book* 155). In ten lines of free verse, Levertov dwells on Rilke's first four lines and last two lines of *The Book*. She concentrates on the monk's experience of receiving the transcendent and poetic gift from a mystical presence: "A certain day became a presence to me" (l. 1). In J.B. Leishman's translation, Rilke's first lines read, "With Strokes that ring clear and metallic, the hour/ to touch me bends down on its way." Neither poet credits God, a creator, as granter of the gift. However, both differ on their interpretation of the significance of the mystical experience. Rilke elaborates the personal consequences of the experience and subsequent receipt of the gift in the next two stanzas. His elaboration, however, does not provide Levertov with any additional insight with the exception that the idea that others besides the poet may be affected by the gift. Thus, Rilke's idea that the monk "know[s] not whose soul it [the mystical/poetic gift] may liberate" (ll. 11–12) becomes, in Levertov's variation, an acknowledged responsibility, an "honor and a task" (l. 7). Clearly, Rilke's monk views the poetic ability as a gift, but differs with Levertov concerning the responsibility the poet inherits. Levertov's speaker considers the seemingly inherent duty of the gift "a task," which is simultaneously bestowed on the poet with the gift (l. 7). Levertov does not elaborate the chance consequence of whom the gift may "liberate"; instead, her speaker emphasizes the momentous occasion expanded into "a certain day" of receiving the gift. Clearly Levertov uses "certain" to modify "day" in order to indicate both special significance and the special enlightenment of the speaker. Thus the lines are given greater emphasis to the transition of the day into a "presence" (l. 1) and a "being" (l. 3). Other meanings of "certain," both "decisiveness" and "conclusiveness," are adumbrated in the first line of the poem and explicitly claimed in the last two lines, "and what I heard was my whole self / saying and singing what it knew: *I can*" (ll. 8–10). Levertov, however, does not allow this significant "certain" day to be denied its natural place during the mystical experience; the day remains a day in the natural order consisting of "a sky, air, [and] light" that "confronts" the speaker (ll. 1–3). Further, Levertov's extension of Rilke's six lines into ten and the uneven rhythm of her blank verse both slow the lines to a contemplative pace and give them more power than is present in Rilke's poem. Rilke's monk says the hour "bends down" (l. 2) at the moment the speaker's "senses" (l. 3) are enlivened with the gift. The image is clearly one of passing time. Rilke's "strokes that ring clear and metallic" are the bells of a clock tower (l. 1). Levertov achieves the same sense of time passing from the highest point on the clock, "height of noon" (l. 4), yet her image is deceptive. Simultaneously, Levertov's passage of time is also the "presence," the "being," the mystical bestower of the gift, that "leaned … and struck," and, thus, delivered to the speaker the "honor" (ll. 4–7). Furthermore, by using the simile, "as if with the flat of a sword" (l. 6), Levertov's speaker invokes the ceremony in which the knight receives both "honor and task" (ll. 6–7). With this image, Levertov's speaker says implicitly that the gift carries with it a duty that must be fulfilled. Rilke's speaker receives the "power" (l. 3) during the striking of the hour. In contrast, Levertov's speaker has experienced an extended mystical visitation in which time, sound, and spiritual experience converge and flow into the speaker in the last four lines of the poem:

> The day's blow
> rang out, metallic—or it was I, a bell awakened,
> and what I heard was my whole self
> saying and singing what it knew: *I can.*

Levertov's speaker is empowered and enlightened; the statement "*I can*" is one of wonder, strength, and willingness to fulfill the "task." While Rilke's monk concludes by speculating about how others may subsequently be "liberated" (l. 12) by his gift, he also demonstrates wonder in his new, enlightened perceptions:

> Not a thing was complete till by me it was eyed,
> Every kind of becoming stood still.

Now my glances are ripe and there comes like a bride
To each of them just what it will. (ll. 5–8)

Both Levertov and Rilke present their respective speakers'/
monks'/poets' deep appreciation of their poetic abilities and belief
that this "gift" is divine.

In Levertov's second "Variation on a Theme by Rilke (*Book I,
Poem* 4)" (*BW* 71), the speaker diverges from Rilke's theme to the
point of disagreement. Levertov's version is not an open declara-
tion of "it is not so," but, more, a gentle articulation of "look at it
this way." Rilke's nine-line poem castigates those who would portray God in graven images (*The Book* 50), and Levertov's twenty-
two lines refute the accusation. Rilke's monk alludes to the Icono-
clastic Controversy, incited by Emperor Leo III, whose edict of 726
demanded the destruction of a revered icon of Christ in Constantinople because he thought the people were worshipping it
and other such images as false idols instead of merely showing the
icons respect. At the same time, Rilke's poem calls not for contemplation of what stands outside and before us, but for self-examina-
tion. Levertov's speaker explores the same issue but sees things
differently. In line 6, Rilke's monk says, "Piously we produce our
images." By placing "piously" at the beginning of the line, its emphasis is greater, thus, calling attention to the threat of religious
enthusiasm getting in the way of authentic piety and meaningful
worship. Indeed, these "images" are portrayed as a barricade of a
"thousand walls" that "our fervent hands" built (ll. 7–9). In Levertov's version, the speaker is an "old," implying wise, monk, who
answers Rilke's monk with loving logic. In contrast, Levertov's
monk says that each of these "depictions" (2) shows the "manifold
countenance" (l. 8) of God. This argument rests upon the fundamental idea that humans cannot truly know God or God's intentions, but the monk soon offers hope.

In lines ten through seventeen, the old monk extends his argument with a comparison of the dependence of the "vaulted
sanctuary['s]" interior, the "shadowy ribs" of the Gothic cathedral;
on the exterior, the "seraph buttress[es] flying" (l. 10) that support
it. He says they are "both" the "form of a holy place" (ll. 13–14)
and implies that without one the other cannot exist. Levertov's
monk next points out the beauty of the stained glass seen from
within but illuminated by the light "from without" (l. 17). With
these architectural images, Levertov's speaker presents a variation
of the issue of graven images and the theme of appearances. Appearances are not necessarily false and, therefore, necessarily bad.

They may convey a purpose not readily conceived of in the viewing, but, nevertheless, these appearances are of vital importance to a larger plan, an in-sight more profound. Additionally, in lines eighteen through twenty, Levertov's monk unites the natural and the mystical and affirms purpose in each "artist's" endeavor. Thus, "[e]ach" (l. 19) is dependent upon, not just the "neighbor" (l. 20), but also upon the "perception" of his neighbor's "work in his art" (l. 19). In the final three lines, Levertov's monk speaks of God's purpose, God's "play" and "grace" (l. 21). This poem clearly ends with a gentle reminder—in contrast to the often vicious portrayal of the graven image controversy of the Eastern church—that one may not be privy to the greater design. Finally, the monk concludes on a whimsical note, suggesting that when God "plays," he offers, "in grace," "clues to His mystery" (ll. 20–22). Standing alone, Levertov's poem is of course complete. But read alongside Rilke's, Levertov's second "Variation" becomes part of a loving debate while it conceives of a world where God is immanence.

In the final "variation," Levertov has added "Reflection" to the title of her poem "Variation and Reflection on a Theme by Rilke" (*BW* 83). Rilke's poem speaks of the yearning all humans feel, the desire for a communion with God in which He can truly be *known* (*The Book* 53). This profound desire is one all seekers, believers or not, understand. It is the need to hold the truth within oneself just long enough to know it—once and for all. Both Rilke and Levertov sing this desire in their poems. Rilke's poem, *The Book of Hours*, "Book I, Poem 7," centers on this desire alone. The speaker says that if everything "for once ... were still" (l. 1), if the noise of living "could be muted" (l. 3), then in such perfect stillness and silence he could perhaps comprehend the incomprehensible. To apprehend God and His truths would require all the human capacity to think, and, therefore, all else that might intrude upon such concentration would have to pause, to stop. That such an occurrence is impossible is implied in the subjunctive mood of the poem's first line, "If only...." Rilke's poem is beautiful in its childlike simplicity and yearning.

Part one of Levertov's "Variation" expands on Rilke's longing. Lines one through seven mimic it in sound and structure:

> If just for once the swing of cause and effect,
> > cause and effect,
> would come to rest; if casual events would halt,
> and the machine that supplies meaningless laughter
> ran down, and my bustling senses, taking a deep breath

> fell silent
> and left my attention free at last ...

The rhythmic repetition and spacing of the phrase "cause and effect" and the evocative white space in line six behind "fell silent," even the trailing off of ellipses following "attention free at last," all embody the yearning that Levertov's speaker describes. Like Rilke's speaker, Levertov's imagines being able to comprehend the truth of God for just one moment. That moment, even if it were "fleeting as a smile" (l. 13), would be more than sufficient to satisfy the speaker's deep longing. Also like Rilke's speaker, Levertov's promises to be satisfied, much as a child promises never to ask again for the thing she desires so keenly if only she may "possess" (l. 12) it one time.

In part two of Levertov's "Variation and Reflection," however, the speaker acknowledges and accepts the impossibility of ever getting what the heart so desires—to know God. By not facing the impossibility squarely, Rilke's monk fails to accept that knowing God in this life will never happen. Consequently, the yearning in Rilke's speaker, although valuable to the soul's journey and consummately expressed, suggests a certain spiritual immaturity, as is made particularly clear in the contrast with Levertov's "Variation and Reflection." While the yearning is still explicitly present in all its tragically beautiful proportions in Levertov's variation, her speaker states flatly, "There will never be that stillness" (l. 15). It is a stark assertion that does not lend itself to dispute. Furthermore, in lines sixteen through twenty-one, the speaker reiterates the statement by acknowledging that "we" are of this world, the world of "dust." This fact is reiterated in the monotonous, hard "t" sounds repeated in "trudge and "turning," the throaty "u" sounds repeated in those same lines. Yet even when admitting the futility of desiring what is not obtainable, Levertov's speaker allows for the beauty inherent in this innate human desire. "We" may be of this world, but it is wonderful, inspirited. Furthermore, within this world, within our place in it, "we" already possess what we desire, even if we are unable to comprehend God in us and in the world around us. Levertov and Rilke agree that the artist does comprehend God in the world in an artistic/mystical process for the poet. The last "Variation" concludes with the stirring words Levertov chose to title the collection: "We must breathe time as fishes breathe water" (l. 23). Thus, the monk reiterates the only recourse available to us that may satisfy our desire to know God—we do this by living.

Denise Levertov was 64 in 1987 when *Breathing the Water* was published. More "recent poems," Gelpi says,

> make it increasingly clear that Levertov's Christian faith is the source of both her inspiration and her politics, her poetry of celebration as well as her poetry of opposition; it informs her sense of tragedy and of transcendence. For her ... mysticism and liberation theology are the double face of the Word in the world. (5)

Rainer Maria Rilke was only 23 when he wrote his *Book of Monastic Life* in 1899. In his later "poetic miracles" (Peters 123), *The Duino Elegies* and the *Sonnets to Orpheus*, the work of Rilke as mature poet, the angel appears as a major figure: "The angel ... symbolizes intensities of feeling that are not directed outward but concentrated in the heart, which, under the impact of their radiance, becomes an angel or, as one might say, experiences pure being" (128). In a way, Levertov has caught him too soon, just beginning the journey towards his mature poetry and beliefs, in her variations on his monk's prayers, as if she is practicing answers she knows he will later find and that have helped her find her own. In contrast to Levertov, he was at the end, only "nominally a Catholic" and wished no last rites, no priests present as intercessors in, as Rilke put it, his "soul's move toward the 'Open'" (Freedman 531). As Zlotkowski reminds us throughout his study of Levertov and Rilke, she approached the numinous always through the sensuous, looked outward; while Rilke looked ever inward. Yet his *Uncollected Poems* (translated by Edward Snow) includes one written in 1924, a year after her birth and only a couple of years before his death, in which he could be speaking for himself as well as Levertov as they come so close together finally in their particular kind of faith in the miracle of poetry:

> As once the winged energy of delight
> carried you over those many first abysses,
> now build the unimagined bridge's
> sternly calculated arc.
>
> Miracle's not only in the unexplained
> outlasting of the threat;
> only in the clear, consummate
> achievement is the miracle *defined*.
>
> There's no presumption in joining in
> on the indescribable relation;
> the meshwork grows more and more ardent,
> mere being-borne is not enough.

Take your practiced strengths and stretch them
until they reach between two
contradictions … For far inside you
the god wishes to consult. (177)

Works Cited

Deutsch, Babette, trans. "Preface." *Poems from the Book of Hours.* Rainer
Maria Rilke. New York: New Directions, 1941; rpt. 1975.

Freedman, Ralph. *Life of a Poet: Rainer Maria Rilke.* New York: Farrar,
Straus and Giroux, 1996.

Gelpi, Albert. "Introduction." *Denise Levertov, Selected Criticism.* Under
Discussion. Ann Arbor: U of Michigan P, 1996. 1–8.

Levertov, Denise. *Breathing the Water.* New York: New Directions, 1987.

———. *Light Up the Cave.* New York: New Directions, 1981.

———. *New & Selected Essays.* New York: New Directions, 1992.

———. *The Poet in the World.* New York: New Directions, 1973.

Mack, Maynard, ed. "Rainer Maria Rilke." *The Norton Anthology of World
Masterpieces.* Vol. 2. New York: Norton, 1995. 1649–53.

Peters, H.F. *Rainer Maria Rilke: Masks and the Man.* Seattle: U of Washington P, 1960.

Rilke, Rainer Maria. *The Book of Monastic Life. Rilke's Book of Hours: Love Poems to God.* Trans. A. Barrows and J. Macy. Riverhead, NY: n.p., 1996.

———. *First Book: The Book of Monastic Life. Rainer Maria Rilke: Prose and
Poetry.* Ed. E. Schwarz. Trans. J. B. Leishman. New York: Continuum,
1984.

———. *Uncollected Poems: Rainer Maria Rilke.* Trans. Edward Snow. New
York: North Point Press, 1996.

Salt and Honey: On Denise Levertov[1]
Sam Hamill

When I was a boy memorizing my first poems, Robert Frost's "The Road not Taken" gave me more problems than almost any other short poem. I never could get the closing couplet right:

> I shall be telling this with a sigh
> Somewhere ages and ages hence:
> Two roads diverged in a wood, and I—
> I took the one less traveled by,
> And that has made all the difference.

It seems that whenever I'd recite the poem, I'd leave out that *by* which makes no real sense and which is there only to fill out the syllabic count and to rhyme. Frost the literary technician traveled roads that might be best described as expressways or thoroughfares, his ear was a conventionally educated ear. He knew his material and he knew his craft. As far as it went. Frost preferred his domesticated snowy woods to the uninhabitable rainy forests of the northwest or to the sun-scorched plains. He preferred Latin iambics to those of the Romantics, and fixed or closed forms to those of his contemporaries, Eliot, Pound, and Williams. He knew his own limitations perhaps as well as any poet of this century, and he pushed against those same limitations perhaps as gently as any.

As an adolescent, I used to take this poem and condense it, sometimes writing a version as brief as two quatrains, but each ending with a version of the poet's closing couplet without that *by*.

Frost's poem touches something in the hearts of each of us—a nostalgia perhaps for a time in which decisions could be made in tranquil deliberation, like the poet as he stops for a moment to

---

[1]This essay originally appeared in *American Poetry Review*, November 1991.

consider a fork in the road, and sees, looking into the blank distance, a future beginning. We Americans are uniform in our passionate defense of individuality. Growing up on Frost, we adopted him as our national literary-curmudgeonly Granddaddy, a flag of white hair waving above a sadly lined face at the inauguration of Camelot. Post-war babies were in their teens and television brought it into their homes so that they were somehow participants in the unfolding drama. Frost spoke our language. A great many of my childhood poems were revisions of Frost. But I never learned to remember "traveled *by*."

These memories of my early struggle with Frost's road were prompted by reading the first poem in Denise Levertov's new book, *A Door in the Hive*.

> To Rilke
>
> Once, in dream,
>   the boat
> pushed off from the shore.
> You at the prow were the man—
> all voice, though silent—who bound
> rowers and voyagers to the needful journey,
> the veiled distance, imperative mystery.
>
> All the crouched effort,
> creak of oarlocks, odor of sweat,
> sound of waters
> running against us
> was transcended; your gaze
> held as we crossed. Its dragonfly blue
> restored to us
>   a shimmering destination.
>
> I had not yet read of your Nile journey,
> the enabling voice
> drawing that boat upstream in your parable.
> Strange that I knew
> your silence was just such a song. (3)

Levertov's poem, like Frost's, presents an archetypal metaphor, but with several profound differences. First, she is journeying in a dream; second, she places herself, both psyche and physical body, completely under the control of another. Where Frost turns alone in a gesture of near invulnerability, Levertov remains particularly vulnerable, her conscious mind given over to the dream, her vision and her body being guided by her Virgil. The experience is transcendent. Finally, like Frost, she has the capacity to enter the future deeply enough to be able to look back into the present. But her insight is not informed by a prescient need to prepare a public utterance. Where Frost foresees himself speaking knowingly, Levertov embraces the silence of completed wisdom, closing her poem in a song of *listening*.

In Levertov's melopoeia, there are no tricks, no Procrustean beds, no learnéd devices. Her language is sincere, pragmatic, and condensed without being compacted; it flows in natural cadences, opening with a five-syllable couplet followed by a seven-syllable couplet followed by a twelve-syllable couplet. The second stanza is, syllabically, less formal, but listen to the echo of "crouched effort" in "creak of oarlock"; listen to the echo of "against us" in "transcended" and again in "destination." Her music is subtle, sophisticated, opening to its own revelation as it develops. Anyone who has sung Frost's "Whose woods / these are / I think I know" to the tune of "Hernando's Hideaway" has learned something about the nature of closed form, of predetermined form. In Levertov's poems, the form is the music revealing itself, the rubbing of syllable against syllable, syllable against silence, her ear alert to syllabic resonance rather than predictable end-rhyme. The whole poem unfolds as naturally as sprout from seed. And what a seed!

The "imperative mystery" and the journey within are the very *stuff* of Levertov's poetry and have been from the beginning. Thirty-five years ago, she wrote a poem, "People at Night" (*CEP* 33–34), which was "derived from Rilke" and in which she spoke of "going up to some apartment, yours / or yours, finding / someone sitting in the dark: / who is it, really?..." The "anybody" she finds is "No one." With Rilke serving as both guide and muse, she has explored the mystery, perfecting her vision.

Levertov journeys into the interior dark in her most social-political poetry as when she returned from the Bach Mai Hospital in Vietnam declaring her intention to "bring the war home." But also in poems like "The Mutes" and "A Wedding Ring," she embraces harrowing experiences of another—although less life-threatening—kind, only to emerge with a profoundly compassionate optimism.

The fourth poem in *A Door in the Hive* again presents the poet as "A Traveler" along a Way:

> If it's chariots or sandals,
> I'll take sandals.
> I like the high prow of the chariot,
> the daredevil speed, the wind

```
a quick tune you can't
quite catch
            but I want to go
a long way
and I want to follow
paths where wheels deadlock.
            And I don't want always
to be among gear and horses,
            blood, foam, dust. I'd like
to wean myself from their strange allure.
I'll chance
the pilgrim sandals. (6)
```

This is another telling of the Road Less Traveled. The "high prow of the chariot" and "daredevil speed" are the "strange allure" of physical—whether personal or national—power. "Pilgrim sandals" lead into a world where such power becomes meaningless, where the pilgrimage follows narrow footpaths of those searching for the authentic sacramental rites of the soul's own transit. In the earlier poem, she addressed Rilke, "You at the prow were the man—" where she now presents only a general masculine image, "I like the high prow of the chariot, / the daredevil speed," declining gracefully the latter's seductive excitement in favor of the more feminine sense of interior abundance, of traveling slowly as though in gestation, wanting to be "weaned" from masculine power.

Neither of Levertov's "road taken" poems is as chatty, as self-consciously *made* as Frost's famous poem. There are no awkward inversions, no formal high-stepping to a pre-determined beat, no sighing for one's self.

In a wonderfully common-sense essay in *Chicago Review* in 1979, later gathered with other prose work in *Light Up the Cave* (New Directions, 1981), Levertov writes "On the Function of the Line":

> What is the nature of the alogical pauses the linebreak records? If readers will think of their own speech, or their silent inner monologue, when describing thought, feelings, perceptions, scenes or events, they will, I think, recognize that they frequently hesitate—albeit very briefly—as if with an unspoken question,— a "what?" or a "who?" or a "how?"—before nouns, adjectives, verbs, adverbs, none of which require to be preceded by a comma or other regular punctuation in the course of syntactic logic. To incorporate these pauses in the rhythmic structure of the poem can do several things: for example, it allows the reader

to share more intimately the experience that is being articulated; and by introducing an alogical counter-rhythm into the logical rhythm of syntax it causes, as they interact, an effect closer to song than to statement, closer to dance than to walking. Thus the emotional experience of empathy of identification plus the sonic complexity of the language structure synthesize in an *intense aesthetic order that is different from that which is received from a poetry in which metric forms are combined with logical syntax alone.* [My italics.] (*LUC* 62–63)

Metrical forms, Levertov observes, also *may* permit such alogical pauses. The use of linebreaks bears directly upon the *melos* of the poem, she says, affecting the poem's *pitch pattern* among other things. And she quotes X.J. Kennedy on the definition of the run-on line: "It does not end in punctuation and therefore is read with only a *slight pause* after it." In other words, the line is a musical structure, not merely the tick-tocking of a metronome. The line carries pitch, breath and pulse, sonic stress, cadence, and rhyme. "On the Function of the Line" ought to be taught in every public school and every college poetry class in the country.

Ben Jonson, dangerously obese, poverty-stricken, imprisoned and released, vents his frustration with the confining nature of rhyme by composing "A Fit of Rhyme Against Rhyme" ("Rhyme, the rack of finest wits, / That expresseth but by fits, / True conceit, / Spoiling sense of their treasure, / Cozening judgment with a measure, / But false weight. / …"), but in a rare example of blank verse has his Lord Lovel say in *The New Inn*,

> The things true valour is exercised about
> Are poverty, restraint, captivity,
> Banishment, loss of children, long disease:
> The least is death. Here valour is beheld,
> Properly seen; about these it is present:
> Not trivial things which but require our confidence.

It is astonishing, reading volume after volume of recent North American poetry, just how little of it relates any sense of social or political responsibility. There is, to be sure, plenty of propagandistic poetry; there is the smug, hip rage of the "politically correct" who speak only to one another; but so much of our recent poetry reflects the general malaise of Yuppie complacency and expediency in the perpetual search for immediate self-gratification, whether in material goodies or in pseudo-self-realization.

Levertov returns us to that greater, more noble tradition with "El Salvador: Requiem and Invocation" in *A Door in the Hive*. A libretto commissioned by the Back Bay Chorale and the Pro Arte Chamber Orchestra for composer Newell Hendricks, it opens with a cacophony of violent words and sounds, then moves from pre-Columbian times through an extremely compacted history utilizing, among other devices, adaptations of Mayan prayers. Arriving in contemporary times, she quotes directly from speeches by the martyred Archbishop Oscar Romero and from letters by the murdered nuns, Sisters Dorothy, Maura, and Ita. Perhaps most powerful is her use of a list of "the week's murdered" made up largely of names of but one extended family, mostly children. This list, and a later one listing the names of murdered priests and nuns, is composed of actual names. Here, "valour is beheld, / Properly seen." The poem closes on a coda, a prayer drawn from the prayers of Archbishop Romero.

There are a great many beautiful lyrical poems in *A Door in the Hive*, and great variety. But it is her gentle, insistent spiritual hunger that most unifies her vision quest. Her sense of spiritual as well as personal accountability has informed her poetry from the beginning. In "Complicity" (63), she says to a hummingbird, having compared it to "a child whose hiding-place / has not been discovered,"

> I saw
> a leaf: I shall not betray you.

and a moment of charm, of poignancy, takes on a much larger emotional complex. "Betrayal" carries a train-load of implication. And how can the child not call up an image from Nazi Germany, especially when we remember that the poet was a young nurse in England during the war? Many of Levertov's poems invite a psycho-analytical interpretation. They engage the reader, making of him or her a participant in the poem itself.

I used to read "The Mutes" to my students in various prisons, many of them batterers themselves struggling with their own phobias and smashed self-esteem. Out of this universal experience, they would come to glimpse another side of their rude behavior and begin to understand how they might transform themselves. Poetry is—or ought to be—that important.

In recent years, we have endured a veritable avalanche of Rilke Industries—multiple translations, scholarly examinations, literary exegesis, biographies, you-name-it—with the inevitable result: more and more bad imitative poems, often picking up Rilke's worst habits at the expense of his best. Levertov has written derivative poems in the very best sense of that often-abused word; she has wrestled with Rilke's vision, adapted it, learned from it; Rilke has indeed been a Virgil to her Dante, leading her deeper into the mystery which so resonates in all of her poetry. There have, of course, been a great many other major influences on her work, figures as diverse as Cesare Pavese and Robert Duncan and Anton Chekhov. Indeed, she remains one of our most "literary" poets in a time when the literary is completely out of fashion: most of our poets often sound like they read nothing at all, almost as though they would apologize for erudition, embarrassed by it.

In "The Life of Art," Levertov begins,

> The borderland—that's where, if one knew how,
> one would establish residence. That watershed,
> that spine, that looking-glass ... I mean the edge
> between impasto surface, burnt sienna, thick,
> > striate, gleaming—swathes and windrows
> > of carnal paint—
> > or, canvas barely stained,
> > where warp and weft peer through,
>
> and fictive truth: a room, a vase, an open door
> giving upon the clouds.
>
> > > (*DH* 85)

She begins by defining a circumstance wherein one may find what John Haines has called "a place of sense," that is, a place where one feels at home, a part, connected to watershed, that spine and mirror which sustains us all. Then, she narrows the focus to her own canvas as she paints. But it may be a vase, it may be the opening door in a poem by Rilke or clouds by Matisse.

> A step back, and you have
> the likeness, its own world. Step to the wall again,
> and you're so near the paint you could lick it,
> you breathe its ghostly turpentine.
> > > But there's an interface,
> immeasurable, elusive—an equilibrium
> just attainable, sometimes, when the attention's rightly poised, ...
>
> > (85)

The poet's attention, rightly poised, becomes numinous just at such an intersection, at the bordering of two or more worlds, each casting light upon the other so that they are one thing,—poets,

worlds, sounds. The melopoeia draws us in. The *a-* sounds of *A,
have, back, again, paint, interface, immeasurable* and *attainable* set up a
resonance. The lines are spoken in almost casual speech. Has anyone ever used "interface" as voluptuously, as sensually? "The Life
of Art" is both philosophy and metaphysics, a poem that brings
the reader into the borderlands where a "looking-glass" slowly
spins.

Levertov has described herself at the beginning as "a British
Romantic with almost Victorian background," and Kenneth
Rexroth introduced her poetry to its U.S. audience in *New British
Poets: An Anthology* forty years ago, saying that her tendency toward "pulsating rhythms, romantic melancholy and undefined
nostalgia" were her "outstanding virtues." Hindsight points not to
pulsating rhythms, but to subtle modulations and a plenitude of
greater spiritual hunger; not to an undefined nostalgia, but to a
sweeping social engagement. In short, she realizes Jonson's ideal.
Many of her poems reveal epiphany located within common,
mundane things without stooping to the trivial. In the elegies for
her mother in *Life in the Forest*, she offers several of the most memorable poems of recent years. She would appear to owe more to
Wordsworth's meditations than to Shelley's flights of fancy, more
to the hard thinking of the English poets of the 17th century than
to the narratives of Browning. Nor has she ever indulged in the
pretty-little-picture poems so often found in *The New Yorker*.

Reading Levertov—as I have: all my adult life—I find myself
turning not to single poems which have moved and inspired me so
much as to whole books, or sometimes a suite of poems within a
book, hungry for the sounds she makes and for the deep quietude
that follows an hour's reading. And there has been a simultaneous
presence of history, the poet's engagement with "poverty, re-
straint, captivity, banishment," and the work of "bringing home
the war." The ambitions are lofty. But they are ambitions, not pre-
tensions. Levertov is a thinker, a pilgrim, not a cheerleader. Now,
when I once again open *The Sorrow Dance*, I return to the murder-
ous summer of 1968, and to a small camp along the Novarro River
where I lived in an old panel truck. I had left my first wife and
daughter—my daughter my only blood relative—to return to
school. I was active in civil rights and anti-war campaigns. So I re-
treated to the real world and spent days walking the river, watching hawks, reading *The Sorrow Dance*.

The Mutes

Those groans men use
passing a woman on the street
or on the steps of the subway

to tell her she is female
and their flesh knows it,

are they a sort of tune,
an ugly enough song, sung
by a bird with a slit tongue

but meant for music?

Or are they the muffled roaring
of deafmutes trapped in a building that is
slowly filling with smoke?

Perhaps both.

Such men most often
look as if groan were all they could do,
yet a woman, in spite of herself,

knows it's a tribute:
if she were lacking all grace
they'd pass her in silence:

so it's not to say she's
a warm hole. It's a word

in grief-language, nothing to do with
primitive, not an ur-language;
language stricken, sickened, cast down

in decrepitude. She wants to
throw the tribute away, dis-
gusted, and can't,

it goes on buzzing in her ear, it changes the pace of her walk,
the torn posters in echoing corridors

spell it out, it
quakes and gnashes as the train comes in.
Her pulse sullenly

had picked up speed,
but the cars slow down and
jar to a stop while her understanding

keeps on translating:
'Life after life after life goes by

without poetry,

> without seemliness,
> without love.' (46–47)

Levertov's "The Mutes" has had perhaps greater import on my life than any other contemporary poem. Its *melos*, its *logos*, its sacred compassionate teaching has brought me to discuss it in essays and classes over two decades. And this is what Rilke is *really* about: that poem changed my life. And the poems gathered in "Life at War" were a poultice for the human soul:

> The disasters numb within us
> caught in the chest, rolling in the brain like pebbles....
> (*SA* 13)

and she quotes Rilke and dares to imagine mercy and joy and peace. And in a "Second Didactic Poem" she says,

> In our gathering, in our containing, in our
> working, active within ourselves,
> slowly the pale
> dew-beads of light lapped up from flowers
> can thicken,
> darken to gold:
>
> honey of the human.
> (*SD* 83)

Maybe the hippies in San Francisco during "The Summer of Love" were lapping up the various honeys of the human, but most of the people I knew were concerned primarily with rivers of blood flowing in Asia and in the still-segregated streets of the U.S. of A.

Nearly a quarter century has passed, and every two or three years, another book of poems by Denise Levertov. I cannot open *The Sorrow Dance* without returning to remembrances of Martin Luther King, David Harris, Eugene McCarthy, and Michael Harrington. And yet with all its grief and darkness, that book, like so many of hers, does indeed include the honeys of hope and joy. History is far more than an accounting of military maneuvers, imperialism, and bloodshed. Denise Levertov's poetry offers a sweeping personal and public vision of our times. Now, reading "Ikon: The Harrowing of Hell," I am drawn into a world where

> there must take place that struggle
> no human presumes to picture:
> living, dying, descending to rescue the just
> from shadow, were lesser travails
> than this: to break
> through earth and stone of the faithless world

> back to the cold sepulchre, tearstained
> stifling shroud; to break from *them*
> back into breath and heartbeat, and walk
> the world again, ...

(DH 105)

Another borderworld. One where the political, the spiritual, and the practical intersect. The road taken is a narrow path through the nearly impenetrable underworld, which is a netherworld. And leads once again to transformation:

> His mortal flesh was lit from within, now,
> and aching for home. He must return,
> first, in Divine patience, and know
> hunger again, and give
> to humble friends the joy
> of giving him food—fish and a honeycomb.

(DH 105–6)

An archetypal parable, it also is a "traveling" metaphor made as it were of salt and honey, bittersweet and sublime. If one insists upon a religious interpretation, it is good to remember that *religion* comes from *re-ligio, to re-bind*. The poem is a journey through Hell in order to find a glimpse of Paradise. A poultice for the wounded soul. The journey itself is a healing. And at the end, there is a feast of human kindness.

Denise Levertov's early books are now being collected into larger volumes. The first volume, *Collected Earlier Poems 1940–1967*, concludes with the poems of *The Sorrow Dance*. Her work has been steady, an accretion rather than an avalanche. She has not gone after the "Big Poem"—which usually is the literary equivalent of the Big Mac anyhow—but has remained a listener, attentive to the poem *as it reveals itself*, whether formally as in a libretto, or in more open structure, whether longer poems, poems-in-sequence, or as small lyrics.

In one of her greatest poems, "The Malice of Innocence" from the 1972 volume, *Footprints*, she says,

> ... Death and pain dominate this world, for though
> many are cured, they still leave weak.

> still tremulous, still knowing mortality
> has whispered to them; have seen in the folding
> of white bedspreads according to rule

> the starched pleats of a shroud.
>   It's against that frozen

> counterpane, and the knowledge too
> how black an old mouth gaping at death can look
>
> that the night routine has in itself—
> without illusions—glamor, perhaps. It had
> a rhythm, a choreographic decorum: ... (52)

remembering her life as a nurse during the war, tiptoeing from bed to bed, "counting by flashlight how many pairs / of open eyes were turned to us" (53), scrubbing lockers, passing out trays of unappetizing food, all the while loving "the knowing what to do" and the orderliness of the night work. But her own remembering propels her into the "death rooms" remembering "just as a soldier or one of the guards / from Dachau might" and sees suddenly that her love of order delivers her the duty of "writing // details of agony carefully into the Night Report" (54).

She has an uncanny ability to connect with all human experience, and to remain, nonetheless, emotionally uncluttered. It is no accident that the leading anti-war poet of our time connects with the psyche of soldiers at Dachau—the love of order is, in part at least, a love of the power to impose one's sense of order. The basic universal impulse of poetry is naming, thereby identifying, and, consequently, ordering experience. In perfecting the poem, the melopoeia, phanopoeia, and logopoeia join seamlessly to present a mythopoeia.

One walks many a road, well-trod and otherwise, in three-plus decades. I have found sustenance and inspiration in the sixteen volumes of poems Denise Levertov has given, and I turn to them now and again as the old friends they are. I am happy I chose the road and the company I did. I'm never inclined to change her lines. I once questioned an inversion in a line from her translations of Jean Joubert, *Black Iris*, and was told, "It's my mid-Atlantic accent; I've only been here forty years and don't quite speak American yet."

There are finally no ornamental flourishes, no dead words, no faked emotion, no public posture. Book by book, I have read her poems for their subtle music, for their deep compassionate intelligence, for their imagination, for their author's dignity and integrity and grace; and, most of all, for the indomitable and humble spirit that hungers there. I have savored them like salt, like honey.

3

the minds of people, the minds of trees
equally remote, my attention then
filled with sensations, my attention now
caught by leaf and bark at eye level
and by thoughts of my own, but sometimes
drawn to upgazing--up and up: to wonder
about what rises
so far above me into the light.

from "From Below" (by Denise Levertov
from *This Great Unknowing*)

Seeing Denise Levertov: *Tesserae*

Denise E. Lynch

When loved ones or treasures disappear from our lives we can retreat to nostalgia or channel memory into acts and words of praise. In the autobiographical volume *Tesserae*, Denise Levertov claims for herself the "universal impulse" to transform loss into praise: "How much of what I feel impelled to write (in prose, though not in poetry) has to do with loss" ("Lost Books" 110). *Tesserae* sketches the development of an imagination that embraces contrast, a tentacled "Connoisseur of continents" that curls into attics or untwines into "unexplored chains of high vaulted throne-rooms" ("The Art of the Octopus: Variations on a Found Theme," *CB* 19). This is the "spiritual imagination" or sense of holiness that Hayden Carruth finds in Levertov's poetry (145), and it is both the subject and generating force of these "memoirs and suppositions." Chronologically arranged, they form a mosaic of love and loss that shows us how Levertov learned to look at the world as her poetic milieu.

Levertov's richly detailed vignettes reflect the poet's persistent efforts to live fully in the moment, past or present. They depict a woman who from childhood was alert to contrasts and patterns and believed she was destined to become an artist. Levertov writes of patterns perceived as a girl and remembered in later life. In "Cordova" (16–19), for example, she recalls the pattern of the iron blanket her mother used as underlay for a flatiron, a pattern of green and beigy cream. When she carried ironed items upstairs for her mother, Levertov saw the same pattern in the interplay of light and shade around her, a "casbah" of the imagination. Later in life she would attach the name of Cordova to this pattern and associate it with the Moorish architecture of Southern Spain. Vivid memories of the ironing board would again be brought back by a 1980s Peter Brown photo, the basis of Levertov's poem "A

Doorkey for Cordova," which evokes the patterns of "the greenish thickwoven cotton tablecover" as a "Septembery casbah" (*BW* 11). The poem links the ironing board to a living pattern as well, since the "doorkey" refers to the tradition of Jewish exiles from Spain taking keys to their houses and passing them along from generation to generation. "Cordova," an "atavistic shred of kinesthetic impressions," connects the poet to a personal and collective past and has the enduring charm of an "ancestral relic" (19).

Another essay, "Meeting and Not Meeting Artists" (74–83), suggests that her training in the visual arts heightened this receptivity to pattern. She recalls with amusement how her parents had taken her to see the London artist Amedee Azenfant in the hope that he would take her on as a student. Azenfant never accepted Denise Levertov as a student, but Miss Eva Noar did. Often taking her young pupil to Kensington Gardens to sketch, Miss Noar taught Levertov how to *see*:

> "Pattern, pattern!" Miss Noar would adjure me—for that word *pattern* was her way of summing up all the essential compositional factors. (She may have meant by it more than mere surface decoration: something closer to Hopkins' term, *inscape*, which became so dear to me later on.) Although she and her dictum lacked for me, at twelve or thirteen, the aura of romance, of Paris and "*Continuez; mes enfants*," yet she succeeded in making me see more. To see—beyond the individual beauties and graces of flower and leaf and cloud, which my mother had revealed to me when I was still almost a baby; or the lacy patterns of bare twigs against pale sky which I'd noticed for myself a little later; or the not dissimilar delicacy of old wrought iron which I had recently discovered at the V. and A.—the complex interaction of three-dimensional objects in space, and their transmutation into compositions: form and colors on a flat surface. I couldn't *do* it, but I did embark upon a lifetime of seeing it. (78–79)

After the war Levertov made another attempt to study art but as she waited to be interviewed by the artist Kokoschka she realized that visual art was not her calling: "My true vocation was and had always been, virtually from infancy, poetry" (81). That was her life of seeing.

Patterns of another sort, rhythmic movement, also appear in *Tesserae*. For example, there are the ballet steps drilled into Levertov by her older sister, Olga. That training yielded the moments of exquisite joy narrated in "By the Seaside" (32–38), which describes the occasion on which Denise Levertov began to dance for herself, feeling the ecstasy of graceful movement: "I leapt, I glided, I twirled, I invented steps and used my whole sturdy seven-year-old body to be at one with the luminous and now fading sky, the soft air, the farewelling of the waves" (35). Dance takes on an aura of mystery when Levertov meets another childhood friend, Margaret Courtwell, and visits her dark, silent house. A striking contrast to Levertov's own house, which pulsates with sound and life, Margaret's house nevertheless contains a player piano. As one of the girls pedals, the other dances to the piano's music. For Levertov the drama of these improvisational dances would be recaptured several years later when she viewed the dark and mysterious landscapes of Salavator Rosa: "… there is an external present where, alternately, Margaret and I, ages forever nine and seven, waltz, and whirl, and strike poses among the ghostly looming of white-draped settees and ottomans, held in the vague greenish stare of a gilt-framed over-mantel looking glass" ("A Dance" 46).

This early pleasure in movement perhaps reinforced Levertov's sense that the rhythms of personal loss and renewal were tied to the deeper rhythms of nature and therefore part of a time-less regenerative cycle. As Edward Zlotkowski has observed, the garden figures prominently in Levertov's prose and poetry as an image of both spiritual and creative power; associated with Beatrice Levertoff, the poet's mother, the garden is an Edenic place that can be lost in time, in the knowledge of evil, or in the betrayal of the imagination ("In the Garden," Gelpi 303–20). Images of gardens in *Tesserae* are also linked with creativity and imagination. In "The Gardener" (47–51), for example, Levertov recalls "Old Day" tending the front gardens hidden from the street. He digs up the wild primroses he has been told not to injure; he watches impassively as other men hired to dig up the lawn cut into her own "special daisy" (49). A mere child, she intuits his "ancient power," yet she secretly likes him:

> Bone and mist, pale, white-haired, grey-eyed, very tall, clothed in colors of ash and earth, a capricious demigod, he still moves in a stately shamble up and down the block, glides unobserved right through certain houses, brings life and blossom, death and burial to the rectangular sanctums closed off from each other by walls of brick and thickets of may, laburnum, apple trees, memory, time. He carries sometimes a spade, sometimes a scythe, and listens in silence to orders he will not obey. He has his own intentions. (51)

Like the improvisational dances of her girlhood, Old Day is an enduring presence for Levertov. In him, as in the engraving of Old
Father Time in her childhood copy of *Parables from Nature*, the
"Active and Passive" (50) forces of nature converge. In this memoir Old Day's misty image takes on a supernatural aura as he
breaks down the barriers of matter and consciousness. A figure of
time and death, Old Day also embodies the imagination that embraces contrast.

Several of the essays in *Tesserae* show the early development of
that imagination. "Janus" (52–56), for example, narrates an adventure with childhood friends that in retrospect represents the paradox of human experience. With her friend Trixie and another
schoolmate, Jean Pilgrim, Levertov climbs the wall surrounding a
boarded up Victorian mansion. When the girls peer over the top of
the wall, they see a magnificent magnolia tree. Just as they exclaim
in delight, an old purple-faced tramp bursts out of the house and
shouts at them: "With shrieks we dropped back down, scraping
hands and knees, landing with a shock in a momentary scramble
of bodies, to pick ourselves up with scared swiftness and race back
to the safety of the street. The devil in paradise!" (55). Looking
back on the episode, which memory imbues with mystery-tale
fascination, Levertov sees in it a marriage of opposites, beauty and
terror. At the moment of "epiphany," when the children glimpse
the unearthly splendor of the magnolia tree, a "raging monster"
(56) emerges and their hearts pound in fear. Levertov recalls the
garden adventure as "a revelation of how intimately opposites
live, their mysterious simultaneity, their knife-edge union: the
Janus face of human experience" (56). "Janus" is reminiscent of
Levertov's poem "The Great Wave," which describes the
childhood experience of being swept up and away from the shore
by a giant ocean wave and being made "unable / to distinguish
terror from delight" (*CB* 106). Both the poem and memoir
transform loss into a synthesis of fear and joy.

"Two Ancients" (39–42) records a similar revelation. In this essay Levertov reflects upon the interwoven memories of two el-
derly men. One was a small, gentle man who regularly appeared
at the sparsely attended weekly service in Holy Trinity church,
where Paul Levertoff was Priest-in-Charge. The Levertoffs called
the old man "The Spiritualist," and to please him they joined in
singing a hymn, "Living Water," whenever he was present. The
image of this frail, bearded man singing a hymn brought to Denise
Levertov a joy intensified by its own ephemerality:

> But there was something powerful in the sight and sound of the
> old man fervently singing in his quavery, reedy voice the words
> he loved, "Living water, living water," and when I think of him I
> not only see the dark, candlelit church (which gave off a certain
> stony chill even in warm weather, a chill that contrasted tantaliz-
> ingly with the sensuous perfume of incense), but also glimpse a
> green pasture with a sparkling fountain at its center. (40–41)

In Levertov's mind "The Spiritualist" is linked with an old man
who played a barrel organ near her home. The music had a
"melancholy charm" (41) for Levertov, who would watch the man
feebly grind his music box then sadly shuffle off. Each of the images is a mix of joy and sadness; each complements the other. "The
Spiritualist" and the organ grinder represent the interplay of light
and darkness in human life, the many colors of the biblical
Joseph's coat:

> Yet how different the two!—one was an image of despondency
> (though his music's charm gave off some faint sense of a world
> of gaiety long past, a gaiety tinged with melancholy, that delicate
> bittersweet mood I was later to recognize in Watteau's *fêtes*);
> while the other, in gentle fervor, testified to a faith and joy that
> seemed to negate his decrepitude. (42)

Another memoir, "A Lost Poem"(147–48), reveals the same syn-
thesizing imagination at work in her poetry. She bemoans the loss
of "Cathedral of Pearls," a poem based on a dream that fused images of a Florentine cathedral with images of jeweled carved saints
in Peru or Brazil. In the dream the cathedral's facade is a cliff entirely encrusted with luminescent pearls that the poor passers-by
affectionately touch. The lost poem captured "the sense of the
murky darkness of the city even in the daylight, the darkness of
the stone in which the pearls were embedded ... and the deep
pleasure that beauty was to those who passed and repassed" (148).
Levertov's memoir attests to her "paradoxical delight" in the moment of vision when darkness enhances beauty.

Levertov also selects and shapes her autobiographical material
to reveal patterns of experience she perceives as an adult. Lost
things and beloved animals are joyfully retrieved from memory.
Two cherished volumes are recalled in "Lost Books" (110–13),
childhood possessions that seem to have augured Levertov's lifetime of travel both real and imagined—*The Griffin*, a story about
three children who recover a "long-lost family treasure" (110–13)
and thereby save the ancestral castle in which they and their im-
poverished mother have been living, and *Heylyn's Cosmography*, a

seventeenth-century text whose maps and descriptions of far-away places she had perused. "Treasure by treasure falls away" (109), writes Levertov in "A Loss"(108–9), where she recalls a suitcase strap given to her by her mother and used by herself in trips all over the world over the course of many years. A tender regard for animals comes to life in "Jinny" (72–73), a memoir of the monkey whose "black and very cold" (72) hand the young Levertov would hold on to in a train: "Jinny gravely passed the hat and I felt as proud to know her personally as if she had been one of the great dancers or actors I was queuing to see. I never saw her again after the war began" (73). In "Mildred" (136–37), Levertov reminisces about the dog she grew up with, a pet whose "expressive eyes" (136) would never be forgotten: "Whatever you are, I enjoyed my encounter with you, and woke from the dream you starred in full of words which would make me remember you" (137).

Also emerging from the memoirs are patterns of relationships forged, broken, and refashioned in later years, such as the one Levertov recalls in "An Encounter—and a Re-Encounter" (65–71). At twelve years of age Levertov walked down to the local Communist Party branch and asked for membership. A party worker named Stan Robertson, who was to fall in love with Levertov's older sister Olga, told the girl that she was too young for membership but that she could sell the *Daily Worker* on Saturdays. Levertov performed the task with gusto. Fifty years later she met Stan Robertson again, and the shadowy memory became a "vivid personality" (71) and friend who would correspond with the poet regularly.

Memoirs of less cordial friendships and acquaintances have surprising poignancy. Levertov's break with her childhood friend Jean Rankin, for example, seems to her in retrospect a loss of innocence, for she titles the memoir "The Last of Childhood—For Jean, In This Life or the Next" (59–65). The friendship with Jean, described as "sensitive, intelligent, imaginative, and a true original" (60), ended abruptly when Levertov with childish self-righteousness lectured her friend for balking at tucking her skirt into her knickers because it was "not ladylike" (61). To the young Levertov "ladylike" meant "kind and proud and honorable," (62) and it had nothing to do with skirts tucked into knickers. She walked away from her friend and refused to forgive her. Over the years Levertov made occasional contact with Jean but lost her address book during the Vietnam War years. The acquaintances Levertov made during her stay in Tonga are conjured up as vividly in "Some

Hours in the Late '70s" (114–36). A motley cast of characters is assembled in this memoir: the two young Australians who have
come to sunbathe, surf, and drink, one of them sick with V.D., and
the "odious" Mrs. Groby, a bigoted woman wrapped in "paranoid
miasma" (122). Thinking about these encounters, Levertov observes "… how fragmented is the human species, and how odd it
is to hold in mind, in some kind of unity of perception, individuals
so mutually unaware" (124). Friendships lost as well as lost oppor-
tunities for friendship find their places in these memoirs.

Even chance encounters, fleeting moments of intersecting
lives, are rendered whole in *Tesserae.* "A Dumbshow" (12–15), for
example, recounts the charming story of Levertov's mother as a
young unmarried woman in Budapest. On the day after her arrival
she waked early at the missionary's flat where she was staying
and, lifting up the newfangled Venetian blinds, spotted across the
way a maid servant airing a featherbed and plumping a feather
pillow on the balcony's balustrade. Along the street came a little
girl and just as she passed under the balustrade the pillow fell in
front of her. The maid had withdrawn; the girl looked up, saw no
one, and ran off with the pillow. For Levertov, the reenactment of
the "dumbshow" her mother had seen again illustrates the poet's
unity of perception. Although Beatrice Levertoff, the little girl, and
the maid brought different perspectives to the event, Levertov's
essay unites their experiences. Writing the memoir, in turn, allows
Levertov to feel a connection to those women: "If that child is
alive, over eighty years old at this moment when I write, I daresay
she remembers the little drama, and whatever events in her life it
may have led to" (14).

"An Early Love" (57–58) similarly captures that sense of life as
an unfolding drama, as when she was "cast as a go-between" (57)
by her sister Olga and a Gypsy suitor. Her "one-line role" telling
the suitor that Olga was looking for him remains with her as part
of an uncompleted script: "I only remember my own regret, my
dreams of writing to tell him—what? Of assuring him *I* was loyal,
I would be glad if he tried again, I would be forever his friend, his
messenger, his ally …" (58). The metaphors of theatre in "A
Dumbshow" and "An Early Love" recall Levertov's poem "The
Chill" (*CB* 5), where a child brought to the theatre for the first time
suddenly realizes in the midst of enchantment that the spectacle
will end. Levertov's stories of loss, like much of her poetry, shiver
with this "chill of patience," the commingled joy and terror with
which the "abyss" of time defines the present moment.

These memoirs are also imaginative "suppositions" of familial life woven into a tapestry of compassion and faith. *Tesserae* confirms the evidence of earlier essays and poems that both Beatrice and Paul Levertoff were a vital part of their daughter's spiritual milieu. Beatrice Levertoff, daughter of Walter Spooner-Jones, M.D., grandson of the Welsh tailor and preacher Angel Jones (*LUC* 238), instilled in Denise Levertov a sense of God's presence in the world. Just before Beatrice Spooner-Jones Levertoff died in 1977, Levertov wrote a brief account of her mother's life. In it she praises her mother's "habits of observation and reflection" (239), her "Tales of Holywell," the Welsh town in which she lived after the age of twelve, and above all, the gift of "vision" she imparted to her daughter ("Beatrice Levertoff," *LUC* 238–43). *Life in the Forest* (1978) sheds additional light on the relationship between Beatrice Levertoff and her daughter. Several poems in that volume seem to be acts of contrition in which Levertov confesses her inadequacies as a grown daughter, a "tower / of iron and ice—love / shrunken in her to a cube of pain / locked in her throat" ("A Daughter (I)," *LF* 27), and bafflement as she witnesses her mother's "laggard death" ("Death Psalm: O Lord of Mysteries," *LF* 40). In the poem "The 90th Year" Levertov writes:

> (It was she who taught me to look;
> to name the flowers when I was still close to the ground,
>   my face level with theirs;
> or to watch the sublime metamorphoses
>   unfold and unfold
> over the walled back gardens of our street....)
>   (*LF* 24)

Implicit in these lines is the child's intuition of her own creatureliness, an insight that would be expressed in Levertov's political poetry as "a sense of the interdependence of all things, a sense of belonging to, rather than dominating, an ecosystem; and of the osmosis, the reciprocal nature, of the sustaining relationship between the parts of an ecosystem" ("Poetry, Prophecy, Survival," *NSE* 152). Although "The 90th Year" acknowledges Beatrice Levertoff's distrust of the flesh as "a shell in which souls were prisoned," it pays tribute to a mother's reverence for life:

> (... with how much gazing
> her life has paid tribute to the world's body!
> How tears of pleasure
> would choke her, when a perfect voice,
> deep or high, clove to its note unfaltering!) (24)

The poem reveals that Beatrice Levertoff kindled her daughter's longing for the "sublime" (24) even as she taught her how to see the evanescent beauty of creation.

The closing lines of "The 90thYear" suggest that the early exposure to Christian mysticism which Levertov acknowledges in *Light Up the Cave* (207) was this essentially Neoplatonic outlook of Beatrice Levertoff. Most telling is the poem's allusion to a work by Teilhard de Chardin, who writes from a tradition of Christian Neoplatonism:

> When I look up
> from her wellworn copy of *The Divine Milieu,*
> which she wants me to read, I see her hand
> loose on the black stem of the magnifying glass,
> she is dozing.
> "I am so tired," she has written to me, "of appreciating
> the gift of life." (25)

A mystical impulse to discover the spirit unifying creation is the maternal legacy in which Levertov maps her grief. The poem honors an imagination which could find great pleasure in natural beauty and yet assert that "'There's nothing less real / than the present'" ("A Soul-Cake," *LF* 41).

That spirituality is evident in the stories Beatrice Levertoff passed along to her daughter. Recounted in memoirs and poems are stories telling of compassionate acts and bringing to life Denise Levertov's maternal ancestors. That Beatrice Levertoff enlarged her daughter's empathy is evident in "Inheritance" (3), an essay in *Tesserae* which sheds light on the poem of the same title. In this memoir, she recalls the story of her mother at five years old being taken by a grandmother in North Wales to a great uncle, a white-bearded fisherman who lived in a tiny cottage. He spoke of having been at Waterloo and having seen Napoleon ride away on his horse. Both a remembering and a re-membering take place as Levertov fits her own life and her relatives into the larger human family: "So I, living in the age of jets and nukes, am separated only by the life span of one person, my mother, from looking into the eyes of a relative who had seen the Emperor at the moment of his defeat; and whose mode of life differed in few respects from that of some ancestor of his (and mine) long before the Norman conquest."

That historical sense also finds expression in "Inheritance" (*DH* 90), a poem that celebrates a maternal legacy of caring and attests to imagination's power to redeem loss. Here the memory of a memory offers Levertov consolation for the loss of her mother. In her nineties Beatrice Levertoff spoke of a village woman who would come down the street to gently cleanse her "grubby face" with soft flannel, while upstairs her stepmother lay in an opiate stupor. The story comes alive in Levertov's poem:

> Those hands, that slow refreshment,
> were so kind, I too,
> another lifetime beyond them,
> shall carry towards my death
> their memory,
> grateful, and longing
> once again to feel them soothe me.

Another memoir in *Tesserae*, "What One Remembers" (138–46), further comments on both the essay and the poem "Inheritance" because it refers to those memorable "proofs of the theory that everyone on earth is only about three people away from everyone else—there being links of some kind between them all" (139). With this idea she remembers how her father would sometimes on joyful occasion break into the Hasidic dancing he had known in his own childhood (144). These "suppositions" of family life bear out Levertov's assertion in an earlier "Autobiographical Sketch" (*NSE* 263) that her early life, more than later intellectual experiences, ignited a desire to write poetry.

The stories of compassion and joy in *Tesserae* reveal the familial roots of Levertov's spiritual imagination. In "A Minor Role" (4) she narrates the story of her Jewish father's conversion to Christianity and marriage to the Welshwoman Beatrice Spooner-Jones. When Paul Levertoff was eight or nine he found a scrap of paper on which he read in Hebrew the story of Christ in the Temple expounding the Scripture to rabbis. He showed the paper to his father who angrily tore it up and told his son to avoid that kind of writing. The boy could not forget the story of the wise child, whom he later recognized at the Jewish seminar and in the free atmosphere of Konigsberg as one of the "false" Messiahs. Turning to the Gospels in German and Hebrew, Paul Levertoff came to believe that Jesus of Nazareth was the true Messiah. After being baptized and living in the house of an Evangelical pastor, Levertoff went to Jerusalem and then to Constantinople, where he met Beatrice Spooner-Jones: "Thus Celt and Jew met in Byzantium" (11). This confluence of traditions left its impression on the Levertoffs' younger daughter. Of Paul Levertoff, she writes:

His religious faith was intense and unwavering—but it was not in order to be absorbed into a Gentile world that he had broken, in sorrow, with his father and mother, but to be, as he believed, the more fully a Jew. In taking, at baptism, the name of Paul, he had expressed his sense of affinity with the most passionately Jewish of the Apostles; he was—and was to so refer to himself all his life—a *Jewish Christian*. (11)

Paul Levertoff's ecumenicism was fertile soil for his daughter's imagination.

Another essay in *Tesserae*, "The Sack Full of Wings" (1–2), supports this view. In the essay Levertov recalls the story of her father's childhood encounter with an old pedlar. Walking through the streets of Orsha, where the poet's father lived, the pedlar always carried a "bulky sack" (1). Paul Levertoff believed the sack was full of wings with which people could fly like birds. Denise Levertov notes that Marc Chagall, born in Vtepsk, painted that same pedlar; like Levertoff he has a sense of the "sack's magic": "Perhaps the constant burden of such a concentration of wings was transmuted into the ability to levitate without stretching and flapping a single pair of them" (1–2). The magic pedlar is the basis of Levertov's poem "Wings in the Pedlar's Pack" (*DH* 89), which recounts Paul Levertoff's discovery of Christianity, and his bold attempt to bring the good news home:

> The certainty of wings: a child's bold heart,
> not, good little *Schul*-boy, Torah or Talmud
> gave it to you, a practical vision:
> wings were needed, why should people
> plod forever on foot, not glide like herons
> through blue and white
> promise unfolding
> over their heads, over
> the river's thawing?
> Therefore the pedlar. (But why did they not
> avail themselves of his wares?)
>
> Later, *ochetz moy*, when you discovered
> wings for your soul, the same bold heart
> empowered you. From Prussia east and
>   southward
> *verst* after *verst* you willed the train to go
>   faster,
> skimming the sails home to the Dnieper valley.
> You bore such news, so longed-for,
> fulfilling a hope so ancient

> it had almost become dry parchment,
>   not hope anymore.
> At the station you hailed a *droshky*,
> greeted the driver like a brother. At last
> there was the street, there was the house:
> but when you arrived
> they would not listen.
> They laughed at you. And then they wept.
> But would not listen.

The pedlar engages the boy's imagination: wings make travelling easier so that people can "glide" rather than "plod." The child does not yet realize that he has grasped the essence of Incarnation, embodied spirit, "vision" made "practical." Christ the "heron" offers the promise of new life ("blue and white" suggest the traditional colors of the Virgin) to those who will accept the pedlar's wings. They acquire a spiritual imagination allowing them to see the spirit dwelling within creation, just as Paul Levertoff sees with certainty wings within the sack.

For Denise Levertov acts of imagination requite divine love and allow the simple acts of everyday life to be imbued with faith. As she observes in the essay "Work That Enfaiths" (*NSE* 249), the spiritual imagination is what links her own pilgrimages of faith and art. Together "The Sack Full of Wings" and "Wings in the Pedlar's Pack" seem a paradigm of those interlocking journeys. The essay links faith to imagination, a boy's vision of wings in a packed sack; the poem narrates his eager journey home with the expectation that his news of the Messiah will be received jubilantly, an expectation denied when no one listens to his message. Paul Levertoff thus takes on the role of prophet in announcing his discovery of the true Messiah; the possibility of being ignored does not even occur to him; nothing deters him from uttering his message. In this sense he represents Denise Levertov's idea of the artist as prophet, one who does not necessarily predict but who stimulates the spiritual imagination of others. As Levertov notes in the essay "Poetry, Prophecy, Survival," some biblical scholars list four types of Old Testament prophecy, "*Threat, Promise, Reproach*, and *Admonition*" (*NSE* 147), and poetry frequently partakes of these utterances. Her conviction that such prophecy must be uttered "powerfully" if it is to move others, that it must "*sing* in some way" (*NSE* 148), suggests that she saw her artistic career as a continuation of Paul Levertoff's ministry. That identification with her father as a prophet who "powerfully" speaks words of witness seems most fully realized in Levertov's mature poetry.

Levertov's "memoirs and suppositions" recount the poet's lifelong efforts to fulfill the demands of *seeing*. Aware of myriad patterns of creation, the child grows into the poet who pays "tribute to the world's body" and in so doing pays tribute to her parents and mentors. Combining intuitive with factual truths, Levertov's "suppositions" implicitly honor the "transformation and activating of conscious and unconscious experience brought about by the Imagination" and sought by the protean poet as father/mother to the word ("Horses with Wings" *NSE* 111). Like Pegasus, Denise Levertov drew her energy as an artist from gifts of her entire being; love and loss alike taught her how to see the world. *Tesserae* is a testament of praise for all who nurtured her creative spirit.

Works Cited

Carruth, Hayden. "What 'Organic' Means?" *Sagetrieb* 4 (1985): 145–46.

Levertov, Denise. *Breathing the Water*. New York: New Directions, 1987.

———. *Candles in Babylon*. New York: New Directions, 1982.

———. *A Door in the Hive*. New York: New Directions, 1989.

———. *Life in the Forest*. New York: New Directions, 1978.

———. *Light Up the Cave*. New York: New Directions, 1981.

———. *New & Selected Essays*. New York: New Directions, 1992.

———. *Tesserae: Memories & Suppositions*. New York: New Directions, 1995.

Zlotkowski, Edward. "In the Garden: A Place of Creation." *Denise Levertov*. Ed. Albert Gelpi. Ann Arbor: U of Michigan P, 1993. 303–20.

Denise Levertov and the Jacob's Ladder

Jerome Mazzaro

I first met Denise Levertov in the Spring of 1962. She had been
invited to participate in what was then known as the Detroit Adventure Series. *The Jacob's Ladder* had been published the year before to both popular and critical acclaim. A friend, the poet Sheila
Pritchard, had been corresponding with her and asked me to join
them and provide transportation for the visit. We picked Denny
up at the airport and almost immediately, the three of us struck up
a long and ranging, warm conversation. Denny filled us in on the
particulars of her flight, and learning that I taught at a college, she
told of friends in Pennsylvania with whom she had a great and
supportive relationship. She also spoke of her visits to William
Carlos Williams and how she often read to the now nearly blind
poet. Despite his condition, he was quick, she said, at detecting
false notes in her work. She related, too, that recently another
young poet, Robert Bly, promised to take the Williamses on an
outing to New York City and that, on the appointed day, they
dressed and waited and waited, and he never showed. At the lun-
cheon for the series participants, Henri Peyre, the distinguished
French critic and a fellow invitee, whispered across the table of his
great admiration for Denny's work. It being a lovely day, we drove
after lunch at Denny's interest to the Botanical Gardens at Belle
Isle. There, among various plants, we came across some Jacob's
ladder (*Polemoniaceae humile*), and being the title of her last collection, we commented briefly on it. She showed previous knowledge
of the flower, although, as she noted in her prefatory note, the Jacob's ladder of the volume had more to do with the biblical account and Martin Buber's *Tales of the Hasidim*. I have long since
found the multiple meanings of the expression ideally suited to the
natural and spiritual leanings, that, in *Light up the Cave* (1981),
Denny associates with her mother and father.

The origin of the angelic or Jacob's ladder lies in Genesis 28:12. It appears in a dream to Jacob, who is fleeing his homeland and his brother Esau's anger. Earlier Jacob had deceived his father Isaac by securing a blessing that by custom should have gone to the first-born Esau. At what is to become Bethel, Jacob takes a stone, places it under his head, and falls asleep. In his dream, he dreams of a ladder "set on the earth" whose top "reached to heaven" and on which "angels of God were ascending and descending." The ladder is, of course, an emblem of hierarchy, an ordering by levels or grades that seems to be deeply ingrained in nature, society, and religion. That the image should appear soon after a religious and social order has been violated makes psychological sense. Much as in Levertov's poetry, the dream is interpreted as "in the midst of ignorance and evil there is still the possibility of a saving revelation." It epitomizes the wonder of Hebrew faith and hope (*Interpreter's* 690). Frequently paired with the incident is—again as it is in Levertov's poetry—a second incident occurring at Jacob's return to his homeland and meeting with Esau. At what is to become Peniel, Jacob meets a supernatural figure, called variously God and an angel (Genesis 32:28, 30 and 48:15–16), and as interpreted by theologians, a figure representing not the Father but the Son of God. The two grapple all night, and just before dawn, the figure asks to be released. Jacob refuses until a blessing has been conferred. Jacob is blessed and given the name Israel ("soldier of God"). In addition to reflecting a spiritual crisis, the struggle indicates a certain gained privileged status and assurance that others will not have destructive powers over one.

With pseudo-Dionysius and John Climacus' *Ladder of Paradise*, "Jacob's ladder" takes on the force of a Christian parallel to the Homeric hierarchic Great Chain of Being. It posits an order for the universe that suits a growing Neo-Platonism. The "ladder" conveys how, through discipline, one may achieve virtues that aid one's spiritual perfection. The idea enters Saint Benedict's *Rule of Monks* and is subsequently taken over by Hugh and the mystical School of St. Victor so that ideally one is encouraged to rise from action to contemplation and from matter to spirit, achieving in the process greater free will and likeness to God. Through sermons and works like Saint Bernard's *Sermons on 'The Song of Songs,'* Thomas Aquinas' *Summa Theologica*, Saint Bonaventure's *The Mind's Road to God*, Dante's *Divine Comedy*, and the pseudo-Bonaventuran *Meditations on the Life of Christ*, the image entered the general imagination, and in Renaissance Neo-Platonism, it attached itself to the person of the poet as *magus* and/or *alter deus*. By special insight and mastery of craft, the poet would rise in vision and understanding above the common outlook. Along with other poets of her generation as well as poets of other generations, Levertov presents herself in this image of the writer. It is an image, moreover, that assumes obligations as well as privileges. Levertov rejects for the most part the false and fictive world that the Renaissance associates with narrative or epical verse. Instead, she chooses the real world of the lyric to uncover God's laws and harmonies and, when finding the world not in compliance, to attack its misconceptions and urge that it reform.

The title poem of *The Jacob's Ladder* presents the ladder as a stairway not "for angels' feet" but of "a rosy stone," whose sheen gains "because behind it the sky is a doubtful, a doubting / night gray" (*Pl* 39). This doubt or questioning of hierarchy will become the focus of two later poems bearing on the apostle Thomas. Situated in a time of terror not only "of what we know" but also "of what we do not know" and "of not knowing," "Mass for the Day of St. Thomas Didymus" from *Candles in Babylon* (1984) indicates that man's "hope lies / in the unknown / in our unknowing" (*CB* 108–9). The "dream" is "of goodwill, of peace on earth" (109). Insisting on the reality of nature and the spirit, modern man, like the saint, both believes and doubts, "interrupt[ing] belief with / doubt" and "doubt with belief" (110). "Blesséd is that which utters / its being" (112), the service goes on to say, and, in the image of Christ as "Agnus Dei," "Mass" ends with a plea to shield that "weak / animal" (114) with "something human" (115). Playing upon *didymus* as "twin," "St. Thomas Didymus" from *A Door in the Hive* (1989) combines versions of the Gospel stories of John 4:46–53 and 20:24–28 into a mirror image for man. Expressing unbelief, "doubting" Thomas responds to suffering which, when alleviated first from a child and then from Christ, allows him the "light" that, while not ending his doubt, gives him "its part / in a vast unfolding design" (*DH* 103). Indeed, in echoes of Matthew Arnold and Friedrich Nietzsche, Levertov appears in these poems to believe that, in the shaking of creeds and questioning of accredited dogma, it is the function of art to interpret, console, and sustain by turning "nauseous thoughts about the horror or absurdity of existence into notions with which one can live" (Nietzsche 60 and Arnold 2).

In "The Jacob's Ladder," this function of art as reaffirming hierarchy is emphasized in the stones of the stairway forming "sharp

/ angles … that the angels must spring / down … and a man climbing / must scrape his knees" (*P1* 39). Levertov makes the ascent "the poem" (39). She thus turns the stone or stones of Genesis 28:11 into something like the Objectivists' association of poetic language with stones that are to be cleaned of their smudges, "washed, dried, and placed right side up" and then made into "parts of nature" (Williams, *Selected Essays* 128 and *Imaginations* 102). Rather than Jacob's "dream," Levertov's stairway is *in nature* and humanly and "solidly built." It implies a pattern of behavior that is as deliberate as that which Benedict prescribes in his *Rule* and that, as Rabbi Moshe of Kobryn indicates, involves "every man." Being of clay and having a soul that "reaches to heaven," man through his actions witnesses adumbrations of Jacob's ascending and descending angels (*P1* 2). However, unlike the "truths" of Objectivist art, "light" is reached not by means of scientific detachment but by the depersonalizations of belief. Most of Levertov's pleas for activism turn into pleas against destruction and destructive reasoning, and her spiritual revelations of God's "vast unfolding design" are linked to artistic endeavors. Like those of medieval writers, her "ladders" occur either, as in Bernard and Aquinas, as movement toward and away from contemplation or, as in Benedict and Dante, as a means of asserting spiritual improvement. *Breathing the Water* (1987), for instance, will begin with a "Variation on a Theme by Rilke." *Evening Train* (1992), in contrast, will begin more straightforwardly in nature and its illuminations and rise to spiritual affirmations and revelations.

The image of the Jacob's ladder will likewise inform "A Calvary Path" in *A Door in the Hive*. In a return of doubt, what earlier had been a "ladder of stone" here becomes a "ladder of roots" (*DH* 94). "Stone steps" have faltered "and come to an end / but the hillside [still] rises." Few come now to the place, but those who do are drawn onward, coaxed to climb "up to the last / cross of the calvary" (94). As with Bonaventure and John Calvin before her, the image has become one of Christ Who is the mediator between man and God. "Where Is the Angel?" pairs this ladder with Jacob's angelic encounter upon his return home. Again angels are linked to the writer's craft. The speaker asks, "Where is the angel // to wrestle with me and wound / not my thigh but my throat, / so curses and blessings flow storming out?" (53). In "Three Meditations" from *The Jacob's Ladder*, an angel had been linked to poetry in the person of Caedmon, the first English Christian poet, and the link is repeated in "Caedmon" from *Breathing the Water*. Relying ultimately for both poems on Bede's account in his *Ecclesiastical History* of the poet's awakening to his calling and privileged status, Levertov relates Caedmon's move from silence to song—called "talk" in the later poem—as having resulted from a capitalized "One" or a "sudden angel" who "affrighted" him (*P2* 31 and *BW* 65). But, lest one conclude that only poets are to be visited by angels, "For Those Whom the Gods Love Less" in *Sands of the Well* (1996) extends these angelic visitations to artists in other fields. The poem asks readers to remember the French painter Paul Cézanne whose Mont Sainte-Victoire is the "tireless noonday angel he grappled like Jacob, / demanding reluctant blessing" (96).

Often, as in the case of the Rilke variations, these "angelic" encounters will be treated by Levertov as indirect or mediated illuminations. Foremost among the sources for these illuminations are incidents taken from the Bible like those involving Jacob, Tobias, and St. Thomas Didymus; but, as indicated, these mediated discoveries can extend to the works and lives of other writers as well as to the works of painters and mystics. "Variations on a Theme by Rilke" (*The Book of Hours*, I, 4) mentions Giotto, Van Eyck, Rembrandt, and Rouault whose images and "inspired depictions, / are true" (*BW* 71). "The Servant-Girl at Emmaus" acknowledges its inspiration from a painting by Velazquez (66), and, even when not citing a specific painter or painting, as in "Nativity: An Altarpiece" and "Annunciation," the poems' debts to art are clear either by title—"An Altarpiece"—or by assertions like "We know the scene: the room, variously furnished, / almost always a lectern, a book; always / the tall lily" (*DH* 86). Dame Julian of Norwich figures prominently among the mystics whose writings Levertov relies on, but they also include other religious people like Thomas Merton and Brother Lawrence. In "Contrasting Gestures," Levertov is careful to distinguish the desire of her mystics for "submersion / to transform them" from the artists' wish not to have "themselves transformed / but their work." Their desire is "to be / subsumed, consumed utterly / into their work" (*ET* 100), and one assumes that this desire for consummation is true, too, for Levertov, at least in terms of God's "vast unfolding design." Interactions with nature and natural illuminations are another matter: They appear to exist directly in what the poet perceives as a full acceptance of "undoubtable being" (*ET* 45).

Levertov makes clear as early as *The Jacob's Ladder* that what she wishes from this acceptance of "undoubtable being" is "joy"— "the recognition, the known / appearing fully itself, and / more itself than one knew" (*P1* 59). In subsequent volumes "being" and "joy" will be linked to "awe" (*ET* 101) and challenged by "tears and sweat" (*BW* 82), greed, exploitation, violence (*DH* 36), and stupidity (*ET* 101). Man's "tragic error" becomes his trying to imagine unassisted by angels an "unhampered" place, "contrived by [himself] … 'outside of nature,'" a triumph of his own reason (*DH* 44). The "place" will be determined by science not art (*ET* 20). In pursuit of it, man will ignore his real "task" which "was to have been / to love the earth, / to *dress and keep it* like Eden's garden" (*ET* 69). This perceived opposition of forces and ignorance feeds into a large "double vision" in which "places / reveal … their longings," giving rise to doubt as well as moments when one comes "to perceive the more that there is" (*SW* 63) as well as "what is fleeting and what remains / outside of time" (*SW* 63). "Our longing," Levertov maintains, "is for Peace and the works of Peace" (*DH* 37). In almost Neo-Platonic fashion, God appears as "the air enveloping the whole / globe of being" (*SW* 107), a "transparency" which "seen for itself … enable[s] / perception not of itself" (*SW* 124). This "transparency" includes "the dead" whose "weight" is both absence and a sense of what was not available to them (*SW* 62). Her inclination is to see life and the things of life increasingly as "gifts," and given the swings of "human passion," the "mystery" is "that there is anything—anything at all" and that God "still / hour by hour sustains it" (*SW* 129).

On that day in 1962, few if any could foresee the direction that either the country or Denny would go in. President Kennedy's assassination, Vietnam, the power of the Civil Rights Movement, Berkeley, El Salvador lay beyond one's imagination, as did Denny's moves away from the projective verse of her early volumes with their emphases on immanence and a natural interaction and magic that she shared with H.D., D.H. Lawrence, and Robert Duncan. Despite the "absurd angel of happiness … dressed for laughs as a plasterer" (*P1* 12) and hints of hierarchy and divine order in some of the epigraphs and phrases, the weight of *The Jacob's Ladder* is decidedly earthbound. The Muse is envisioned at a lake in "The Well" and "The Illustration," and there is a sense of depth psychology lurking in the probings of those poems as well as in "Clouds" and in the volume's surreal imagery. While not "common speech," the book's language certainly did not appear to be headed toward "the uncommon speech of paradise" (*P1* 5). Bears pissed, groans drove through windows, children were murdered. For a young poet trying to learn his craft, the book's appeal was its descriptive power, its attention to voice patterns, and its depictions of urban life, landscape, and animal behavior. "The Rainwalkers," "From the Roof," "The Tide," and "The Depths" struck me as remarkable poems, and "Night on Hatchet Cove" with its lively language was a textbook. There was profundity as well in "During the Eichmann Trial," and despite a similarity to Dylan Thomas' work "'… Else a great Prince in prison lies'" seemed a very successful effort. Like other poets of her generation, she appeared to be expanding and redefining the form and subject matter of verse away from the formalism and pseudo-logical imitations of the Metaphysicals that I had been exposed to at the Iowa Workshop. The book was a revelation that only slowly and incrementally I was able to adapt to aspects of my own vision.

Sheila and I and others hoped that *The Jacob's Ladder* would get that year's Pulitzer Prize for poetry. It did not, and rumor was that Richard Wilbur had prevented its being so honored. That fall I moved to Cortland, New York, and was fortunate to meet with and hear Denny again in Ithaca when she read at Sage Chapel. Later, in the Spring of 1963, she offered me her and Mitch's flat on Greenwich for the summer. They would be away, and she wanted someone to take care of her plants. I visited her once at the apartment to decline the offer. There were plants, but the apartment was not overwhelmed by them. I had received a grant from the Research Foundation of the State University of New York to complete my Juvenal translations. I had put off work on them to finish my Ph.D., and I felt that by staying in Cortland away from distractions I might complete the project. About this time, I wrote a poem, "The Visiting Poet," that recalled her visits to Detroit and Ithaca. The poem was later published in John Logan's *Choice* and reprinted in my collection, *The Caves of Love* (1985). I remember that Denny objected to my depiction of her as a refugee, perhaps as imprecise or as having hit a sore spot. She was a British war bride. I had meant to suggest that, in America at that time, all poets were displaced people, especially one deplaning in Detroit. She did not object, however, to the poem's emphasis on flowers or to my casting her as a kind of Flora who, like the poem's flowers, profoundly touches the lives of those who hear her. Nor did I see then that the two settings—Belle Isle's Botanical Gardens and Sage Chapel—were to become the poles of nature and "vast unfolding design" that describe her later vision.

"The Visiting Poet" is written in the formal manner of much of my early poetry, and since it is not widely accessible today, I reprint it here:

The Visiting Poet
(for Denise Levertov)

Magically where you move
flowers spring to blossom. So from the first,
   in Detroit, alighting from the plane,
      your corsage giving sign
of all the varied flowers yet to burst—
      iris, daisy, foxglove—
         you stunned reason.

You stood nervous, intent,
marked off by strain from the hard traveler,
   like a refugee just orphaned
      by a journey, in hand
your books as tag, and we two, too eager,
      armed with our compliment,
         played being friend.

First at Belle Isle, among
the Jacob's ladder and red slipperwort,
   we went searching ferns and cacti
      as a makeshift family
who tested through the hours of that trial visit
      how we might get along,
         and proved happy.

Again in Sage Chapel
in Ithaca, as the stained-glass windows
   burst like gardens in our seeing,
      voiding a year's being,
we breathed old fragrances in new echoes
      of a thudding footfall,
         still agreeing.

Proved by these cases, caught
like those charmed, rooted trees of Orpheus
   or David's Saul, our beings stir
      like an ending winter
to flowers of your rich, mind-seeding voice,
      whose nurtured words, grown taut,
         move as aster. (16–17)

After 1963, I did not see Denny again, though I felt I was in touch by following reports of her doings and reading her volumes when I could.

Works Cited

Arnold, Matthew. "The Study of Poetry." In *Essays in Criticism: Second Series*. London: Macmillan and Co., 1888.

The Interpreter's Bible. Vol. I. New York: Abington-Cokesbury Press, 1952.

Levertov, Denise. *Breathing the Water*. New York: New Directions, 1987.

———. *Candles in Babylon*. New York: New Directions, 1984.

———. *A Door in the Hive*. New York: New Directions, 1989.

———. *Evening Train*. New York: New Directions, 1989.

———. *Poems 1960–1967*. New York: New Directions, 1983.

———. *Sands of the Well*. New York: New Directions, 1996.

Mazzaro, Jerome. *The Caves of Love*. Aptos, CA: Jazz Press, 1985.

Nietzsche, Friedrich. *The Birth of Tragedy and the Case of Wagner*. Trans. Walter Kaufmann. New York: Vintage Books, 1967.

Williams, William Carlos. *Imaginations*. New York: New Directions, 1979.

———. *Selected Essays*. New York: Random House, 1954.

Setting Denise Levertov's High Drama to Music for High Liturgy

Karen Marie Fuchs

A composer faces many challenges of interpretation when setting someone else's words to music, even if the words are organized into a poem. Although poetry involves many elements common to music, like tone, rhythm, stress, themes and phraseology, the composer must also consider other building blocks particular to music. Such concerns as time values, instrumentation, key signatures, harmony, melody, musical genres and dynamics (fluctuations of loud and soft) come into play when creating organized sound. When working with a poem by Denise Levertov, who writes in organic form rather than regular, traditional meters, the composer faces additional problems when interpreting the rhythmic patterns. Fortunately, Levertov has written extensively and lucidly, often in musical images, about her poetic techniques. Her essays, as well as other means of interpreting poetry, helped me compose a musical setting for Levertov's "On a Theme from Julian's Chapter XX," from her 1987 collection *Breathing the Water* (68–69).

The setting for which I conceived this piece is the Roman Catholic liturgy for Good Friday. Knowing the rituals involved in this rite makes immediately clear why I seized upon this particular Levertov poem as the perfect verbal expression of what this ritual is supposed to evoke in the assembled "body of Christ." The altar is stripped and bare of any ornamentation or decoration. There are no plants or floral bouquets. The crucifix is draped in a crimson red shroud. Everyone observes silence in preparation for the most solemn night of the Catholic church's liturgy. The preceding evening on Maundy Thursday the Blessed Sacrament has been removed from the church to an altar of repose in another building. On Good Friday the priests and deacons enter solemnly and silently, process down the central aisle, and prostrate themselves on the floor before the bare altar.

When the Blessed Sacrament is returned to the sanctuary, we do not celebrate the full liturgy of the mass; only the Lord's Prayer is spoken; and only one element is offered, Christ's body in the bread. A somber hymn closes this starkest of liturgies. No moment is more poignant in Catholic ritual, and it is at this point that the Levertov poem is offered up musically. No setting could form a more reflective backdrop for her words drawn from St. Julian's twentieth chapter. No more suitable liturgical framework exists in which to hear her terse, compact, yet sweeping apprehension of the problem of pain inherent in the human condition and Christ's complete embrace of it and us.

Basic questions the composer must ask before translating the poem to music are those the reader must also consider in interpreting the poem: What is the tone? What are Levertov's themes? How are these conveyed? "On a Theme for Julian's Chapter XX" is the perfect verbal expression of what the Good Friday liturgy should evoke. The tone of the poem is dark and somber, with dramatic undercurrents and searing lines ("immemorial branding iron, / electric prod" [ll. 11–12]). The poem deals with two of Levertov's major themes, pain and suffering, as the speaker raises *the* central question of Christianity: Why does Jesus' suffering matter when considered beside all the pain and torment human beings have suffered and still suffer? To suit the tone and themes of the poem, I chose a dark, somber minor key, G minor, for two reasons: the first one a practical musical consideration and the second purely subjective. First, I had to accommodate limitations of range (that is, the lows and highs of pitch possible for the human voice) because the piece would be performed by a traditional, four-part choir of mixed men's and women's voices serving in the capacity of a Greek chorus and musical backdrop for a dramatic soprano soloist. Secondly, I *like* G minor because its flavor suggests drama and pathos to my ears, a subjective choice that suits my own ways of expressing and hearing things. I chose a sparse, but important accompaniment, a synthesized sound that combines the clarity of piano with ethereal strings that swell and fade. The desired effect is for the listener to float in time: to be at Golgotha and "in the hospital ward they reserve / for the most abused" (ll. 14–15) simultaneously. The basic musical plan is to use the choir as an austere musical background for startling, shocking musical leaps by the soprano soloist.

Levertov's essay "On the Function of the Line," from *Light Up the Cave*, is especially helpful in understanding her techniques and translating her poetry to music. Levertov compares the poem to a musical "score," as it provides, in particular through the linebreaks, "visual instructions for auditory effects" (64). Linebreaks contribute to both the rhythm and the "*melos* of the poem" (63). Linebreaks, indentions, and "other devices of scoring" establish and control the rhythm of the line by "record[ing] the slight (but meaningful) hesitations between word and word that are characteristic of the mind's dance among perceptions but which are not noted by grammatical punctuation" (62). Levertov uses the linebreak as an "alogical, parallel (not competitive) punctuation" or "a form of punctuation *additional* to the punctuation that forms part of the logic of completed thoughts" (62). The interaction of the "alogical counter-rhythm" and "the logical rhythm of syntax" produce "an effect closer to song than to statement, closer to dance than to walking" (62–63). Levertov also uses the linebreak to create melody in a different way. Where the line ends influences the pitch patterns: "The intonation, the ups and down of the voice, involuntarily change as the rhythm (altered by the place where the tiny pause or musical 'rest' takes place) changes" (65). Like anyone else who wants to get the full effect of the poems, the composer can hear the rhythm and melody Levertov has created by reading the poems aloud.

Drama in music does not happen by chance; musical effects are evoked both by inspiration and design. Musical components such as rhythm and pitch create physical and emotional reactions in listeners that to some degree can be predicted. How well a composer anticipates those responses is an indication of how skillful (and/or inspired) she is at her craft. Guided by Levertov's dicta, I was able to create musical phrases. For instance, because the first and third lines describing Christ's suffering on the cross end with "yes," in an odd positioning of a word that usually begins a sentence, the meat of these phrases is introduced starkly and without accompaniment by the soprano soloist. The choir then sings that last word "Yes" as a kind of musical exclamation point.

The choir as "chorus" is chosen to sing portions of text that comprise a cohesive section of thought, such as the passage beginning in line 6 with rhetorical questions:

In this context the choir is representing the universal community of believers with their doubts about the meaning of Christ's crucifixion, which continue:

> Torture then, torture now,
> the same, the pain's the same,
> immemorial branding iron,
> electric prod.

The word "torture," repeated in line 9 to stress the agony, begins on the same note both times for emphasis and for the heavy effect that word demands.

At the end of the passage the soloist inserts shock value, which seems appropriate for the phrase "electric prod," with the jarring, huge, and extreme leap of a ninth.

"Electric prod" is a quintessential Levertov choice of words, not a term a listener expects to hear couched among spiritual thoughts and certainly not in a religious setting. The soloist's shriek undergirds this poet's drama.

In the passage beginning with "This air we're breathing" in line 16 and continuing through line 25, Levertov hammers away at the sweeping idea of all the pain, suffering, and injustice the human race has endured since its beginning. She points over and over to our collective grief and agony as if to minimize the torment of just one person, Christ. One touch that seemed especially fortuitous was fitting two lines in this section—"and in the ancient dust of the world / what particles / of the long tormented"—to the first two lines of the "Pange Lingua," an ancient chant used musically to allegorize the ancient remains of those long dead.

This entire ten-line passage, given to the choir, again acting as the community of believers, ends the series of faith-questions on suffering.

The second half of the poem introduces Julian's understanding of the uniqueness of Jesus' suffering: "One only is 'King of Grief.'" With that line the choir becomes a more active participant and continues in dialogue with the soprano to convey Julian's insight:

> *The oneing,* she saw, *the oneing*
> *with the Godhead* opened Him utterly
> to the pain of all minds, all bodies
> . . . .
> empowered Him to endure
> inside of history,
> through those hours when He took to Himself
> the sum total of anguish and drank
> even the lees of that cup....

To contrast the pathos and sad quality of the minor key of the rest of the passage, the word "cup"—a powerful image for Catholic Christians, a reminder of Christ's blood-sacrifice—ends on a major tonality, which because of its construction produces an open, expansive, final, affirmative sound.

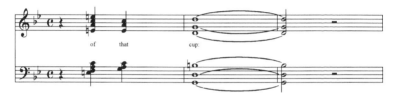

Levertov's final stanza, set off by double spacing, contains the loveliest, most comforting images in the poem: The phrase "within the mesh of the web, Himself / woven within it, yet seeing it, / seeing it whole." The phrase "within the mesh of the web," sung harmonically by the choir, is sustained while the soloist interjects "Himself"—musically picturing someone enmeshed in a web. Then the soloist breaks away to illustrate that while He is in the web, He can still see it "whole," as from a distance.

The piece ends with Levertov's final exquisite lines describing Jesus' complete union with us in our humanity: "*Every sorrow and desolation / He saw, and sorrowed in kinship.*" The soprano sings "in kinship" in the minor key, and then the choir enters, ending the piece by repeating the same two chords in a G *major*, an uplifting major tonality intended to convey the hope and comfort to listeners that serve as a possible answer to Levertov's earlier searing questions.

It is fitting that Levertov chose the Roman Catholic liturgy in which to express her conversion to Christianity; reading her "On a Theme from Julian's Chapter XX" helps us understand a slice of Levertov's personal faith-journey. Her words and understanding are the finale, the coda, the great Amen, so to speak, to this moment of high drama remembering and celebrating the Lord's unspeakable gift of His humanity in suffering.

Wisdom Hath Builded Her House

Anne Waldman

> who wouldn't want
> to put their lips to the true chalice?
>
> from "The Cult of Relics" (*SW* 72)

Myriad questions are asked of this poet, even after her death, about her faith, her conversion, her "belief in the physical resurrection of Jesus," as she titles a late poem. Questions concerning the efficacies of such fiercely humble faith, how transubstantiation affirms language (can it?), how language might suffer at the edge of conviction, content, message, at the foot of a deity one kneels before, diminished, *subjected* towards. Submissive. Isn't this a private matter? What is the prejudice? Is it a pre-conceived male god she imagines she experiences, one asks? Is that Denise Levertov's imago? Her Grail? Muse? She whose political conviction & poetry inscribed & thereby seemingly transcended gender, who was reckoned primordially feminist by nature. The powers of faith run deep—they say—so that one might possibly lose sense of perspective, rational reference point & intellect. The poem won't abide props, is that it? It must dwell always in a perpetual state of Negative Capability. (This poet certainly accepts this condition). But isn't true faith beyond an irritable reaching after fact and reason? No room for Absolute Reality! All poets are "sinners" anyway.

> As if the world were a thought
> God was thinking and then
> not thinking. Divine attention
> turned away.
> from "The Danger Moments"
> (*SW* 10)

233

What are the contradictions for us as witness to Levertov's rare
poetic gifts, spanning a long life, particular & generous, whose
personal conviction in her poetry—especially during the Vietnam
War period—already led to dissembling among the post-modern
ranks. Levertov was never to waver in her strong social-political-
environmental conscience. However, during the 1960s as she
became more active, the poetry was perceived as strident,
righteous, and content-driven. Of course the perennial rub is: what
is poetry's role? May the making of it really ever be subsumed by
an overriding purpose, agenda, theism. Doesn't poetry by its
nature, as something "made," both mirror a greater creation and
subvert divine origin? Is the poet, on the other hand, a mere vessel,
a conduit, for a higher power & inspiration, which might
conceivably be a stubbornly fixed mentality, praxis, belief system?
Did Pound's obsession with usury make him any less a poet?
Doesn't the current trend and fashion away from confessionalism,
first person narrative and an embrace of language for language's
sake also suggest a kind of subversive dogma? Who are the
religious poets? What is the "cost" there? Does one's religion
ultimately count/ matter to the poetry? Or is the poetry an
expression of possession, faith, ecstasy, as in the case of the Sufi
mystic Rumi or passionate Hindu Mirabai? Julian of Norwich,
Dante, John Donne ("Holy Sonnets") and all the lush
metaphysicians, John Clare, T.S. Eliot, St. John Perse, the Buddhist
Allen Ginsberg. And what about all the romantic pantheists?
Examine less secular forms: psalm, hymn, *doha* (Buddhist poem of
"realization"), proverb, allegory, litany. Study the probing
"intellectus" of Sor Juana. Levertov saw her own poetry, her
"song" as a salutary act:

> an equalization of
> hazards
> bringing the poet
> back to song
> as before
>
> to sing of death
> as before
> and life, while he
> has it, energy
>
> being in him a singing,
> a beating of gongs, efficacious
> to drive away devils.
>   from "Three Meditations" (*JL* 31)

What is the problem, after all, with a religious "gaze" for the work? None, I would suggest if the poems succeed as kinetic universes, as life-in-language, not begging questions, preaching, proselytizing (she never does proselytize). Perhaps the needling questions continue because Levertov seemed to be something else for much of her poetic life—radical, freethinker, a New American Poet who kept company with Robert Duncan, Robert Creeley. Her essays "Some Notes on Organic Form" (1965) and "On the Function of the Line" (1979) were, and continue to be, defining post-modernist texts.

> The beginning of the fulfillment of this demand [to make a poem] is to contemplate, to meditate; words which connote a state in which the heat of feeling warms the intellect. To contemplate comes from "*templum*, temple, a place, a space for observation marked out by the augur." It means not simply to observe, to regard, but to do these things in the presence of a god.
>
> from "Some Notes On Organic Form" (*PW* 8)

Levertov herself in an extremely cogent essay "A Poet's View" (1984) addresses these very questions concerning the relation between her "religious and intellectual position" and whether it is satisfactory to her. She first defines her intellectual creed:

> I believe: that the primary impulse of the artist is to make autonomous things from the materials of a particular art; and in the obligation of the artist to adhere to a particular vision, to the inspired experience, and not make merely cosmetic "improvements." I believe in the obligation to work from within. (*NSE* 240)

She then moves from the aesthetic into the ethical:

> I believe: that artists, particularly writers, have social responsibilities, at least of a negative kind, i.e., even if incapable of undertaking social actions related to the implications of their productions, they should refrain, at least, from betraying such implications. (*NSE* 240)

She concludes her affirmation with a belief in the artistic obligation to nurture the creative gift "in a degree proportionate to the strength and demands of the gift" (which, paradoxically, when the very fact of life itself, of the existence of anything at all, is so astounding may mean imbalance and sacrifice "in other areas of life").

Her treatise moves into a discussion of the inviolate "mystery" that accompanies the creative act:

> Why, why—I asked myself—should I withhold my belief in God or the claims of Christianity until I am able to explain to myself the discrepancy between the suffering of the innocent, on the one hand, and the assertions that God is just and merciful on the other? Why should I for one moment suppose that I or any other human mind can comprehend paradoxes too vast to fit our mental capacities and, thus, never perceived in their entirety? Wasn't it as if I were scolding the Almighty, refusing my acknowledgement until provided with guarantees? What if I began to act as if I did believe, without waiting for intellectual clarity—that is, what if I prayed, worshipped, participated in the rituals of the Church? Might not faith follow? (*NSE* 242)

and then on, in spite of her reluctance to *define* her religious beliefs, into a more personal narrative—which includes the "emotional influence" of her "Jewish-Christian roots"—of a gradual coming to God and "the claims of Christianity." She finds that "an avowal of Christian faith is not incompatible with my aesthetic nor with my political stance." Levertov never joined a political party. She remained ecumenical. She would choose "works over faith." She was drawn to the radical element in the Catholic Church, however—the Catholic Worker movement, Liberation Theology. "I simply cannot enter a ready-made structure." "I am by nature, heritage, and as an artist, forever a stranger and pilgrim." Peregrinations shaped her faith.

She has cited "The Thread," an early poem (1960s), testifying to the presence of a force she was conscious of but unable to name:

> Was it
> not long ago this thread
> began to draw me? Or
> way back? Was I
> born with its knot about my
> neck, a bridle?

The last section from her book *Sands of the Well*, entitled "Close to a Lake," is a cluster of her late, extremely straightforward religious poems. Yet "On Belief in the Physical Resurrection of Jesus" thrums with questions, including:

Are some intricate minds
                    nourished
                              on concept,
as epiphytes flourish
                high in the canopy?
                              Can they
subsist on the light,
              on the half
                      of metaphor that's not
grounded in dust, grit,
              heavy
                  carnal clay?

                              (*SW* 115)

Rhetorical questions. Yes, she affirms. It can be that simple, an act of living that feeds on spiritual light. Simple, these late works, yet the poems of a pilgrim with an intricate mind, like a tropical orchid or staghorn fern that needs must grow upon another plant or system to survive, but exists up high, in the air. In another poem she identifies with the prayer plant that folds and raises its "many pairs of green hands" in the darkness. No easy answers. I am not sure the poems "succeed" in the sense of a brilliant marriage of form & content, or a balance amongst the *poeias* (logo-, phano-, logo-), but they are the grammar of her mind settled in its assured faith. These later poems remain open for our own mediation or meditation and provoke the curious reader with modesty & conviction:

> Lord, I curl in Thy grey
> gossamer hammock
>
> that swings by one
> elastic thread to thin
> twigs that could, that should
> break but don't
>   from "Psalm Fragments
>   (Schnittke String Trio)" (*SW* 118)

and from "The Beginning Of Wisdom" which refers us to Proverbs 9–10:

> I am so small, a speck of dust
> moving across the huge world. The world
> a speck of dust in the universe.
>   *
> Are you holding
> the universe? You hold

onto my smallness. How do you grasp it,
how does it not
slip away?
                    *
I know so little.
                    *
You have brought me so far.

The Proverbs are a complex read. A syncretic text from Solomon
gives "good doctrine" to the children of Israel, yet bristles with
gnosticism, back of which is the female ur-goddess Sophia, Wisdom. A lot of imagery here of mouth, lips, tongue and the outcome
or fruition of words these vocalizing organs pronounce. A judgment is meted out on their efficacy, their righteousness. The words
of Denise Levertov often concur with this view & carry a similar
responsibility. She was a compassionate woman, a warrior for justice, an exemplary human poet-being.

The mouths of the just bringeth forth wisdom...
from Proverbs 10

Rapt

in memoriam, Denise Levertov

The human clock, the heart and its ally, the lungs, give
unimpeachable testimony of ongoing life.

from "A Prose Summary *First Dream*," Sor Juana
trans. Alan S. Trueblood

liturgy her
        kind ritual
in feedback
of life
        kneels
in art
    audacious
all we can make of it

        never in isolation
but in action with her
    tread

world, whirl
step to
a trans-
formation
she chants
acute detail

spirit flower
a stick, a drum
sacred or secular
to
energize form
to
rhythm
tongued
movement of
creedance

"moonray on a
passing cloud"

in performance
of resistance
you start from scratch
born to the
attritions of time
century of war

where
madness valorizes
discourse

& she speaks out
for a
a wound extrapolated
not a
word not a planet
without dance
or song
never

we go mad in a thinking
     commerce-body
   mark her
    ghostlines
   for
faith
    all's *communitas*

   bow down

Anne Waldman

Wanderer and Pilgrim;
Poet and Person

Paul A. Lacey

"… that there is indeed, in so many writers and readers, that 'deep spiritual longing' Jorie Graham speaks of, seems to underscore the irrelevance to literature, for both writer and reader, of the kind of criticism currently prevalent in the academic world—a criticism which treats works of art as if they were diagrams or merely means provided for the exercise of analysis, rather than what they are: testimonies of the lived life, which is what writers have a vocation to give, and readers … have a need to receive." (*NSE* 20–21)

While I work on this essay, the days grow shorter, long, dark shadows stretch across the harvested fields, bare trees and underbrush turn amber in the waning afternoon light. The winter solstice, the first anniversary of Denise Levertov's death, is approaching and I find myself determined not to write that kind of conventional literary criticism she calls irrelevant to literature. What I would most like to do is to write her a letter, full of comic incident, so I could imagine hearing her delighted cackle once again. Failing that, I would like to write reflectively and personally about her effect on me over the thirty-five or more years I have been reading her work and the nearly twenty years we have been friends, to celebrate and mourn her as a maker, as a witness, as a model, as a companion and friend in life's journey. But to do any of that well, I have to find the right theme, the right images and metaphors to let me use what craft I have as a student of literature. A number of critics, most notably Joyce Lorraine Beck and Denise Lynch, have illuminated Levertov's theme of pilgrimage (Gelpi 268–302).[1] I want only to touch on a few poems over her career, to suggest something of the personal cost, as well as the reward, it was for her to live "on pilgrimage."

In her 1967 essay, "A Sense of Pilgrimage," Denise Levertov leads us into an exploration of an initially unconscious, dominant, recurring theme in her life, "some traces, at least, of *a* myth running through all my work from the very beginning" (*PW* 62). From early childhood, faeryland was "a world very real to me." "… In an infantile way it introduced the theme of a journey that would lead one from one state of being to another …" (*PW* 63). She cites such early and life-long influences as John Bunyan, Hans Christian Andersen, Charles Kingsley, George MacDonald and Andrew Lang, writers who have in common that they create mythic worlds, dream-like places of origin, archetypal figures and patterns of relationships, "images of inner knowledge," which engage the deep "Imagination" (*PW* 75–76). This kind of tale or story is especially resonant for Levertov in later life, when she examines them from Jungian perspectives.

"… the idea of pilgrimage is essentially that of passage from one spiritual state into another …" (*PW* 71). The quest itself may be marked by stages of pre-vision or inspiration where the seeker gains glimpses of a secret, quickly forgotten or hidden again, which will bring him or her closer to a goal. Themes of remembering and forgetting, recurrence and revelation, appear frequently throughout Levertov's poetry. In "Some Affinities of Content" (1991) she says, "… more and more, what I have sought as *a reading writer* is a poetry that, while it does not attempt to ignore or deny the ocean of crisis in which we swim, is itself 'on pilgrimage,' as it were, in search of significance underneath and beyond the succession of temporal events …" (*NSE* 4).

"Pilgrim" and "wanderer" recur often in her poetry, with overlapping but distinguishable meanings. The archetypal pilgrim is someone called to a hoped-for goal, a destination more or less known. The pilgrim makes mistakes, experiences delays and painful tests, but each set of tests prepares her for entering a new spiritual state, a stage of knowing important in itself and preparatory for subsequent tests and gifts of knowing. For these reasons,

---

[1]Joyce Lorraine Beck, "Poetics and *Oblique Prayers*"; Denise Lynch, "Denise Levertov in Pilgrimage," in *Denise Levertov: Selected Criticism*, ed. and intro. Albert Gelpi (Ann Arbor: U of Michigan P, 1993).

in the "Olga Poems" Levertov must comprehend her sister Olga's years of alienating her family, hiding among strangers, "trudging after your anguish ... soberly, soberly ..." as nonetheless a pilgrimage, "the pilgrim years" (*P1* 209).

The pilgrim also discovers guides along her way. There is a dependable reality underlying the quest; what is to be tested is the pilgrim's valor, intention, determination, steadfastness, ability to overcome discouragement, her readiness to follow the master, to learn and grow. Bunyan's hymn, which, as children, Denise and Olga Levertov would sing aloud when walking through the darkness, captures the essence of the pilgrim's life:

> He who would valiant be
> 'Gainst all disaster,
> Let him with constancy
> Follow the Master.
> There's no discouragement
> Can make him once repent
> His first avowed intent,
> To be a pilgrim.

By contrast, the wanderer seems more driven from than toward something, lacking either guide or goal. "Poem" begins "Some are too much at home in the role of wanderer, / watcher, listener...." It is significant that she thinks of wanderers as engaged in a very different kind of search from the pilgrim:

> The undertone of all their solitude
> is the unceasing question, 'Who am I?'
>   (*CEP* 7)

The image of the wanderer seems to appear more frequently and carry a heavier burden in her poetry from the time of the Vietnam War on. In *Footprints* , she describes "The Wanderer" thus:

> The chameleon who wistfully
> thought it could not suffer
> nostalgia
>
> now on a vast sheet of clear glass
> cowers, and prays for vision
> of russet bark and trembling foliage.
>   (*P2* 232)

And in "The Old King" she speaks of the *"Soul's dark Cottage"* throwing off a red glow, while

> Far-off a wanderer
> unhoused, unhouseled,
> wonders to see
> hearthblaze:
> fears, and takes heart.
> (P2 235)

In "A Wanderer," the wanderer "has taken his sorrow / away to strangers." The poet (who is also a pilgrim), separated from this lover and complementary self, wants to lie alone, dreaming about how the wanderer and his sorrow were received in a circle of song and dance:

> I don't know how to sing,
> that language
> strangers talk to him in,
> speaking runes to his sorrow.
> (LF 122–23)

This section of the book, titled "Life in the Forest," is tightly interwoven, and "A Wanderer" is a close companion-work to the two poems which follow it, "A Pilgrim Dreaming" and "Metamorphic Journal"—both further exploring the landscape of dream to speak of loneliness and the hunger for the Imagination's power,

> those instants
> when the Creative Spirit, sisterly,
> takes a Wanderer's cold and burning hand
> in hers
> and they enter the dance.
> ("Metamorphic Journal," LF 134)

Both pilgrims and wanderers make inconvenient companions. That Levertov knows this about herself is illustrated in "Poet and Person." The poet's readers love her for how they see themselves in the poems: "Your solitudes / utter their runes, your own / voices begin to rise in your throats." When she arrives, they welcome her, for she "sing[s]" all the "messages" they have learned by heart, "and bring[s] / as housegifts, new ones." But soon, she says, they love her less, because she brought too much with her for a visit, including her infirmities,

> my crutches, and my spare crutches,
> my desire to please, and worse—
>
> my desire to judge what is right.

> I take up
> so much space.
>
> (*CB* 6)

"Poet and Person" shows a sad self-awareness of how difficult an acquaintance or friend she could be, but it is also a commentary on an artist's audience. For Levertov, the artist always has a prophetic, truth-telling duty, which means speaking politically, judging what is right and speaking out against what is wrong. How often we go to a reading, exhibit or performance, however, wanting only what we have already learned to love from the artist and seeing each departure from the nostalgic and familiar as a let-down, a falling-off from a previous accomplishment. Levertov has recorded one such experience in "The Day the Audience Walked Out On Me, and Why" (*P2* 220–21). Even sophisticated critics writing about living artists want them to remain predictable, ful-filling only the promise they have predicted; otherwise, they take up too much space. "Though I own a house and have steady work, I am by nature, heritage, and as an artist, forever a stranger and pilgrim" ("A Poet's View," 1984, *NSE* 245).

> When I leave, I leave
> alone, as I came.
>
> (*CB* 6)

The trajectory of Levertov's life as poet and person might be very simply sketched as from hopeful, confident pilgrim, led by a guide or muse in her early career, to baffled and despairing wan-derer—"… And now the arrival / the place of pilgrimage … / is this the place? / This is not the place / The spirit's left it."—in the middle years ("The Cold Spring," *P2* 8), ultimately achieving a tested, resilient blend of pilgrim/wanderer, formed by a provi-sional religious faith, always aware of the darkness, always prone to despair, but persisting in obedience to the guides she has found. Two poem-parables written more than twenty years apart, "To The Muse" (*P1* 98) and "The Spirits Appeased" (*BW* 8) serve to frame this evolution.

In "To The Muse" the poet has learned from a wise man that the muse, the spirit of inspiration, always inhabits her own house, so when she appears to have gone away she is merely hiding in secret rooms. The muse has not failed, "the host, the housekeeper, it is / who fails you" by forgetting to make room at the hearth or table. Like a gold ring lost in the house, the muse is always there.

The poet can invite the return or rediscovery of the muse, who waits to be found:

> No more rage but a calm face,
> trim the fire, lay the table, find some
> flowers for it: is that the way?

The tone of this poem is serious, but also joyful and utterly confident; becoming aware, taking care of the simplest domestic tasks, waiting in patience seem both possible and productive, for the muse, the guide for the artist's journey, is always at home.

"The Spirits Appeased" has two movements; the first an extended parable in the form of a mythic "once-upon-a-time" fable, and the second a personal reflection and application of the parable to the poet's life. In the fable, a wanderer comes to a forest hut "where it was promised / someone wise would receive him. / And there's no one there...." Though "[n]o human eyes meet his" the hut contains all the requirements for hospitality: food set to keep warm by glowing logs, "fragrant garments to fit him," and a bed of heather. The wanderer remains: "He stays there waiting."

Now the magical element of the story becomes more explicit. "Each day the fire / is replenished, the pot refilled while he sleeps." In this kind of fable, which is deliberately dream-like, the magical or miraculous is taken for granted, but the reader— whether of poem or dream—finds the work demanding questions. We start by wondering how the fire gets replenished and the pot refilled, but there are more pressing questions. How, under these strange circumstances, can the wanderer sleep? How can he trust the food that fills the pot? How can he be sure the garments are safe for him to wear? Why does he wait, when his accustomed role is to wander? The story raises these questions in us but answers none of them.

There are other puzzles to the story. The magical room-service is not perfect: food and fire are provided in the night, but the waiting wanderer has to draw up his own water from the well. In fact, his waiting is occupied by three activities: "He draws up water from the well, / writes of his travels, listens for footsteps." So he remains occupied for an undetermined length of time, engaged in a curious mix of activity and passive acceptance. Food, clothing, warmth are there for him, if he will trust their source. Water he must draw up for himself, but the rest of his time can be given over to writing up his travels and listening for someone from outside. Under these conditions, the story concludes,

> Little by little he finds
> the absent sage is speaking to him,
> is present.

The completed story now invites additional questions. When did the absent sage arrive? What brought him to the hut? Were the wanderer's actions, and passive waiting, necessary to bring about the sage's presence? By contrast with the far-simpler "The Muse," the fable in "The Spirits Appeased" acts as what Denis de Rougemont calls a "trap for meditation," setting up within us resonances to its magical images and archetypes. The wanderer's work, to draw water, write his travels and listen for footsteps, can be understood as three forms of the same activity. The writing reaches into and records the past, while the listening reaches into the immediate future, but each is also a way of reaching into the depths of the self, often imaged in dreams and fables as a deep well from which the water of life can be drawn. Reflecting on where one has been, waiting to hear what will lead one into the future, are both ways of drawing knowledge into consciousness from the deep wells of the unconscious.

From this reading, we can conclude that the sage was never absent, but became present only as the wanderer did the work of waiting and reflection which prepared him to discern that presence. The wanderer's nature had to be transformed before he could be spoken to. The logic of the fable is that he must once again go on his travels, but now as finder as well as seeker, pilgrim as well as wanderer. As the fable makes clear, the sage is found within, little by little, but the poet's commentary adds a layer of meaning.

> This is the way
> you have spoken to me, the way—startled—
> I find I have heard you. When I need it,
> a book or a slip of paper
> appears in my hand, inscribed by yours: messages
> waiting on cellar shelves, in forgotten boxes
> until I would listen.

"The Spirits Appeased" also rewards comparison with another earlier poem, "A Soul-Cake" (*LF* 41–42) which begins: "Mother, when I open a book of yours / your study notes fall out into my lap." Reading those notes, and her mother's underlinings in books, the poet comments,

> What hurts is not your absence only,
> dull, unresonant, final,
> it's the intimate knowledge of your aspirations,
> the scholar in you, the artist reaching
> out and out.

"A Soul-Cake" reaches only to poignant reminiscence. The words her mother has left have no particular significance except as they reflect that dull, unresonant absence.

> There's too much grief. Mother,
> what shall I do with it?
> Salt grinding and grinding from the magic box.
> *(LF* 41–42)

In "Visitant" her mother returns only to pay a visit and is preoccupied with other concerns. There the poet speculates of the dead, "… their own present / holds them intent. Yet perhaps / sometimes they dream us" (*CB* 44).

In "The Spirits Appeased," that familiar experience of finding a passage underlined in a book, or an old, forgotten letter by a parent or a dead friend which directly addresses our immediate needs, is more than fortunate coincidence—it is a link with living spirits, beloved forerunners, mentors and guides. (When I first visited Denise Levertov's West Somerville home, she showed me where all the important books and documents were—her whole lifetime's notebooks in a fire-trap attic, and in the basement, on shelves protected from dust by clear plastic covers, her father's books and her mother's diaries. She would let none of these things be more safely stored: they had to be kept close by, for they were all of present help to her life and her art.)

Levertov always took the messages from her dream-life seriously, but as her spiritual life came to have more focused reality for her in Christian belief, the dream-visitations—from her parents, from her dead, once-estranged friend Robert Duncan, from Rilke—become more than messages from her unconscious or wish-fulfillment. They are encounters with the loving companions of the spirit-world. "The Change" (*SW* 62) describes the difference.

> For years the dead
> were the terrible weight of their absence,
> the weight of what one had not put in their hands.
> Rarely a visitation—dream or vision—
> lifted that load for a moment....

The grief from absence and failure was a continual burden, which the poet needed for grounding: "How flimsy to be without it...." Eventually, however, the dead begin to return,

> but not as visions. They're not
> separate now, not to be seen, no,
> it's they who see: they displace,
> for seconds, for minutes, maybe longer,
> the mourner's gaze with their own.
>
> (*SW* 62)

What *appeases*, gives peace to, the spirits, is that the poet now *"is looking ... now she begins to see."* Their return is parable and miracle, blessing, and guide to a renewed vision.

The scope of this essay does not permit anything more than briefly noting another rich aspect of life "on pilgrimage," the many kinds of landscape to be traversed and the analogues between "the journey of art and the journey of faith" ("A Poet's View," *NSE* 249), among them the sacred parks of her childhood, deserts and waste places, "Imagination's holy forest," Keats's "Vale of Soulmaking," "no man's land," "the Valley of Transformation," "the language-root place," "the Almost Island." Levertov says of Rilke as her mentor that his "'mutual bordering and guarding of two solitudes' ... became a cardinal point in my map of love" (*NSE* 234). "The Life of Art" (*DH* 85) encapsulates much of what is most compelling to her about the borderland: "— that's where, if one knew how, / one would establish residence. That watershed, / that spine, that looking-glass...." She celebrates that in-between as "interface," "equilibrium," and "exquisite balance." It is the point where we can see the brush-strokes or "pencilled understrokes," smell the turpentine, delight in the craft itself, and at the same time discern the large patterns, the fictive truths, the whole world of vision (*DH* 85). "The Hymn" records a dream of a beautiful and wonderfully detailed landscape, which she experiences as "this hymn, this ecstatic paean, / this woven music / of color and form, of the sense / of airy space—." She asks,

> was the dream
> showing forth the power
> of Memory, now, today, or at any
> moment of need? Or the power
> of the inner eye, distinct
> from Memory, Imagination's power,
> greater than we remember,

> in abeyance, the well in which
> we forget to dip our cups?
>
> (*SW* 97)

But this dream does not derive its power or significance from allegory; no parable informs the scene; it is clear *seeing*, epiphany, pure gift.

As Denise Levertov travels more deeply into faith, she discovers a special affinity for a particular kind of Christian seeker, represented by Caedmon, St. Peter, and Brother Lawrence. The first is a "clodhopper" with "clumsy feet," who has no place in the dance of language until the angel touches him with flame and gives him the gift of poetry. She tells us that "Caedmon" is a companion-piece to "St. Peter and the Angel," which retells the story from The Acts of the Apostles of Peter's being miraculously rescued from prison by an angel and left "alone and free to resume / the ecstatic, dangerous, wearisome roads of / what he had still to do ..." (*OP* 79). Peter, we are reminded in "Poetics of Faith," impetuously tries to walk on water. Though he can only sustain a few steps, "years later, / his toes and insteps, just before sleep, / would remember their passage" (*SW* 110). Brother Lawrence is a "[c]lumsy footman" until his opening, "*By the Grace of God*." Then he is sent out from his work, "by untold ways, by soldier's marches" to the monastery kitchen. He is lame, clumsy,

> ... though your soul felt darkened, heavy, worthless,
> yet God, you discovered, never abandoned you but walked
> at your side keeping pace as comrades had
> on the long hard roads of war. You entered then
> the unending 'silent secret conversation',
> the life of steadfast attention.
>
> (*SW* 111–12)

What these three exemplars have in common is that they are clumsy pilgrims who nonetheless persist in their walking. Sometimes they appear to be on their own in the journey, sustained only by memory, or brief ecstatic visions, or the examples of comrades. In "For Those Whom the Gods Love Less," Denise Levertov applies that example to her journey of art. When "your new work travels the ground you had traversed / decades ago, you wonder, panicked, / 'Have I outlived my vocation? Said already / all that was mine to say?'" The only remedy is to "[r]emember the great ones" who doggedly pursued the same motifs and themes all their lives—Paul Cézanne, Henry James— "Each life in art / goes forth to meet dragons that rise from their bloody scales / in cyclic rhythm...." Though these are the ones the gods love less—why we do not know—they *are* loved, and they catch glimpses of "radiant epiphanies" which confirm that "You can, you must / proceed" (*SW* 96). Was Denise Levertov one of those the gods loved less? Perhaps the question is foolish to raise, but reading *The Sands of the Well* again in these past few months I have been saddened at the valedictory tone of a number of the poems. Certainly as she completed the book she knew her health was failing, that "the certainty of return / to this imprinted scene ... / can not be assumed" ("In Question," *SW* 6). How much more poignant, then, that question she put to herself whether she had outlived her poet's vocation.

Having asked the question, however, I feel compelled to try to offer the beginnings of an answer. Here is a poet who spent her life "on pilgrimage," inviting the muse, the sage, the spirit, finally the Holy Spirit to lead her. Again and again, when the inner voice was silent, she blamed herself for being absent. Again and again she tried to open herself so that the voice of poetic inspiration and ethical action could speak to her again. Denise Levertov did many kinds of walking: she loved to dance, its aesthetic expression, out of conviction she went on marches, its political form, and she cherished above all long meditative explorations of the world around her. In daily life, often all she could manage was, in one of her favorite words, to "trudge" along. There are deep wells of sadness in her poetry, grieving, loss, depression, despair, the agony of being speechless. Her poetry is also full of deep joy, both wells and fountains of joy.

In Spring 1999 a final book of her poetry appeared, named *This Great Unknowing*, from a line in one of the poems. Two brief quotations from that book seem to offer a fitting close to this essay. Reflecting on paradise as a paradigm for how to live on earth in "A Clearing" she concludes

> ... paradise
> is a kind of poem; it has
> a poem's characteristics:
> inspiration; starting with the given;
> unexpected harmonies; revelations.
> (*TGU* 54)

In "First Love" she recalls seeing a flower so early in her life that she could barely ask its name. Her mother tells her it is "convolvulus." She and the flower look at one another with delight, she says, "*And there was endlessness.*"

> Perhaps through a lifetime what I've desired
> has always been to return
> to that endless giving and receiving, the wholeness
> of that attention,
> that once-in-a-lifetime
> secret communion.
>
> (*TGU* 8–9)

That is her final description of life on pilgrimage, her testimony of the lived life. It reminds us that the winter solstice is also the time of Advent, the promise of new life, giving and receiving. Those who have known Denise Levertov's complex, difficult, sometimes outrageous, loving, generous companionship— through her writing and her public witness and (a fortunate many) as a friend—are better equipped for their own journeys. "Let us enter into ourselves," she quotes Brother Lawrence. "Time presses."

Works Cited

Beck, Joyce Lorraine. "Poetics and *Oblique Prayers.*" *Denise Levertov: Selected Criticism*. Ed. Albert Gelpi. Ann Arbor: U of Michigan P, 1993.

Levertov, Denise. *Breathing the Water*. New York: New Directions, 1987.

———. *Candles in Babylon*. New York: New Directions, 1982.

———. *Collected Earlier Poems 1940–1969*. New York: New Directions, 1979.

———. *A Door in the Hive*. New York: New Directions, 1989.

———. *Life in the Forest*. New York: New Directions, 1978.

———. *New & Selected Essays*. New York: New Directions, 1992.

———. *Oblique Prayers*. New York: New Directions, 1984.

———. *Poems 1960–1967*. New York: New Directions, 1987.

———. *Poems 1968–1972*. New York: New Directions, 1987.

———. *The Poet in the World*. New York: New Directions, 1973.

———. *Sands of the Well*. New York: New Directions, 1996.

———. *This Great Unknowing*. New York: New Directions, 1999.

Lynch, Denise. "Denise Levertov in Pilgrimage." *Denise Levertov: Selected Criticism*. Ed. Albert Gelpi. Ann Arbor: U of Michigan P, 1993.

What/Calm

by Ralph Mills

—for Denise Levertov   (Variation on Jaccottet)

what
calm—
         grass &
dropped leaves,
                  willow whips

shining
on water
      /
            this shadow of
       shadows, call
       it,
             lies lengthwise in november sun's
flat whiteness,
                  spreads like
wood smoke or vapor
                        then widens to
include a
blue dust between trees
                        which is

sky—

Index